THE BETTER BEGINNINGS, BETTER FUTURES PROJECT: FINDINGS FROM GRADE 3 TO GRADE 9

Ray DeV. Peters, Alison J. Bradshaw, Kelly Petrunka, Geoffrey Nelson, Yves Herry, Wendy M. Craig, Robert Arnold, Kevin C. H. Parker, Shahriar R. Khan, Jeffrey S. Hoch, S. Mark Pancer, Colleen Loomis, Jean-Marc Bélanger, Susan Evers, Claire Maltais, Katherine Thompson, and Melissa D. Rossiter

W. Andrew Collins
Series Editor

MONOGRAPHS OF THE SOCIETY FOR RESEARCH IN CHILD DEVELOPMENT

Serial No. 297, Vol. 75, No. 3, 2010

WILEY-BLACKWELL   *Boston, Massachusetts   Oxford, United Kingdom*

Andrew Fuligni
University of California, Los Angeles

Susan Graham
University of Calgary

Elena Grigorenko
Yale University

Megan Gunnar
University of Minnesota

Paul Harris
Harvard University

Susan Hespos
Vanderbilt University

Aletha Huston
University of Texas, Austin

Lene Jensen
Clark University

Ariel Kalil
University of Chicago

Melissa Koenig
University of Minnesota

Brett Laursen
Florida Atlantic University

Eva Lefkowitz
Pennsylvania State University

Katherine Magnuson
University of Wisconsin, Madison

Ann Masten
University of Minnesota

Kevin Miller
University of Michigan

Ginger Moore
Pennsylvania State University

David Moshman
University of Nebraska

Darcia Narvaez
University of Notre Dame

Katherine Nelson
City University of New York

Lisa Oakes
University of California, Davis

Thomas O'Connor
University of Rochester

Yukari Okamoto
University of California, Santa Barbara

Robert Pianta
University of Virginia

Mark Roosa
Arizona State University

Karl Rosengren
University of Illinois, Urbana-Champaign

Judith G. Smetana
University of Rochester

Kathy Stansbury
Morehouse College

Steve Thoma
University of Alabama

Michael Tomasello
Max Planck Institute

Deborah Vandell
University of California, Irvine

Richard Weinberg
University of Minnesota

Hirokazu Yoshikawa
New York University

Qing Zhou
Arizona State University

THE BETTER BEGINNINGS, BETTER FUTURES PROJECT: FINDINGS FROM GRADE 3 TO GRADE 9

CONTENTS

ABSTRACT

Although comprehensive and ecological approaches to early childhood prevention are commonly advocated, there are few examples of long-term follow-up of such programs. In this monograph, we investigate the medium- and long-term effects of an ecological, community-based prevention project for primary school children and families living in three economically disadvantaged neighborhoods in Ontario, Canada. The Better Beginnings, Better Futures (BBBF) project is one of the most ambitious Canadian research projects on the long-term impacts of early childhood prevention programming to date. Bronfenbrenner's ecological model of human development informed program planning, implementation, and evaluation.

Using a quasi-experimental design, the BBBF longitudinal research study involved 601 children and their families who participated in BBBF programs when children were between 4 and 8 years old and 358 children and their families from sociodemographically matched comparison communities. We collected extensive child, parent, family, and community outcome data when children were in Grade 3 (age 8–9), Grade 6 (age 11–12), and Grade 9 (age 14–15).

The BBBF mandate was to develop programs that would positively impact all areas of child's development; our findings reflect this ecological approach. We found marked positive effects in social and school functioning domains in Grades 6 and 9 and evidence of fewer emotional and behavioral problems in school across the three grades. Parents from BBBF sites reported greater feelings of social support and more positive ratings of marital satisfaction and general family functioning, especially at the Grade 9 follow-up. Positive neighborhood-level effects were also evident. Economic analyses at Grade 9 showed BBBF participation was associated with government savings of $912 per child.

These findings provide evidence that an affordable, ecological, community-based prevention program can promote long-term development of children living in disadvantaged neighborhoods and produce monetary benefits to government as soon as 7 years after program completion.

I. INTRODUCTION

Increased interest in early childhood development has prompted renewed attention to the positive effects of preventive interventions on development in children and their families, particularly those living in high-risk, socioeconomically disadvantaged neighborhoods. The long-term effects of these programs are of particular interest, especially the effects on academic, health, and social functioning in children and their families, which in the long term may result in decreased rates of unemployment, delinquency, welfare participation, and illness. Recent reviews have found that there is substantial evidence that preventive interventions can have large short-term effects on children's cognitive development, as well as on social and emotional functioning, behavioral problems, and school competence (grade retention, special education placement) in elementary school (e.g., Brooks-Gunn, 2003; Karoly, Kilburn, & Cannon, 2005; Webster-Stratton & Taylor, 2001). Although program effects on cognition typically diminish over the elementary school years (Karoly et al., 2005; Nelson, Westhues, & MacLeod, 2003), effects in other domains such as school competence and social functioning are often observed through adolescence (Brooks-Gunn, 2003; Camilli, Vargas, Ryan, & Barnett, 2010; Karoly et al., 2005). Further, it is evident that early childhood prevention programs can have large effects into young adulthood on important societal outcomes, including educational attainment, criminal activity, employment, earnings, and use of social services (Boisjoli, Vitaro, Lacourse, Barker, & Tremblay, 2007; Karoly et al., 2005; Reynolds et al., 2007; Schweinhart et al., 2005).

In this monograph, we investigate the long-term effects of a universal, comprehensive, community-based prevention project for primary school children and families living in three disadvantaged communities in Ontario, Canada—the Better Beginnings, Better Futures (BBBF) project—1, 4, and 7 years after the end of program participation. Three major questions are addressed.

1

1. What are the medium- and long-term effects of participation on social, emotional, behavioral, cognitive, and physical development of children and youth?

2. To what extent does participation positively affect parent health, parenting behaviors, family functioning, and community involvement?

3. Do the long-term economic benefits of participation outweigh the project costs?

We report findings from longitudinal analyses of the BBBF project. The original study cohort involved 601 children and their families who participated in the BBBF project when children were between 4 and 8 years old and 358 children and their families from two sociodemographically matched comparison communities. Based on a quasi-experimental design, differences between project and comparison groups were analyzed. We collected extensive child, parent, and community outcome data from children, parents, teachers, and school records when children were in Grades 3, 6, and 9.

This study differs from previous evaluations of the effects of early preventive interventions in five key ways. First, we comprehensively investigate the long-term effects of a preventive intervention. Although there are several notable U.S. exceptions (e.g., Chicago Child–Parent Centers [CPCs] [Reynolds et al., 2007] and Perry Preschool Project [PPP] [Schweinhart et al., 2005]), many early childhood programs to date have reported no long-term follow-up. In a meta-analysis of 34 longitudinal preschool prevention programs (Nelson et al., 2003), only 10 of the programs followed children past Grade 8; no studies reported long-term outcomes for parents or families of the children. Much of the current knowledge about the long-term effects of prevention programs for young children rests on a limited number of U.S. studies carried out 20–30 years ago with small samples or samples involving only African American children. Because the theoretical assumption is that children provided with enriched experiences at a young age will develop more positively than children without those experiences, it is essential to collect long-term follow-up data.

Second, this study has a strong focus on community development. Local parents and residents were involved in all aspects of the BBBF project planning and implementation, such that each project site delivered programs based on locally identified needs. Collaboration, integration, and partnerships with other community organizations were considered crucial to project success. These aspects distinguish this project from almost all other prevention projects in North America (Durlak et al., 2007).

Third, the large sample size of the BBBF cohort and the cultural diversity of the three participating communities (Anglophone, Francophone, recent immigrants) increase the likelihood that our findings will be generalizable across Canada. In contrast, most early preventive interventions in Canada (and the United States) have been single-site studies with relatively homogeneous samples. Those samples are unlikely to be representative of Canada's children (Brooks-Gunn, 2003).

Fourth, we present a rigorous economic analysis. No other early childhood prevention project in Canada and very few in the United States have comparable economic analyses (Karoly et al., 2005; Waddell, Hua, Garland, Peters, & McEwan, 2007). Cost-benefit analyses are important for three reasons: First, economic benefits relative to costs are relevant to policy development; second, an economic analysis converts program effects on multiple outcomes to comprehensible monetary terms; and third, cost-benefit analyses emphasize longer term effects of programs (Reynolds & Temple, 2008).

The fifth distinguishing characteristic of this study is that we investigate effects for parent, family, and community outcomes. Although prevention and intervention programs are often expected to have effects on families (Reynolds, 2000), most studies do not investigate these outcomes but instead focus primarily on child/youth outcomes, such as cognitive development, deviant behavior, or educational attainment. Our inclusion of broad outcome measures reflects the ecological framework of our research. From an ecological perspective, development must be understood in context. As such, it was crucial to include both child outcomes and outcomes that capture the context in which the child lives (parent, family, school, and neighborhood settings).

Contemporary ecological perspectives emphasize that changes among children, families, communities, and societies over time are interdependent and that development must be understood within these broader contexts. Bronfenbrenner's ecological model (1979, 1986a) has been widely used to frame developmental research and programs for healthy youth development. This model formed the theoretical basis of the BBBF project.

THE DEVELOPMENTAL ECOLOGICAL PERSPECTIVE

The ecological perspective posits that child development is directly and indirectly influenced by the quality and context of the child's environment, including parent, family, school, neighborhood, and sociocultural settings. More specifically, development is a function of the reciprocal interactions between both the immediate and distal environment and the developing child (Bronfenbrenner & Morris, 2006; Tolan, Guerra, & Kendall, 1995).

According to Bronfenbrenner (1979), the ecological environment consists of four nested, interconnected systems that affect the developing child. The innermost level, referred to as the microsystem, consists of the immediate settings with which the child has contact including family, preschool, school, and neighborhood environments, as well as the relationships and interactions the child has in each of these settings. The second level, the mesosystem, is the interconnections between settings that contain the child. That is, the mesosystem is "a system of two or more microsystems" at a particular point in the child's development (Bronfenbrenner & Morris, 2006, p. 817). Interconnections or relationships between settings could include, for example, the number and quality of the relations between family and school or between family and neighborhood. These are important to investigate because events in one setting have the potential to influence the child's behavior and development in another (Bronfenbrenner, 1977). The third level of the ecological environment, the exosystem, is the settings and interconnections among settings that do not contain the developing child. Thus, settings within the exosystem have an indirect influence on the child and may include the parent's workplace or community group. The outermost level, the macrosystem, refers to the larger sociocultural context within which the three aforementioned systems are located.

Almost a decade later, Bronfenbrenner (1986b) recognized that development is influenced by changes within the child and the environment *over time*. Thus, he added a temporal dimension to the ecological model, the chronosystem, to acknowledge this interplay over time. The chronosystem encapsulates the "dynamic relation" between the processes of change within the child and her environment over time (Bronfenbrenner, 1986b, p. 724). In short, the chronosystem describes the developmental and life transitions that occur throughout the life span. These transitions, such as entry into preschool or elementary school or graduation from high school, are developmentally important for two reasons. First, they involve a change in role (e.g., from child in preschool to child in elementary school); second, because they invariably involve more than one setting, reciprocal processes occur between those settings. Thus, transitions have developmental effects on the child and also effects on ecological systems, such as family, peer group, or school. For example, the child's transition to school (a normative transition) can affect family interactions and processes; a parents' divorce (a nonnormative transition) can affect the mother–child relationship or the child's behavior at school or with peers (Bronfenbrenner, 1977, 1979, 1986b).

In the context of early prevention and intervention programs, a developmental ecological perspective informs program development and implementation, as well as program evaluation and analysis of long-term program effects. Indeed, the ecological approach aids researchers in establishing more effective programs because the classroom, school, family, and community characteristics are important components of the project development and evaluation. Given the research confirming multiple

4

influences on child and youth development, a number of organizations have recommended that preventive interventions/strategies for youth take an ecological approach, and involve families, peers, schools, neighborhoods, and policies (Carnegie Task Force on Meeting the Needs of Young Children, 1994; Institute of Medicine, 2000; National Research Council Panel on Research on Child Abuse and Neglect, 1993).

EFFECTIVE PREVENTION INTERVENTIONS FOR PRESCHOOL AND EARLY PRIMARY SCHOOL CHILDREN

Early childhood prevention programs are designed to intervene at a young age in order to improve the developmental trajectories of at risk children. There are two major types of preventive interventions—targeted and universal. In a targeted approach, individual children or subgroups of at risk children are identified in two ways: by characteristics that are outside the child (e.g., sociofamilial or environmental factors) or by individual characteristics (e.g., aggressive or disruptive behavior). These classifications reflect two targeted approaches, selective and indicated, respectively (Institute of Medicine, 1994). Universal preventive interventions focus on all children within a geographic area or setting (e.g., a neighborhood or school) and do not identify children on the basis of any type of risk (Offord, Kraemer, Kazdin, Jensen, & Harrington, 1998).

There have been numerous published reports of early preventive interventions that show short-term improvements in cognitive, behavioral, or school functioning outcomes. Unfortunately many of those programs have not been evaluated by following children into late adolescence or early adulthood (Brooks-Gunn, 2003; Karoly et al., 2005; Nelson et al., 2003; Russell, 2002). Thus, we focus our review on the results of four well-researched preventive interventions with long-term follow-up—the PPP (Schweinhart, Barnes, & Weikart, 1993), CPCs (Reynolds, 1997), Fast Track project (Conduct Problems Prevention Research Group [CPPRG], 1992) and the Montreal Prevention Experiment (Tremblay et al., 1992) relevant to the current study. The results from these four studies are the best evidence of the long-term outcome effects of preventive interventions for preschool and early primary school-aged children. Table 1 summarizes the characteristics and outcomes for the four programs.

The PPP

The High/Scope PPP (Schweinhart et al., 1993) began in Ypsilanti Michigan in 1962 and is the most frequently cited early childhood program in reviews of the literature (Reynolds, 2000). This study was initiated

TABLE 1

CHARACTERISTICS AND OUTCOMES OF FOUR PREVENTIVE INTERVENTIONS FOR PRESCHOOL OR EARLY PRIMARY SCHOOL-AGED CHILDREN

Program	Sample Size	Age of Children (Years)	Program Type	Length of Intervention (Years)	Format of Intervention	Age at Last Follow-Up	Results[a] Short Term (Child/Youth)	Results[a] Long Term (Adult)
High/Scope Perry Preschool Project (Schweinhart et al., 1993, 2005)	I = 58 C = 65	3–4	Targeted Selective	1–2	Classroom-based cognitive and social skills training; child skills training; parent skills training and home visits	40	IQ, achievement test scores; special education; teen pregnancy	High school graduation; employment, earnings; use of social services; arrests
Chicago Child–Parent Centers (Reynolds, 1997; Reynolds et al., 2007)	I = 974 C = 565	3–9	Targeted Selective	1–6	Classroom-based language and social skills training; parent involvement half day per week; home visits and outreach services; also half or full-day kindergarten and G1-3 program	24	Achievement test scores; special education; grade retention; social competence; delinquency	High school graduation; highest grade completed; attendance at 4-year college; arrests
Fast Track Prevention Trial (Conduct Problems Prevention Research Group, 1999, 2002b, 2007)	I = 445 C = 446	6–16	Targeted Indicated	10	Classroom-based skills training; tutoring, and social skills training for children; individual and group parent training	15	Social cognition; conduct problems	
Montreal Prevention Experiment (Tremblay et al., 1996; Boisjoli et al., 2007)	I = 43 C = 123	7–9	Targeted Indicated	2	Lunch time child social skills training; home-based parent skills training	24	Special education; disruptive behavior; delinquency	High school completion; criminal record

Note.—C = Control or comparison group; I = Intervention group.
[a]Improvement in all listed outcomes was statistically significant at $p < 0.05$, versus control or comparison group.

around the same time as the Head Start federal preschool program for low-income children in the United States and was influenced by studies showing the importance of the preschool years for children's cognitive development. The PPP was the first study to report preschool program effects on high school graduation, employment, earnings, use of social services, and arrests up to age 40 years (Schweinhart et al., 2005). Although the results of this study are often cited as evidence of the positive effects of early preventive interventions, the PPP was a small-scale, model project involving 123 African American children with low IQ (<85) from very low socioeconomic status (SES) families. The intervention involved 1 or 2 years of preschool and weekly home visits during the school year; no other family- or community-based programs were offered. Children were randomly assigned to either the PPP intervention group ($n = 58$) or the comparison condition, in which children received no preschool ($n = 65$) in five waves between 1962 and 1967. Over the 5-year period, 45 children entered the PPP at age 3 and attended for 2 years, and 13 entered at age 4 and attended 1 year before entering public kindergarten. The preschool intervention consisted of daily 150-min center-based classes and weekly 90-min teacher home visits, both delivered from October to May each year. The in-class teacher–student ratio was 1–6; all teachers were certified public school teachers trained in early child development.

Evaluations of the children were performed annually until the children reached 11 and again at ages 14, 15, 19, 27, and 40. By age 10, only 17% of the preschool children had been placed in special education, compared to 38% of children who had not attended the PPP, demonstrating a large effect of the PPP intervention on school functioning (Schweinhart et al., 1993, 2005). These results are impressive because effects were sustained over time. The PPP resulted in long-term savings in costs associated with crime and remedial education, as well as increased projected tax revenues for preschool participants (Schweinhart et al., 2005). The large benefit-cost ratios estimated when the participants were age 27 and 40 have often been cited in arguments for increased preschool funding (e.g., Lynch, 2005). The PPP was initiated nearly 50 years ago, before substantial research attention was focused on the developmental context.

Although the PPP included weekly home visits by the teacher, other aspects of the child's ecological environment, such as the neighborhood, were not targets for change. Consequently, long-term outcomes for parents, families, or neighborhoods have not been reported. In contrast to the PPP, the BBBF project focused on multiple influences on the child's development, including parents, peers, schools, neighborhoods, and social programs. Accordingly, in this monograph, we report long-term results for a wide range of outcomes at the microsystem and mesosystem levels of the child's environment, such as child and parent social functioning, child emotional and

7

behavioral problems, child school functioning, child–parent relationships, and child and parent community involvement and satisfaction.

CPCs

Another well-researched preventive intervention that was initiated in the 1960s is the CPCs program (Reynolds, 1995, 1997, 2000). This ongoing large-scale program serves predominantly African American children (93%) who reside in Chicago's economically and educationally disadvantaged neighborhoods. From 1967, the preschool program in 11 Chicago public schools provided a structured half-day program during the 9-month school year for 3- and 4-year-olds and was designed as an early education program to prepare children for school through promotion of language and reading skills. The program also provided comprehensive services including health and social services, and parent involvement. In 1978, the program was expanded to continue programs and services for children through third grade, including full-day (6 hr) kindergarten. The primary grades program provided reduced class sizes, parental involvement activities, and instructional coordination. Other comprehensive services at each age included free breakfasts and lunches and health screenings. The CPCs were integrated with the primary schools, and the preschool and kindergarten programs met in buildings of their affiliated elementary schools.

The long-term goal of the CPC program was to facilitate social competence in adolescence and beyond. In CPC, social competence refers to indicators of school performance, social skills, grade retention, special education placement, delinquency, and crime (Reynolds, 2000). These outcomes for one cohort of CPC children have been studied extensively in the Chicago Longitudinal Study (Reynolds, 1997, 2000; Reynolds et al., 2007). The Chicago Longitudinal Study consists of a single age cohort of 1539 low-income minority children (95% African American, 5% Hispanic). Children entered the CPC program at age 3 or 4 (1983–1985) or kindergarten (1985–1986), graduating from kindergarten in the spring of 1986. Some children continued to participate in the CPC through Grade 3 (age 9, 1989) for a total of up to 6 years in the CPC program.

In a rigorous conceptual application of the ecological perspective, Reynolds (2000, 2004) outlined the key constructs and pathways through which CPC preschool participation is hypothesized to improve long-term social competence behaviors. The five pathways are: *cognitive advantage, motivational advantage, social adjustment, family support,* and *school support*. These pathways include elements of the microsystems (family, school, peers) and mesosystems (child–parent and parent–school interactions) that are fundamental to ecological theory. Reynolds (2000, 2004) hypothesized that the

8

pathways to social competence begin in early childhood with preschool program participation. At this age, the characteristics of the prevention program (timing, duration, and intensity) interact with socio-environmental risk and neighborhood attributes as well as the gender of the child in influencing the success of the program. The effects of the early prevention program are subsequently transmitted in middle childhood through developed cognitive abilities, social development and adjustment, parent behavior and family support, children's motivation, and the quality of school characteristics postprogram. Thus, the hypothesized pathways leading from preschool participation to social competence behaviors in adolescence and adulthood are diverse.

Numerous follow-up evaluations of CPC participants have demonstrated the benefits of preschool on elementary and secondary school performance, outcomes at age 21, and, most recently, outcomes at age 24. CPC preschool participants had higher achievement test scores in elementary school, were less likely to be retained in a grade, were more likely to graduate from high school and attend a 4-year college, and had lower rates of felony arrests, convictions, incarceration, and depressive symptoms relative to the comparison group (Reynolds, 1997; Reynolds et al., 2007). Effect sizes in cognitive outcomes decreased over time, as is typical for early intervention programs (Aos, Lieb, Mayfield, Miller, & Pennucci, 2004; Brooks-Gunn, 2003). Reynolds (1997) found that children in the CPC outscored their comparison group counterparts on math and reading tests at Grades 3, 5, and 8 but that the differences in scores decreased over time and, as in the PPP, in some cases became statistically insignificant. The benefits of early intervention may improve school readiness for poor children but cannot fully compensate for the environmental risks that they face. Intervening variables that affect child development after they enter school have a large impact on whether the benefits of intervention will be maintained. For example, parent involvement in the CPCs played a significant role in ensuring the long-term continuity of effects of preschool (Reynolds, 1992).

Results of structural equation modeling of the CPC program data have indicated that all five pathways outlined by Reynolds (2000, 2004) contributed to long-term social competence behaviors to some extent. The three primary mediators for outcomes such as high school completion and delinquency, however, were cognitive advantage (e.g., literacy skills in kindergarten, avoidance of grade retention), school support (e.g., attendance in high-quality elementary schools and lower mobility), and family support (e.g., parent involvement in school and avoidance of child maltreatment) (Reynolds, Ou, & Topitzes, 2004).

Although the CPC program affected child, family, and preschool functioning in order to improve children's later social competence behaviors, these researchers did not include broader neighborhood and social contexts

9

as targets for change. There is, however, consensus in the prevention literature that communities can provide important protective resources and developmental opportunities for children (e.g., Kohen, Hertzman, & Brooks-Gunn, 1998). From the inception of BBBF, a healthy neighborhood was conceptualized as enhancing the developmental opportunities for children and families. The BBBF project sites invested substantial effort in increasing the availability of supportive resources for children and families, and fostering the development of civic engagement and leadership.

The U.S.-based Fast Track project and the Canadian Montreal Prevention Experiment are two more recent intervention studies for high-risk early primary school children designed to assess program effects on antisocial delinquent behavior, school performance, and mental health problems in adolescence and young adulthood.

Fast Track

The Fast Track project (CPPRG, 1992), initiated in 1991, was an early intervention within which developmental ecological perspectives were embedded (Hinshaw, 2002). The project was based on the premise that "early starting" antisocial behavioral development is a function of the interaction of multiple influences such as child characteristics, family stressors, school characteristics, and, in early adolescence, deviant peer group influences (CPPRG, 1992, 2002a). Thus, the intervention addressed "home and school settings, and included key socializing agents, such as parents, teachers, and peers, along with targeted high-risk children" (CPPRG, 2002a, p. 3). The Fast Track program was intensive in both duration (Grades 1–10) and intensity and focused on building skills in multiple systems in addition to strengthening relations among these systems. This randomized controlled trial for high-risk primary school children was implemented in four U.S. sites in Durham, NC; Nashville, TN; Seattle, WA; and rural Pennsylvania.

Three successive cohorts of approximately 10,000 kindergarten students from 54 elementary schools were rated on a disruptive behavior scale between 1991 and 1993 by their teachers and their parents. All schools served predominantly high-poverty neighborhoods where community risk factors were concentrated. Each school was assigned to either the intervention or control condition because one component of the intervention was a universal school-based program. A total of 891 highly disruptive children who scored in the top 20% on both the teacher and parent screening measure were assigned to the Fast Track intervention ($n = 445$) or to a "treatment as usual" control group ($n = 446$).

The Fast Track investigators have emphasized that that interventions must focus on age-related stressors and strategic points in development (i.e., transition periods), such as school entry and transition to middle school

(CPPRG, 1992). The intervention continued across these developmental periods, with the greatest intensity at school entry (i.e., Grades 1–3) and again at the transition to middle/high school (Grades 6–10). According to Tolan et al. (1995), intervening at key transition points can increase the chance of modifying developmental trajectories.

The Fast Track intervention began in 1992 when the first cohort was in Grade 1. During the elementary school phase of the intervention project (i.e., Grades 1–5) all high-risk children were offered social skills training; this was coupled with home visiting for parents. Group meetings for both children and parents were provided every other week in Grade 1 (22 sessions per year), every third week during Grade 2 (14 sessions per year), and monthly during Grades 3–6 (9 sessions per year). By Grades 5 and 6, the monthly group sessions for both youth and their parents covered how to successfully negotiate the transition into middle school as well as skills in resisting drug use and adjusting to sexual development. From Grades 1 through 10, individualized intervention plans were developed and implemented with each youth based on assessments of risk and protective factors that were collected three times during the school year (CPPRG, 2007).

In addition to these intervention activities targeted to the highly disruptive children, a universal classroom intervention was provided by the teacher two or three times a week in Grades 1–5. This intervention was designed to promote social and emotional competence and a less aggressive classroom climate. Fast Track staff provided teachers with weekly consultation concerning effective use of the curriculum materials and classroom behavior management.

A report after the first year of the intervention indicated positive effects on child social cognition and reading, peer relations, four measures of conduct/behavior problems, and two measures of parenting behavior (CPPRG, 1999). Some of these positive effects were still evident after 3 years of Fast Track programming, including three measures of child conduct/ behavior problems and two measures of parenting behavior (CPPRG, 2002a). The most recent evaluation of Fast Track (CPPRG, 2007) investigated measures of various types of antisocial problems including conduct disorder (CD), oppositional defiant disorder, attention-deficit hyperactivity disorder (ADHD), and antisocial behavior (ASB) when the intervention and control children were in Grades 3, 6, and 9. Results from the report indicated that at all three grade levels, the children in the Fast Track program who had been at highest risk before the program began—that is, had the highest 3% of disruptive behavior scores for the entire kindergarten population (the "high-risk" intervention group; $n = 70$)—showed significantly lower scores on measures of CD, ADHD, and ASB than children in the "high-risk" control group ($n = 72$). Conversely, in "moderate risk" children—that is, those who initially scored below the top 3% in disruptive behavior scores in kindergarten—there was no difference between the Fast Track intervention ($n = 375$) and control ($n = 374$) conditions at any of the three grade levels. Further, when compared to a normative sample of 384 children, the disruptive children (i.e., those in high-risk and moderate risk intervention and control groups) showed higher scores on all the externalizing measures at all three grade levels.

These findings suggest that the Fast Track program had its greatest impact on a relatively small sample (72 out of a total intervention sample of 445, or 16%) and that the externalizing behaviors of 84% of the original intervention sample of disruptive children were unaffected by the Fast Track program, at least through Grade 9. However, as has been the case in several other studies including the Montreal Longitudinal study (Vitaro, Brendgen, Pagani, Tremblay, & McDuff, 1999) and the CPC program (Reynolds et al., 2007), some positive intervention effects may not be manifest until later adolescence and early adulthood, such as high school completion and criminal behavior. These later findings underscore the importance of following children who have experienced preschool and early primary school prevention programs through to late adolescence and early adulthood. Because the Fast Track program has been estimated to cost US$58,000 per child over the 10-year intervention period from Grade 1 to Grade 10 (Foster & Jones, 2005), it will be particularly important for the study to follow their intervention and control samples into young adulthood (to at least age 24) to determine the potential financial benefits of the program resulting from lower costs of incarceration and rehabilitation and funding to victims of crime.

The Fast Track investigators are clearly committed to an ecological perspective. They emphasize the importance of the broader social context, such as neighborhood violence, in influencing children's development (Coie & Jacobs, 1993; Lochman, 2004) and the developmental importance of "protective contextual supports" (CPPRG, 2002a, p. 3). Although there is a focus on mesosystemic change in terms of "the development of a healthy bond between the family and school, child and family, and child and school" (CPPRG, 1992, p. 513), there is no attempt to foster systemic changes at the neighborhood or community level (such as community involvement, community activities, and sense of belonging in neighborhood). In contrast, in the BBBF project, neighborhood capacity and community development were seen as essential components of healthy child development.

Montreal Prevention Experiment

This 2-year Canadian intervention began in 1984 and was designed to determine the outcome effects on antisocial behavior and school adjustment

12

of an intervention program for aggressive, low SES boys and their parents in Montreal, QC. It was hypothesized that delinquency and antisocial behavior develop as a result of a chain of events in three developmental domains including child characteristics, parental disciplinary practices, and associations with deviant peers in adolescence (Vitaro et al., 1999; Vitaro, Brendgen, & Tremblay, 2001). The intervention addressed parenting and child disruptive behavior and attempted to change the boys' home and school environments through parent and social skills training, respectively.

The Montreal Prevention Experiment (MPE) intervention was implemented for 2 school years when the boys were in Grades 2 and 3 (i.e., ages 7–9). Based on a rating of disruptive behavior by kindergarten teachers in the lowest SES schools in Montreal, 166 White French-speaking boys from low SES homes who scored above the 70th percentile on teacher ratings of disruptive behavior were randomly assigned to an intervention ($n = 43$) or control group ($n = 123$). The 2-year intervention consisted of three components: (a) in-school social skills training in small groups consisting of a ratio of three prosocial boys for one aggressive boy; (b) in-home parent-training in effective childrearing practices based on Patterson's (1975) social learning program for parents of aggressive boys; and (c) information and support for teachers concerning highly aggressive boys and how to deal with them effectively in school. This third component was not particularly successful, however, with only 50% of the teachers participating in at least one meeting with a project clinician. The boys have been followed through adolescence and into young adulthood as part of the larger Montreal Longitudinal Experiment Study.

Interestingly, no treatment effects were observed during the first year following the intervention (Tremblay et al., 1992). Normally, such disappointing outcomes would bring a program evaluation study to an end. The boys in both the program and control groups, however, were part of a much larger, ongoing longitudinal study, and in the second follow-up year at age 11 positive outcomes began to appear in the boys who had experienced the 2-year program compared to those from the control group. Boys in the intervention group showed better school adjustment (less special education and less disruptive behavior at school) in their last 2 years of primary school (age 11 and 12), and a lower percentage reported being gang members and being involved in delinquency between 11 and 15 years of age than boys from the control group. Other positive outcomes for the boys from the treated group only began to appear later when the boys were between ages 13 and 15. These were seen on measures of being drunk, using drugs, being arrested, and having sexual intercourse (Tremblay, Masse, Pagani, & Vitaro, 1996).

Long-term results from the MPE have indicated that participants in the intervention group were less delinquent through later adolescence than those in the control group and less likely to drop out of school before the age of 17 (Lacourse et al., 2002). At age 24, a higher percentage of the boys who had been assigned to the intervention group had completed high school and a marginally lower percentage had a criminal record than those originally assigned to the control group (Boisjoli et al., 2007).

As with the preventive interventions reviewed above, the MPE focused on a limited number of settings and outcomes. In response to the narrow focus adopted by most early childhood prevention programs to date, BBBF researchers were committed to an ecological project model and a comprehensive view of children's development. Our ecological–developmental perspective encompassed children's physical, social–emotional, and cognitive development, as well as an awareness of the multitude of parent, family, neighborhood, school, and cultural/societal factors that directly and indirectly influence children's development.

Limitations of Current Prevention Programs

Although the studies reviewed above provide strong evidence of positive long-term outcome effects of preventive interventions for preschool and early primary school children, we note three key limitations of these programs. First, the programs were not designed to assess the impact on the health and well-being of children in the general population, as all of the four programs targeted only very high-risk children. In the CPC, enrollment was reserved for those in most educational need (as determined by a screening interview with center staff), all children were from ethnic minority families (93% were African American; 5% were Hispanic), and all resided in Chicago's most economically and educationally disadvantaged neighborhoods (Reynolds, 2000). The PPP was offered only to Black children with low IQ from very disadvantaged families, and the Fast Track and MPE programs were available only to highly disruptive or aggressive children from disadvantaged schools or neighborhoods. Thus, these preventive interventions probably had limited impact on the rates of early childhood difficulties in the general community.

Canadian research indicates that the vast majority of children who are vulnerable to poor developmental outcomes do not live in severely economically disadvantaged families (McCain, Mustard, & Shanker, 2007). Data from the Canadian National Longitudinal Survey of Children and Youth (NLSCY) show that although there is a socioeconomic gradient for child vulnerability, more than 70% of young children manifesting serious cognitive, emotional, and behavioral problems do not come from "high-risk" or poor families but rather from two-parent families with adequate income and parental education (Willms, 2002). As an alternative to the high-risk targeted approach, the universal approach, employed in the

BBBF project, has the potential to reach a greater proportion of vulnerable children and have a larger effect on the population as a whole (Offord et al., 1998).

The BBBF project model was unique in that it defined "high-risk" by the characteristics of neighborhoods rather than by characteristics of children or their parents. The neighborhoods selected for project implementation were characterized by socioeconomic disadvantage, but all children in the designated age range living in the neighborhood and their families were eligible for program involvement. Thus, the BBBF project was designed as a universal intervention to improve developmental outcomes in all children and their families living in a high-risk neighborhood environment.

A second limitation of the programs reviewed above is the focus on a limited number of developmental contexts and settings, suggested as important based on Bronfenbrenner's ecological model. The programs focused on children and parents, primarily within the school setting and, to a lesser extent, within the home setting. With the exception of the CPC (Reynolds, 2000), no long-term family or parent outcomes have been investigated, despite the inclusion of home visits or parent training components in all of the programs. The Fast Track, PPP, and MPE programs have focused exclusively on child outcomes, such as cognitive development or disruptive behavior in the short term and high school graduation or criminal activity in the long term. None of the programs aimed to change the neighborhood or the broader social or cultural context that surrounded the children and their families, and none investigated neighborhood or community outcomes (such as parental community involvement or neighborhood satisfaction).

Although there has been little research into the processes by which neighborhood factors affect children's development (Benson, Leffert, Scales, & Blyth, 1998; Connor & Brink, 1999), it is widely held that child and adolescent well-being requires the active engagement of multiple community constituencies and resources (Benson et al., 1998). Accordingly, one of the key aims of the BBBF project was to enhance neighborhood capacity. Project strategies included local resident involvement in all aspects of planning and implementation; the development of partnerships among service providers and between the service providers and local parents and residents; and the creation of voluntary leadership roles along with new participatory structures in the neighborhoods. To quantify the neighborhood/community effects associated with the BBBF project, we assessed a variety of community-related measures when children were in Grades 3, 6, and 9.

Finally, the preventive interventions reviewed above offered few opportunities for local community members to become involved in the development and implementation of the programs. Further, the programs did not appear to be well integrated with other local services or organizations. A

15

lack of community engagement is common among preventive interventions (St. Pierre & Layzer, 1998). In the four studies reviewed above, program development and implementation were carried out by public school boards (CPC and PPP) or university-based clinicians and researchers (Fast Track and MPE), with little or no input from parents or other local residents. For example, although the principal investigators of the Fast Track program acknowledged that community engagement was critical to the long-term success of programs, they were nonetheless "committed to a theoretical model that prespecified the desired change targets, change agents, and change methods" (CPPRG, 2002a, p. 2). Thus, the establishment of collaborative partnerships with schools and families occurred within a highly prescriptive, researcher-led program model. MPE researchers have commented that even if a preventive intervention program is intensive, multimodal, and long term, it can have only a limited protective effect under the conditions of chronic disadvantage (Boisjoli et al., 2007).

Although there is growing interest in the potential value of "community building," particularly in disadvantaged neighborhoods (e.g., Barnes, Katz, Korbin, & O'Brien, 2006; Coie & Jacobs, 1993), there have been very few evaluations of primary prevention programs for children that have examined community-level outcomes. In a review of 526 outcome studies of universal, competence-promotion programs for children, Durlak et al. (2007) found only two studies that examined community-level outcomes, and the outcomes in those two studies were bonding with adults in the community. The lack of attention to community-level outcomes is not surprising given that the vast majority of primary prevention programs for children have been more narrowly focused on child, parent, and family impacts. More recently, however, the potential limitations of narrowly focused programs have been noted, and there has been increased interest in more ecologically focused prevention programs that target the child, parent, and family, as well as formal and informal community organizations and service providing agencies. These programs have been variously called comprehensive community initiatives (Schorr, 1997) and complex multilevel interventions (Hawe, Shiell, & Riley, 2004; Nastasi & Hitchcock, 2009). We are aware of two large-scale prevention programs for young children that have targeted and evaluated community-level outcomes: 1, 2, 3 GO! in Montreal and Sure Start Local Programmes (SSLPs) in England. Both of these programs involve very young children ages birth to 3.

Beginning in 1995, the 1, 2, 3 GO! initiative was implemented in five low-income Montreal communities and in one nearby rural community (Bouchard, 2005). The underlying premise of this initiative was that local-level consortia of partners can collaborate to plan and offer high-quality activities for young children and families that would improve child, parent, and family outcomes. The particular activities and programs chosen depended upon what the community partners saw as most important for their community. Increased participation of parents and children in these activities was hypothesized to lead to enhanced perceptions of community cohesion and collective efficacy, improved social networks, individual self-efficacy and empowerment for parents and improved development and well-being for children. Using a quasi-experimental design, the six 1, 2, 3 GO! communities were compared with six comparison communities that did not have a 1, 2, 3 GO! initiative. Data were collected from parents and front-line workers every 2 years, with four waves of data collection in all.

The researchers (Bouchard, 2005; Cormier, 2005) reported that during the first two waves of data collection, service providers in 1, 2, 3 GO! communities reported a significantly higher level of formalization of partnership activities than did service providers in comparison communities. On the other hand, the development of a shared vision was more likely to occur in comparison communities at the second period of data collection. Perception of service coordination did not change significantly over time for either group, and both groups reported a significantly improved climate in the communities over time. Parent perceptions of the communities were significantly more positive in the comparison communities than in the 1, 2, 3 GO! communities, although this was due in part to the fact that parents in 1, 2, 3 GO! communities experienced significantly more risk factors in their lives.

The other program, SSLP, is a similar initiative that began in the U.K. in 1999, but it has been implemented on a much wider scale than 1, 2, 3 GO! (Belsky, Melhuish, Barnes, Leyland, Romaniuk, & the National Evaluation of Sure Start Research Team, 2006). By 2004, more than 500 SSLPs had been implemented across England. It is similar to 1, 2, 3 GO! in many ways. First, SSLPs are aimed at families of children ages birth to 3 years, who reside in low-income communities. Second, while there is a core of services (e.g., home visitation) that must be offered, each SSLP has considerable autonomy in how services will be delivered and which ones will be emphasized. Third, the participation of parents and service providers in partnerships that oversee the SSLPs is central to this initiative. Fourth, SSLP's theory of change is that enhancing local services for children and families and changing the community will lead to beneficial outcomes on parents and children. Fifth, Sure Start also used a quasi-experimental design to examine the effects of the SSLPs.

The early evaluation of Sure Start compared more than 16,000 children living in SSLP areas with 2,600 children living in comparison areas. Unfortunately, the mothers in the SSLP areas rated their communities more negatively as a place to live and raise children than mothers in the non-SSLP neighborhoods. Overall, the SSLPs were less effective for the highest risk than for the lower risk families (Belsky et al., 2006). A second evaluation was undertaken after the SSLPs became more sharply focused in their activities and targeted the most vulnerable children and families in the communities. In this evaluation, Melhuish, Belsky, Leyland, Barnes, and the National Evaluation of Sure Start Research Team (2008) compared 5,883 children from SSLP areas with 1,879 children selected from the British Millenium Cohort Study who did not reside in SSLP areas, but with similar demographic characteristics to the lower risk families from the SSLP areas. Unfortunately the researchers could not find an adequate sample of high-risk families in the Millenium Cohort Study to match with those in SSLP areas. In this study, mothers in SSLP areas reported significantly higher use of services than mothers in non-SSLP areas but nonsignificant differences in their ratings of their neighborhoods as a place to live and raise children.

Barnes (2007) examined changes in SSLP communities from 2000–2001 to 2004–2005 and reported the following:

> Many changes chronicled suggested that communities were growing in terms of the number or proportion of children, improving in terms of less income deprivation, fewer births to teen-age mothers, fewer young children living in homes dependent on benefits, less property crime and fewer severe behavioral problems in schools, although some indicators also suggested otherwise (for example, more violent crime). While some of these changes were greater than those taking place across England, this was not routinely the case. (pp. 180–181)

As Barnes (2007) suggests, some of the positive changes in the SSLP communities may have resulted more from general societal influences rather than from the SSLP programs. The results from these two programs on community-level outcomes are disappointing. The SSLP study is following the children and families in their research sample longitudinally through school entry, and these results may yield more positive findings regarding community outcomes. Nonetheless, these two studies do underscore the difficulty in demonstrating positive program outcomes on neighborhood or community-level measures. In the BBBF project, the ecological approach required a focus on community-related influences on child development, including influences of formal and informal neighborhood organizations and service providing agencies.

The BBBF project, initiated in 1991 by the Ontario provincial government, was designed to address some of the limitations associated with early childhood prevention programs.

BBBF PROJECT MODEL

This study evaluates the long-term effectiveness of an ecological, community-based, early prevention project. In 1990, the BBBF project was

announced by the Ontario government as "a 25-year longitudinal prevention policy research demonstration project to provide information on the
effectiveness of prevention as a policy for children" (Government of Ontario, 1990). The project was designed to include the following characteristics in the program model.

Ecological and Holistic

In the BBBF project, child development was conceptualized using
Bronfenbrenner's (1979, 1986a, 1986b) ecological model, which recognizes
the many influences on the growing child, starting within the family and
expanding outward to the local neighborhood and broader community.
The BBBF programs addressed a multitude of different areas of children's
functioning, including school readiness and primary school adaptation;
children's physical, social, and cognitive development; and children's mental health. In addition, the family, school, and neighborhood contexts were
targets for change.

Universal

All children in the selected age group (described below) living in the
neighborhood and their families were eligible for program participation,
not just those seen to be at highest risk. In contrast, most prevention programs have targeted a narrow range of children who are exposed to factors
that are deemed to place them at risk for future problems (Waddell et al.,
2007).

Community Driven

The model allowed the project sites considerable freedom and respon-
sibility to tailor programs to local needs, within budget limitations, and the
overall mandate of the project. Residents comprised at least 51% of the
major decision-making bodies and committees of the three BBBF projects
and actively participated in a variety of different roles in these projects,
including project governance, program planning, advocacy and public relations, program delivery (as paid staff and volunteers), and research
development. Thus, parents and neighborhood residents were not only the
targets of change, as they are in other prevention initiatives, but they were
also the agents of change because they were involved in developing, implementing, and sustaining prevention efforts.

Collaborative and Coordinated

The BBBF project sites were to develop partnerships among existing
neighborhood and community organizations that provide services for

19

young children and families and to improve coordination among community-based programs (e.g., sharing resources, equipment, and space).

Conceptual Model

The conceptual model of the BBBF project is presented in Figure 1. There were three major outcome goals of the project, as announced by the Government of Ontario (1990): (a) to reduce the incidence of serious long-term emotional and behavioral problems in children; (b) to promote social, emotional, behavioral, physical, and educational development in children; and (c) to strengthen the ability of disadvantaged communities to respond effectively to the social and economic needs of children and their families.

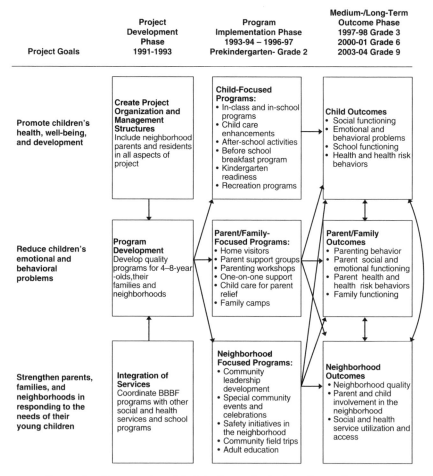

FIGURE 1.—Conceptual model of the Better Beginnings, Better Futures project.

The first phase of the project occurred between 1991 and 1993 when each of the funded project sites were to create organization and management structures, develop quality programs available to all children between 4 and 8 years of age and their families living in the project site, and begin to coordinate these new programs with other existing programs.

The project implementation phase began in 1993, when 4-year-old children entered half-day prekindergarten operated throughout Ontario by the local boards of education. As outlined in Figure 1, the programs were to focus on children ages 4–8, their parents and families, and also their neighborhoods. Based on an ecological model and comprehensive view of child development, programs were implemented in each of the three BBBF sites focusing directly on the children, including in-class, in-school, before- and after-school, and holiday/vacation programs. Also, a variety of programs were implemented to provide support for parents and some for other family members. Finally, a range of programs focusing on the entire neighborhood was implemented, including special events, safety initiatives, and community development activities.

The child-focused programs were designed to facilitate healthy child development and well-being in all areas of children's functioning with the strongest emphasis on social and academic functioning. The parent-focused programs were expected not only to have positive, direct effects on the children's parents, in terms of improved social and emotional functioning and general family functioning, but also to yield positive direct as well as indirect effects on the children themselves, as well as on the community in general as parents developed greater social supports and interest in community activities. Likewise, the programs that were communitywide and focused on all community residents were expected to improve the quality of the neighborhood in terms of greater satisfaction as a place to live and raise children, greater knowledge about and access to existing services, and increased involvement in community activities. As outlined in Figure 1, the BBBF programs were designed to have not only positive outcome effects, both directly and indirectly on children, families, and their neighborhood, but also reciprocal positive effect influences among the three general outcome domains.

It is important to realize that the BBBF project is neither a service nor a program. In reviewing the BBBF project in 2000, Lawrence Schweinhart, from the High/Scope PPP longitudinal study, commented that BBBF was a "meta-program." Given the variety of child, parent/family, and community focused programs in each project site, BBBF can be best viewed as an initiative for mobilizing disadvantaged neighborhoods around early child development and prevention. In practice, some children and families were touched directly by these improved resources (e.g., home visitors, classroom programs, before- and after-school programs, parent support, play groups, safer parks and streets, community participation). Some attended

21

programs on a regular basis, others on a very random or part-time basis. Some did not attend any programs but were touched indirectly, for example, by a neighbor who attended programs and offered advice or support or by safer streets and parks.

Thus, the BBBF programs were expected to have not only direct, positive influences on parents and children through active participation in programs but also multiplier effects due to indirect influences similar to the social contagion effects on obesity, smoking, and more recently on individual happiness described by Christakis and Fowler (Christakis & Fowler, 2007; Fowler & Christakis, 2008). These researchers have examined the influence of social networks in the Framingham Heart Study. They observed that prevention and early intervention programs typically aim to improve well-being by targeting individuals and estimating success in terms of program impact. However, helping one individual may make a difference on a collective level, and the effects of a prevention program may spread through social networks creating a positive impact on individuals who never directly participated in the program. They further suggest that these contagion effects might become an intentional part of a more coherent prevention strategy and in the process enhance efficacy and cost effectiveness (Fowler & Christakis, 2008). Similar effects of the BBBF child, parent/family, and community programs were expected to spread through social networks. This is why child and parent social behavior and social support programs as well as community development activities were so prevalent in the BBBF sites.

THE BBBF PROJECT: OVERVIEW OF MONOGRAPH

BBBF is a universal, ecological, community-based prevention program. This approach holds considerable promise in mobilizing change in multiple settings, promoting healthy child and family development in the long term, and enhancing the abilities of disadvantaged communities to provide for young children and their families.

The developmental ecological perspective underlies all aspects of the BBBF project, including design, implementation, program evaluation, and longitudinal analysis of long-term effects. A strength of this perspective is the ability to view the family, school, and community as "evolving social systems susceptible to significant and novel transformation," rather than "eternally fixed and unalterable" systems (Bronfenbrenner, 1977, p. 528). A key aspect of the research presented in this monograph is that it was designed to allow an analysis of effective microsystem and mesosystem changes. In a review of efforts at social systems change in 526 positive youth development interventions, Durlak et al. (2007) described the BBBF project as "unique in our review as a large-scale community based intervention that used participatory research methods to target all three microsystems: families, schools, and community-based organizations ... and collected information in terms of mesosystemic change" (pp. 276–277).

In the next chapter, we describe the methodology of the BBBF project in detail, including the selection of project sites, range of programs offered in each site, recruitment and maintenance of the research cohort over 11 years, measures collected at each follow-up, and statistical analyses. In Chapters III and IV, we present results related to the microsystematic and mesosystematic changes associated with the BBBF project. The microsystems are the settings surrounding the child, including parents, family, peers, school, and community, whereas the mesosystems are the interconnections among these settings, such as family involvement with the community. Further, we investigate these systematic changes associated with the BBBF project at three distinct developmental periods (Grades 3, 6, and 9). In Chapter III we present the results for measures related to child development in four domains, including social functioning, emotional and behavioral problems, school functioning, and health. We focus on three critical developmental transitions: (a) adjustment to primary school (Grade 3); (b) transition to middle school and pubertal onset (Grade 6); and (c) transfer to high school (Grade 9). In Chapter IV, we present results for parent, family, and community-related measures at the same three time points. In both of these chapters, we also assess mesosystematic change associated with the BBBF project with measures of parent–child relations, family functioning, degree of parent and child community involvement, and parent ratings of neighborhood satisfaction.

In Chapter V, we report on the monetary costs and savings of the BBBF project for the Ontario government, up to the Grade 9 follow-up. Recently, there has been growing interest in determining whether early prevention programs are a wise societal investment and whether resources invested in implementing prevention programs for young children and their families will return monetary benefits to society that exceed the value of their original investment (Aos et al., 2004; Coffey, 2003; Heckman, 2006; Karoly et al., 2005). To date, however, few preventive interventions in the United States, and none in Canada, have reported such economic analyses, partly because the outcomes that demonstrate economic dividends often do not begin to occur until mid- to late adolescence or beyond. In the final chapter of the monograph, we discuss the broader relevance and implications of our findings for both prevention research and public policy.

II. PROJECT DESCRIPTION AND RESEARCH METHODOLOGY

In this chapter we describe the selection of the three Better Beginnings, Better Futures (BBBF) project sites/neighborhoods and the range of programs offered; recruitment and maintenance of the longitudinal sample over 11 years; outcome measures used to investigate program impact; and statistical analyses used to address the major research questions.

BBBF PROJECT SITES

Three communities were funded by the Ontario government to develop a local prevention project that would (a) reduce emotional and behavioral problems and promote the healthy development of young children; (b) strengthen parents, families, and the neighborhood in responding to the needs of their children; (c) develop a local organization to provide programs for children from 4 to 8 years of age and their families that respond effectively to local needs; (d) encourage neighborhood parents and other citizens to participate as equal partners with service providers in developing and carrying out programs; and (e) establish partnerships with existing and new service providers and schools and to coordinate programs with these partners.

The lower age limit of 4 years was chosen because it is at this age when children in Ontario enter Junior Kindergarten (JK), a free 1-year, half-day prekindergarten program for all 4-year-olds. The JK year is followed by a half-day Senior Kindergarten year (SK) for 5-year-olds, then full-day learning in Grade 1 for 6-year-olds and Grade 2 for 7-year-olds. Thus, BBBF programs were offered for the 4 years between JK and Grade 2.

The project was developed in response to the Ontario government's release of a Request for Proposals in the spring of 1990. The first step in the process of application to the BBBF project was designed to ensure that potential program sponsors had a minimal level of integration already in place and were prepared to implement the local project in a low-income,

24

high-risk community. Applicants needed to demonstrate that their neighborhood was very economically disadvantaged and that there was very high risk for poor child development. Economic disadvantage was defined in terms of unemployment, high numbers of families below the poverty line, high numbers of children in families on social assistance, and high numbers of children living in subsidized housing. Indicators of risk for poor child development included factors such as low birth weight, infant mortality, single parenthood, teen pregnancy, low maternal education, high school drop-out rates, and immigration. Proposal development grants of approximately $5,000 were awarded to 55 initial applicant communities to offset expenses incurred in gathering information and obtaining expertise, administrative support, and community involvement. The second step was the submission of a full proposal, describing the local model and community plans for meaningful, significant involvement of community residents, integration of services, and high-quality programming. Forty-eight proposals were submitted in July 1990 and reviewed by a 15-member Proposal Review Panel that had expertise in implementing health, education, and social service programs in economically disadvantaged communities. Three members of the review panel met in person with the local groups that submitted the top 20 proposals; following these site visits, final selections were made (see Cameron, Pancer, McKenzie-Mohr, & Cooper, 1993, for more details on this process). The three selected communities that focused programming on children 4–8 years old were announced on January 29, 1991, and the Ontario government launched a 25-year longitudinal, prevention research initiative, the BBBF project. The review panel also chose four communities to implement another version of the BBBF project for children ages 0–4 years old (see Peters et al., 2000, technical report for more details about this model).

The three socioeconomically disadvantaged sites that provided programs for children and their parents, families, and communities were located in Cornwall (Eastern Ontario), Highfield (Greater Toronto Area), and Sudbury (Northern Ontario). The Cornwall site included four Francophone primary schools, the Highfield site focused on the Highfield Junior School neighborhood, and the Sudbury site focused on two downtown neighborhoods. All three project sites experienced socioeconomic disadvantage. For example, among those interviewed at the sites before programs were in place, 36% of families were headed by a single parent and 64% of the families reported annual income below the Statistics Canada Low Income Cut Off level, widely treated as Canada's poverty line. However, all children 4–8 years old and their families living in the geographically defined project neighborhoods were considered as potential project participants, regardless of the socioeconomic characteristics or structure of the family.

Although the three sites all demonstrated significant levels of socioeconomic disadvantage, they differed from one another in terms of language

25

and culture. The Cornwall site consisted mostly of Franco-Ontarians, in a city with an Anglophone majority and much intermarriage between Francophones and Anglophones. The Sudbury site included one traditionally French-speaking and one English-speaking neighborhood and served a mix of Anglophone, Francophone, Native, and multicultural families. At the Highfield site, 88% of parents who participated in the research were born outside Canada, with the two largest places of origin from India and the Caribbean. Those participating in the Highfield programs came from many different countries and language groups. It has been estimated that more than 40 different languages are spoken in the homes of children living in the Highfield neighborhood, making it one of the most multicultural communities in the country.

Program Descriptions for the Three Sites

Each local BBBF project site was mandated to develop a set of high-quality programs that were appropriate for the unique needs and character of its community. Programs were based on the key principles of the project model; that is, they were to be ecological, universal, community driven, and collaborative. The programs that were offered can be placed into three different categories—child focused, parent/family focused, and community focused. Each site provided several programs, with an average of 20 different programs implemented in each site (see Appendix A for a description of all the programs offered at each of the sites during the period in which the research cohort was in JK to Grade 2 (i.e., 1993–1994 to 1996–1997).

Many of the programs were offered at all three sites, though variations in the nature of these programs occurred from site to site. Table 2 provides a list of programs common to the three sites. All three BBBF sites operated child-focused group programs that emphasized social skills and positive social interaction with peers and adults, problem-solving and learning experiences, and recreation programs. All sites offered breakfast programs, toy lending, and crafts programs. With the exception of the *Lion's Quest Skills for Growing Program* (Quest International, 1990) in the Highfield site, none of these programs was highly structured or manualized; none had a fixed curriculum or a specified number of sessions. Child programs were run by BBBF professional staff members who were predominantly child- and youth-care workers or community volunteers. Parent-focused programs were also offered in all three sites. Home visiting by BBBF staff provided emotional and social support to parents as well as information concerning child development and community resources. Each site also offered parent programs that provided opportunities for discussions of parenting problems, improving parent skills, and socializing and planning family activities. A variety of family- and neighborhood-focused programs were offered in

26

TABLE 2

BETTER BEGINNINGS, BETTER FUTURES PROGRAMS COMMON TO THE THREE SITES

Program Type	Program Description
Child-focused	In-class and in-school programs
	Child care enhancements
	Before and after-school activities
	School "breakfast club"
	Recreation programs
Parent-focused	Home visitors
	Parent support groups
	Parenting workshops
	One-on-one support
	Child care for parent relief
Family- and community-focused	Community leadership development
	Special community events and celebrations
	Safety initiatives in the neighborhood
	Community field trips
	Adult education
	Family camps
	Outreach to families

each site, including active community outreach, social activities, environmental programs, economic development initiatives, and cultural celebrations.

The BBBF programming had two unique features compared with other large-scale prevention initiatives: comprehensive programming and matching programs to community needs. Rather than focusing solely on the child in school or on parenting or community development, programs were provided at all ecological levels—the individual, family, school, and community. Programs were customized to fit the needs and desires of the communities in which they were provided. For example, Sudbury, the community with the highest levels of unemployment and lowest family income, focused some of its programming in the community development area establishing programs, such as Grassroots Economic Opportunities Development and Evaluation to provide economic development opportunities to community residents. It is important to note, however, that this study was designed to evaluate the effects of a universal, community-based intervention strategy, as exemplified by the nature of the competition to become a BBBF site, not of specific program components.

Project Staffing and Budget

In Table 3, we provide information on the number of staff at the three sites. The number of staff ranged from 17 at Highfield to 26 in Cornwall.

27

TABLE 3

NUMBER AND TYPES OF STAFF AT THE THREE BETTER BEGINNINGS, BETTER FUTURES SITES

	Site		
	Cornwall	Highfield	Sudbury
Total number of staff	26 (8 residents)	17 (11 residents)	24 (18 residents)
Number of project coordinators	1	1	1 (resident)
Number of other managers	4 (1 resident)	3	1
Number of front-line staff	21 (7 residents)	13 (11 residents)	22 (17 residents)

Many of these positions were part-time or contract for a limited time period. Community residents constituted the majority of staff at Highfield and at Sudbury but not at Cornwall.

Because each site was able to develop programs to best meet local needs, there were differences in the programs offered and in the balance of programs focused on children and families, parents, schools, and communities. In Table 4, we provide direct government costs (in Canadian dollars) for the three BBBF sites for the years 1995/1996 and 1996/1997; the BBBF

TABLE 4

DIRECT GOVERNMENT COST FOR THREE SITES (IN CANADIAN DOLLARS), BY PROGRAM AND YEAR, ONTARIO BETTER BEGINNINGS, BETTER FUTURES (BBBF)

	Program			
Site and Year	Child-Focused	Family/Parent-Focused	Community Development	Total
Cornwall				
1995/1996	$297,926	$86,564	$191,953	$576,443
1996/1997	384,527	92,327	104,084	580,938
Total	682,453 (59%)	178,891 (15%)	296,037 (26%)	1,157,381
Highfield				
1995/1996	200,761	165,520	143,711	509,992
1996/1997	186,292	175,669	150,205	512,166
Total	387,053 (38%)	341,189 (33%)	293,916 (29%)	1,022,158
Sudbury				
1995/1996	439,808	105,631	94,748	640,187
1996/1997	419,109	125,009	113,824	657,942
Total	858,917 (66%)	230,640 (18%)	208,572 (16%)	1,298,129
All sites				
1995/1996	938,495	357,715	430,412	1,726,622
1996/1997	989,928	393,005	368,113	1,751,046
Total	1,928,423 (55%)	750,720 (22%)	798,525 (23%)	3,477,668
			Average cost/site	$579,611

Note.—Direct government costs were based on audited financial statements from each of the three BBBF project sites.

28

programs funded directly by the Ontario government were implemented and operated under three major categories: child focused, family/parent focused, and community development. As shown in Table 4, just over $1.7 million was spent on these programs by the three sites combined each year. The average annual budget for each of the three sites was approximately $580,000, with Highfield having the smallest budget ($512,166 in 1996/1997) and Sudbury having the largest budget ($657,942 in 1996/1997). The site budgets were determined based on the number of children served in the area and services already existing in the neighborhood/community. The Sudbury BBBF site received more government funding than the other two BBBF sites because the site had fewer existing services in the neighborhoods or schools. Resources were most heavily focused on child programs: child focused (55%), community development (23%), and family/parent focused (22%). Cornwall invested the majority of its resources into in-school programs and other child-focused programs (59%); considerably less of the budget (15%) was allocated to family/parent-focused programs, while community development–focused activities received 26% of the budget. Highfield had the most equally divided budget of the three sites, reflecting its commitment to a balance of in-school programs for children, parent and family support, and community development. Nearly 66% of Sudbury's budget was spent on child-focused programs, such as before- and after-school and holiday programs; 18% of the Sudbury's budget was allocated to family/parent-focused programs and 16% to community development.

The following is a more detailed description of the programming at each of the sites.

Cornwall

In Cornwall, BBBF programming focused on four Francophone schools, of which two were operated by the Catholic Separate School Board and two were operated by the Public School Board. Children were transported to the latter two schools from all over the city because they are the only Francophone schools operated by the Public School Board. Owing to transportation of students, the Cornwall BBBF site worked within less sharply defined boundaries than the Highfield and Sudbury sites did. The large geographical area and population (approximately 29,000 in 1996) of the Cornwall BBBF site was not problematic because the site's major programs were school based and focused on four Francophone schools.

As shown in Table 4, child-focused programs accounted for 59% of Cornwall's annual budget. Each of the four schools had a full-time educational assistant who helped the teachers of children in JK through to Grade 2 to provide activities designed to improve children's thinking and learning skills, promote social skills, reduce behavioral problems, and build French language skills and cultural identity. The educational assistants, hired by the Cornwall BBBF site, spent a half to 1 full day per week in each classroom. All children in the class were involved, although additional time was spent with children who, in the view of the assistant, required more attention. A school breakfast program was provided every morning for children from JK to Grade 2.

Two home visitors conducted family visits to provide support and give information about child development and community services and resources. This site started a toy-lending library to make toys and other educational and fun resource materials available to parents for a nominal fee. The Cornwall site also offered a family vacation camp experience to families during the summer and school breaks, a summer tutoring program, and homework help service for children and families.

Highfield

The Highfield Community Enrichment Project was focused on the Highfield Junior School in the City of Toronto. The surrounding neighborhood is densely populated and very diverse. In 1996, when the longitudinal research cohort was involved in BBBF programs, there were about 8,500 residents, many of whom were recent immigrants (60% were born outside Canada) from a variety of cultures. The 1996 Census identified nine major languages including English, Arabic, Chinese, Hindi, Italian, Polish, Punjabi, Spanish, and Urdu. Also, as mentioned earlier, more than 40 different languages were spoken in the homes of families participating in the BBBF longitudinal research from this site.

Unlike the Cornwall and Sudbury sites that each contained four primary schools, the Highfield site was able to concentrate its resources in a large, single school catchment area. This site adopted a unique approach to programming during the period in which the longitudinal research cohort was in JK to Grade 2 (1993–1997), wherein considerable effort and resources were concentrated on this cohort of children and their parents (i.e., those children born in 1989 and entering JK in 1993). These children and their families were the focus of more frequent, intensive, and wide-ranging attention than families at the other two sites. The educational assistants provided continuous individual and group support to children in the longitudinal cohort from JK to Grade 2. They lowered the adult-to-student ratio in the classroom to about 1:10; provided assistance with language, social, and self-help skill; and offered summer activities. The assistants also visited families in their homes before the children started JK. Other children who attended Highfield Junior School also benefited from the BBBF project; for example, the *Lion's Quest Skills for Growing* social skills program (Quest International, 1990) was introduced in all primary grades. Additionally, there was a focus on health and nutrition programming. Initially, a free snack program was implemented three times a week; later, a twice-weekly breakfast and hot lunch program was added.

Family support and community programs strengthened the links between the school and the families and between the families and their community. Enrichment workers visited parents in their homes, provided them with information about programs, and encouraged them to get involved in their children's school and to attend community activities. In addition to home visiting, family support services included a family drop-in for parents with children up to age 4, playgroups for children in JK, a toy-lending library, activities for children outside school hours and during holidays, parent peer-support groups, and child care for parent relief. These programs were designed to help reduce the isolation of parents and promote self-esteem and personal growth.

Sudbury

This site included the two downtown neighborhoods of Donovan to the west and le Moulin à Fleur (The Flour Mill) to the east, with a combined population in 1996 of approximately 13,800. Until 1997, there were four Anglophone and two Francophone schools serving this area. Owing to school closures, there are now three Anglophone schools and one Francophone school in this area. In contrast to the Cornwall and Highfield sites, the Sudbury project did not originate within the school system. Project staff and families in Sudbury were very interested in community development and came together under the aegis of the Native Friendship Centre. The evolution of the project progressed toward greater community ownership, broader community development efforts, and the securing of additional funds for programs and activities that fell outside the BBBF mandate. Program staff were hired to work with Aboriginal, Anglophone, Francophone, and multicultural populations at the site.

The Sudbury site focused the highest percentage of its budget resources on child-focused programs (66%). The in-school programs included peaceful playground and Native cultural and multicultural programs. The peaceful playground program focused on the prevention of bullying and aggressive behavior and was implemented by part-time BBBF staff members during school hours. The Native cultural program, facilitated by a full-time BBBF Native community worker, focused on teaching Native children traditional stories and crafts. The multicultural program, operated informally by a part-time BBBF staff person, focused on teaching children positive aspects of other cultures. The before- and after-school and holiday programs included a breakfast and games program, after-school activities (such as crafts, games, and reading activities) held in locations off school grounds, and summer recreation programs. These three programs promoted problem solving and conflict resolution. Other programs included a Francophone mom and toddler drop-in center, a family visiting and support program, and a weekly meeting for parents to discuss parenting problems and solutions and organize community events.

Community Development and Resident Participation

All of the three sites had an emphasis on both prevention programs for children and families and community development to change the larger neighborhood context. At the Cornwall site, there was an evolution toward greater partnerships with other organizations and efforts were made to provide programming initiatives that fell outside of the BBBF mandate. For example, the Cornwall site created the incorporated Community Action Group that helped to develop prevention initiatives beyond the BBBF mandate (e.g., a youth center for teens, a municipal skate park for teens, development of a disposal of toxic waste education program). The Cornwall site was also active in the community in promoting French language and culture and increasing awareness of child development issues. Initiatives included conferences on prevention issues, National Child Day activities, and monthly breakfast discussions for local agencies.

At Highfield, community development emphasized activities and events that increased resident participation and built community leadership, provided opportunities for residents to get to know each other, increased neighborhood safety, and promoted respect for ethnocultural diversity. A variety of cultural celebrations were held at the Highfield site, and there was an emphasis on helping parents to learn English as a second language.

The focus on community development processes in creating the project organization and programming and working with the neighborhood was very strong at the Sudbury site. Community kitchens, community gardens, community economic development, environmental enhancement, as well as other community initiatives all reflected the strong community development orientation at this site. Building better relationships among the Francophone, Anglophone, and First Nations members of the community was another priority at the Sudbury site.

Central to each of the sites was an emphasis on resident participation. Residents participated in a variety of ways at each of the sites: in project governance (e.g., sitting on the projects' Steering Committees and other committees); in program planning, advocacy, and public relations (e.g., speaking at different events); in program delivery (e.g., child care, parent groups); as paid

32

staff; and in research (e.g., on research committees and as research assistants). Resident participation led to positive outcomes for the residents, the programs, the projects, and the communities (Pancer & Cameron, 1994).

Each of the three sites experienced barriers to resident participation. There were both individual barriers (e.g., lack of awareness of the project, language and culture, financial barriers, child care, and work overload) and structural barriers (e.g., formality of meetings, too many intimidating professionals, school resistance). Strategies that the sites used to overcome these barriers included the following: offering community outreach to inform people about the projects, providing translation services, providing child care and financial honoraria for participation, hiring staff from different cultural backgrounds, providing residents with many ways for residents to participate, developing a climate of informality that often included food, recognizing volunteers, maintaining 51% resident participation on all committees, providing training to residents in how to chair meetings and other leadership activities, and developing partnerships with the schools (Nelson, Pancer, Hayward, & Kelly, 2004).

Program Exposure and Participation Rates

Although program activities offered varied depending on a local community's decisions, there were three indicators across all sites that provided information about the amount of exposure children and families had to BBBF programs (see Table 5). The first indicator is the number of months a child lived in a BBBF site during the 4 years (from JK to Grade 2, 1993–1997) that the BBBF programs were offered. By the end of the target period of BBBF program delivery, in Cornwall, 96% of the longitudinal

TABLE 5

BETTER BEGINNINGS, BETTER FUTURES (BBBF) PROGRAM PARTICIPATION OF THE
LONGITUDINAL RESEARCH SAMPLE

	Cornwall	Sudbury	Highfield
Percentage of research children who lived in a BBBF site for at least 3 of the 4 years of programming	96	53	72
Percentage of research children who participated 80 times or more in BBBF programs between JK and Grade 2 as rated by BBBF program staff	97	55	100
Percentage of research parents who participated 40 times or more in BBBF programs when their children were in JK to Grade 2 as rated by BBBF program staff	15	16	62

Note.—JK = Junior Kindergarten.

research sample of children had lived there for at least 3 of the 4 years; in comparison, only 53% of Sudbury's sample of research children had lived there for at least 3 years and in Highfield, 72% had. The BBBF program staff were asked to indicate how involved each of the research families and children were with BBBF programs over the 4 years using a range of fewer than 20 times to more than 80 times. Ninety-seven percent of the research children in Cornwall and 100% of the research children in Highfield participated in BBBF programs 80 times or more over the 5-year period compared with 55% of the research children in Sudbury. A higher percentage of parents in Highfield participated in BBBF programs 40 times or more over the 4 years; in Highfield 62% of the parents participated in programs 40 times or more versus 15% of parents in Cornwall and 16% of parents in Sudbury.

Program Implementation Challenges

In a qualitative study of the BBBF programs, we examined challenges in implementing the programs at the sites (Pancer, Cornfield, & Amio, 1999). First, there was the challenge of limited time, space, and resources. Though the sites were given 2 years to develop a broad range of high-quality programs, a number of other tasks (e.g., engaging residents in the process, hiring and training staff, developing an organizational infrastructure, working with community partners) had to be undertaken within this 2-year period. All of the sites experienced considerable pressure and stress to get the programs launched. As well, some sites had difficulty finding enough space to operate the programs. For example, the vice-principal of a school in one of the sites lost his office because it was needed to accommodate a school snack program, and the space previously used was too small for the snack preparation. Many of the programs experienced rapid growth as they attempted to meet the needs of the community. As programs grew, they attracted more participants, stretching staff resources.

A second challenge was learning how to work with a variety of people from different backgrounds. The BBBF project sites hired many staff members from the local community. While these people brought many valuable skills from their life experiences, many did not have experience in planning programs. This lack of experience meant that the projects had to provide considerable support and training to new staff. Individual staff also had different working styles, with some wanting to develop detailed program plans and procedures before beginning the programs, and others wanting to start programs with minimal structure to allow programs to develop in a manner that was more flexible and responsive to participant input.

Ethnocultural diversity in the BBBF communities was a third challenge. Many of the participants in each of the three communities spoke a first language other than English. Thus, staff needed to be hired who spoke the different languages that were used in the communities. But not all language groups could be accommodated because of the limited number of staff. There were also cultural differences that needed to be taken into consideration when programs were implemented. Finally, racial, ethnic, and national groups with a history of mistrust and conflict often lived within the same community, making it difficult to attract members of all backgrounds.

A fourth challenge was related to issues of resident participation. Many residents had not previously participated in program development and governance and consequently reported feeling intimidated working with professionals. As a result, a considerable amount of work needed to be done to establish trust among residents and to make them feel comfortable contributing their ideas for programs. Political issues were a fifth challenge. Funding for BBBF was provided for a 5-year demonstration project. Near the end of the funding period, staff and residents at each of the three sites were quite anxious about the impending loss of funding and devoted considerable time and effort to the development of plans for alternative funding. Permanent funding for each of the sites was eventually obtained but not before the sites spent time planning alternative scenarios, with staff worried about losing their jobs and community residents anxious about losing their project and programs. Provincial policy decisions to cut benefits to people on social assistance and a teacher strike also occurred during the demonstration phase, and both of these events created a challenge for programming.

Each of the sites also experienced challenges working with existing community agencies, which was a sixth challenge. Other new program initiatives were introduced by the provincial and federal governments during the demonstration phase. Therefore, programs needed to be coordinated with existing BBBF programs. As well, BBBF sites were sponsored by host organizations (e.g., school board, children's mental health), which meant that program policies and procedures needed to be harmonized with those of the sponsor agency. A difference in philosophy and operating procedures between BBBF projects and sponsor agencies was an ongoing challenge.

The final challenge stemmed from the low-income communities themselves. Residents living in poverty, often without reliable transportation or child care and sometimes experiencing violence in their families, had a difficult time using programs because of so many competing stressors in their lives. The programs had to find ways to reduce the barriers for the participation of these low-income residents.

RESEARCH COORDINATION UNIT (RCU)

An independent RCU was selected by competition in 1990 to carry out the evaluation of the BBBF project. Seven Canadian universities were part

35

of this consortium, led by Queen's University. Owing to the ecological nature of the BBBF project, a research team with interdisciplinary expertise in psychology, education, sociology, social work, criminal justice, and applied nutrition was formed.

Objectives for the short-term research period (1991–1998) were to determine how effective a reasonably financed and community-supported project can be in the short term, document the costs of the project, and investigate process and organizational issues associated with implementation of the project in each site. The focus of this monograph, however, is the longitudinal follow-up phase from 1998 onward, when children were in Grade 3 (typically age 8 years), Grade 6 (11 years), and Grade 9 (14 years). The key objectives of this study were to investigate (a) the medium- and long-term effects of participation on children's social, emotional, behavioral, cognitive, and physical development; (b) the medium- and long-term effects on parent health, parenting behaviors, family functioning, and community involvement; and (c) the economic benefits of the project up to Grade 9.

METHOD

Sample

BBBF Cohort

As depicted in Figure 2, the BBBF longitudinal research cohort consisted of a *focal* cohort and a *following* cohort. Children in the focal cohort ($n = 363$) were born in 1989 and were recruited into the longitudinal study between JK and Grade 3. To ensure adequate sample size for long-term analyses, an additional cohort of children (*following* cohort; $n = 238$) was added later. Children in the following cohort were born in 1990 and were recruited into the longitudinal study when they were in Grade 3. Children in the focal and following cohorts were eligible for BBBF programming between JK (age 4 years) and Grade 2 (age 8 years). We tested each outcome variable at Grades 3, 6, and 9 for statistical differences between focal and following cohorts. Data from both cohorts were combined for analyses reported in this monograph due to the absence of statistically significant differences between focal and following cohorts.

Comparison Site Cohort

Because the three BBBF sites were chosen by competition, comparison sites could be selected only after the demonstration sites had been

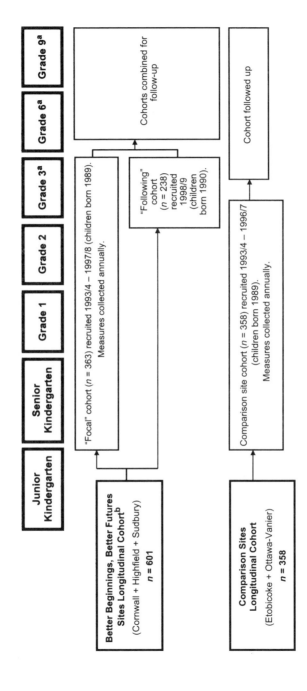

FIGURE 2. — Recruitment of longitudinal cohort. [a]Outcome measures collected at the end of Grades 3, 6, and 9 are reported in this mono-graph; [b]Children recruited to the Better Beginnings, Better Futures (BBBF) cohort (focal and following) received BBBF programming between Junior Kindergarten and Grade 2, whereas children recruited to the comparison cohort did not receive BBBF programming.

announced. The comparison site research cohort ($n = 358$) consisted of children born in 1989 and their families who were recruited from one of two sociodemographically matched comparison site neighborhoods between JK and Grade 2 (1993–1997). The inclusion of two comparison sites (Ottawa-Vanier and Etobicoke) provided an estimation of the changes among children and families who did not receive BBBF programming yet lived under broadly similar societal conditions. The Ottawa-Vanier site served as the comparison for the BBBF sites in Cornwall and Sudbury; the Etobicoke site served as the comparison for the Highfield BBBF site.

The selection of the Ottawa-Vanier and Etobicoke sites was the result of a multistage process to identify the most desirable potential comparison sites. Recognizing the distinctiveness of the three BBBF sites, the RCU took a systematic approach to identifying comparison sites. Initially, data for all Census Metropolitan Areas and Census Agglomerations in Ontario were examined with the intent of identifying Census Tracts or Enumerator's Areas (EAs) that met a set of basic eligibility criteria: their median incomes must fall below the provincial median, at least 20% of households with children must be led by a single parent, and adjacent tracts (or EAs) must contain an average of 100 children per birth year in the age range from 5 to 9. For areas meeting these basic criteria, it was necessary to check the proportion born outside Canada and the proportion speaking English and French at home to see if there was a rough match to one of the BBBF sites.

At this point, data were needed beyond what the census could provide; for example, the Highfield BBBF was an immigrant reception area, whose cultural composition can sometimes change significantly in a few years as new refugee groups arrive or as members of an earlier group, having established themselves, move elsewhere. Interviews were held with school personnel, public health staff, and other service providers to try to clarify the current cultural mix at each site. For sites not yet eliminated, further interviews were held with municipal planners (who were likely to know about rezonings or signs of redevelopments to come), community information center staff, public health nurses who worked in the area, and others likely to know of unusual aspects of the community service system. After these interviews were completed, two members of the RCU visited each site still being considered to see if there were hints of beginning gentrification not detectable by other means. As the set of potential sites was being developed, the BBBF sites were informed of progress and asked for their reactions to the sites being proposed; no preferred alternatives were suggested and all agreed that the proposed comparisons were reasonable. As a final step, in order to check for initial site differences between the three BBBF sites and the two potential comparison sites, the RCU gathered Grade 2 teacher ratings on several scales of behavioral problems and social skills. If scores on these scales had been very different, they would have suggested that child development at the various

TABLE 6

KEY SITE CHARACTERISTICS BASED ON CANADIAN CENSUS DATA 1991

Site	Percentage of Single Parent Families	Mean Family Income ($)
Cornwall	16.8	44,778
Sudbury	26.6	36,191
Ottawa-Vanier comparison	22.4	41,417
Highfield	22.8	43,841
Etobicoke comparison	23.1	48,938

sites was following different courses. Fortunately, neither of the comparison sites needed to be rejected at this final stage.

Through this multistep search process, sites in the former borough of Etobicoke (now in the enlarged city of Toronto), and in the town of Vanier, with adjacent areas of Ottawa, were chosen. Had workable sites been more plentiful, and funding less restricted, it would have been helpful to have more than one comparison site for each BBBF site. However, for most sites it proved difficult to find two workable alternatives, and funding did not allow us to pursue the option. Using data from the 1991 Canadian Census, the three BBBF sites and their comparison sites are compared on two key demographic variables, mean family income and percentage of single parents (see Table 6).

According to Statistics Canada Census data, approximately 22% of the Ottawa-Vanier sample was led by a single parent compared with approximately 17% in Cornwall and 27% in Sudbury; the mean family income in Ottawa-Vanier was $41,417 compared with $44,778 in Cornwall and $36,191 in Sudbury. Therefore, on both variables Ottawa-Vanier lies between Cornwall and Sudbury. Both the comparison site in Etobicoke and the project site in Highfield had approximately 23% of families led by a single parent; the mean family income in Etobicoke was $48,938 compared with $43,841 in Highfield. Because point-by-point precision matching of sites was impossible, it was important to use covariates to control for observable site differences (see the description later in this chapter for further details on the covariates used in all analyses).

Sample Recruitment

The longitudinal samples at the BBBF sites and comparison sites were recruited largely through the school system. Some parents were asked to participate through personal contacts, for example, at parent-teacher information nights. However, most of the parents were reached through recruitment letters sent home with their children. Each letter was accompanied by documents explaining the research. A parent who was willing to participate in the study returned a consent form to the school with the child. When a consent form was not returned, it was not known whether the parent had not received the letter or had received the letter but did not want to participate; therefore, the reasons for nonparticipation cannot be described. The RCU continued to recruit families up to Grade 3, to maintain sample size and to ensure that families that might have been missed before were brought into the sample if possible. Comparisons have been done between those recruited at JK and those recruited later, between those recruited up to SK and those recruited later, and between those recruited up to Grade 1 and those recruited later. The variables used in comparison included gender of respondent and child, respondent's year of birth, number of siblings, number of parents at home, years in the neighborhood, respondent's education, family income, food and housing costs, residence in public housing, respondent's labor force status, partner's labor force status (if applicable), and cultural group. Altogether, 20 variables were tested, on three occasions, with only one difference significant at $p < .05$. In the absence of differences between the focal and following cohorts, all members of the longitudinal cohort were analyzed together for this report, regardless of when they were recruited into the sample.

Participation levels were compared with the estimated number of eligible children. Annual principal's reports provided the number of children enrolled for each school in the study area; based on these data, we determined that the longitudinal research cohort represented 50%–60% of the entire birth cohort of children in their neighborhood. Potential sample bias was assessed by obtaining teachers' ratings for behavioral problems and social skills of all children in their classrooms, then comparing ratings for children in the research sample and those outside it. Comparisons were made using four behavior problems scales and three social skills ratings scales. These analyses were carried out for each year of data collection from 1993–1994 to 1997–1998. No significant differences in teacher ratings of behavioral problems or social skills were found, indicating that the research sample was representative of the entire population of children in the birth cohort for each site.

Attrition

We considered attrition to have occurred when no data were gathered from a family in a particular data collection period (see Table 7). At Grade 9 after 11 years of data collection, 280 of the 959 (29.2%) families did not participate; there was significantly more attrition in the two comparison sites (35%) versus the three BBBF sites (26%; $p < .01$). As a test for attrition bias, we employed logistic regression to examine sociodemographic differences in children and families ("cases") who dropped out of the research cohort between Grades 3 and 6 and between Grades 6 and 9, and families

TABLE 7

ORIGINAL SAMPLE SIZE AND ATTRITION UP TO GRADE 9 IN THE BETTER BEGINNINGS, BETTER FUTURES (BBBF) PROJECT

	BBBF Sites[a] n (%)	Comparison Sites[b] n (%)	Total n (%)
Focal cohort families recruited between JK and Grade 2	363	358	721
Cornwall	85	—	85
Sudbury	147	—	147
Highfield	131	—	131
Etobicoke comparison	—	132	132
Ottawa-Vanier comparison	—	226	226
Following cohort families recruited in Grade 3	238	0	238
Cornwall	67	—	67
Sudbury	76	—	76
Highfield	95	—	95
Total original longitudinal cohort	601[c]	358	959
Cornwall	152	—	152
Sudbury	223	—	223
Highfield	226	—	226
Etobicoke comparison	—	132	132
Ottawa-Vanier comparison	—	226	226
Families participating in follow-up			
Grade 3	529 (88)	316 (88)	845 (88)
Cornwall	135 (89)	—	135 (89)
Sudbury	209 (94)	—	209 (94)
Highfield	185 (82)	—	185 (82)
Etobicoke comparison	—	117 (89)	117 (89)
Ottawa-Vanier comparison	—	199 (88)	199 (88)
Grade 6	488 (81)	269 (75)	757 (79)
Cornwall	135 (89)	—	135 (89)
Sudbury	163 (73)	—	163 (73)
Highfield	190 (84)	—	190 (84)
Etobicoke comparison	—	110 (83)	110 (83)
Ottawa-Vanier comparison	—	159 (70)	159 (70)
Grade 9	447 (74)	232 (65)	679 (71)
Cornwall	113 (74)	—	113 (74)
Sudbury	175 (78)	—	175 (78)
Highfield	159 (70)	—	159 (70)
Etobicoke comparison	—	103 (78)	103 (78)
Ottawa-Vanier comparison	—	129 (57)	129 (57)
Reasons for attrition at Grade 9			
Unable to locate	70 (12)	92 (25.4)	161 (17)
Declined to participate	84 (14)	33 (9)	117 (12)
Child death	0 (0)	2 (.6)	2 (.2)
Total attrition up to Grade 9[d]	154 (26)	126 (35)	280 (29)

Note.—JK = Junior Kindergarten.
[a]Children and their families who participated in BBBF programs between 1993/1994 and 1997/1998.
[b]Children and their families who did not receive BBBF programming.
[c]BBBF cohort consisted of *focal* and *following* cohorts (see Figure 2 for details).
[d]The difference in attrition between BBBF and comparison groups is statistically significant ($p < .01$).

("cases") who completed all years of data collection. These analyses indicated no significant differences in sociodemographic variables between the retained and lost cases. That is, the characteristics of the longitudinal cohort remained similar despite attrition of 105 families between Grades 3 and 6, and 79 families between Grades 6 and 9 (results of the Grades 6–9 regression analyses are included in Appendix B).

The overall drop-out rate of 29% in this study compares favorably to the drop-out rate in the corresponding wave of data from Statistics Canada's National Longitudinal Survey of Children and Youth (NLSCY; Statistics Canada, 2005), which studied children of a similar age to the BBBF cohort. The total NLSCY cohort included 16,903 families in the first wave of data collection. After 10 years (six waves) of data collection, the attrition was 33.9%; that is, 5,730 families did not participate in that wave.

Retention of families in the BBBF research also compares favorably to other longitudinal studies. For example, the Chicago Child–Parent Centers program reported an overall attrition of 29.5% at age 15 (Reynolds, 2000), and the Fast Track project had a 20.4% attrition rate at Grade 9 (Conduct Problems Prevention Research Group, 2007). Further, a meta-analysis of 34 preschool prevention programs indicated that over half of the programs had an attrition rate of >20% at the first follow-up (Nelson et al., 2003). Capaldi and Patterson (1987) reviewed major American longitudinal studies with follow-up periods of 4 to 10 years; the average attrition rate was 47%.

Design

Owing to the process adopted by the government for selecting project communities, a randomized controlled trial design was not feasible. Thus, a quasi-experimental longitudinal comparison site design was developed, wherein cohorts of children and their families were recruited in three project sites and two sociodemographically matched comparison neighborhoods. Longitudinal follow-up analyses contrasted outcomes from Grades 3, 6, and 9 children and their families from the BBBF sites relative to children and their families in the comparison sites. Quasi-experimental approaches are common in applied research (Cook & Campbell, 1977; Reynolds & Temple, 1995), particularly when testing ecological or community-level models (Black & Krishnakumar, 1998).

Measures

A range of measures was collected from the entire research cohort in Grade 3 (1997/1998), Grade 6 (2000/2001), and Grade 9 (2003/2004) to examine the longitudinal outcomes in children and their families from the BBBF sites compared with those among research participants in the comparison sites. In accordance with the developmental ecological approach, we collected research information on many different aspects of developmental

42

TABLE 8

MEASURES COLLECTED AT GRADES 3, 6, AND 9

Level of Ecological Model	Measure
Child	Social functioning
	Emotional and behavioral problems
	School functioning
	Academic achievement
	Use of special education resources
	Physical health and nutrition
	Health risk behaviors
Parent and family	Social and emotional functioning
	Parenting
	Family stress
	Physical health
	Health risk behaviors
Community	Parent social activities
	Parent activities in neighborhood
	Sense of community involvement
	Neighborhood satisfaction
	Health care and social services use

changes in children, their families, and their communities. Information about children, parents, families, and neighborhoods was obtained by parent and child interviews, teacher questionnaires, and Canadian Education Quality and Accountability Office academic achievement test results.

A summary of the 61 outcome measures employed at Grades 3, 6, and 9 is provided in Table 8. Further detail on the specific measures employed is included in chapter III (child-related measures), and chapter IV (parent, family, and community measures).

Assessment of Psychometric Properties of Scales

For assessment of program effects to be meaningful, the same construct must be measured by the same scale in the same metric, across sites and cohorts. We employed confirmatory factor analysis to assess the stability of scale behavior using methods described in Meredith (1993). The confirmatory factor analyses (Mplus, version 3; Muthén & Muthén, 1998) allowed us to determine whether the scales had equal factor loadings across sites (BBBF vs. comparison), and across cohorts (focal vs. following). The goodness of fit of models was assessed with (a) the χ^2-test of model fit; (b) the Comparative Fit Index (CFI: Bentler, 1990); (c) the Tucker and Lewis Index (TLI, also known as Non-Normed Fit Index, NNFI: Tucker & Lewis, 1973); (d) the root means square error of approximation (RMSEA: Steiger, 1990); and (e) the standardized root mean square residual (SRMR: Hu & Bentler, 1999).

Hu and Bentler (1999) recommended that for the CFI and TLI, co-efficients above .95 are required for a model to be deemed well fitted. For the RMSEA and SRMR, values of .06 and .08, respectively, were suggested. For 15 of the 29 scales we tested, a single-factor model met Hu and Bentler's standards without any modifications required. When a single-factor model did not meet Hu and Bentler's standards, theoretically meaningful correlations between item pairs were tested, and were added to the models if they were significant. For the 14 scales where such pairs were added, eight pairs received one correlation, five received two, and one pair received three correlations. Note that when interitem correlations must be introduced to the model, they do not suggest that a scale based on a single-factor model will yield biased estimates of the underlying construct. The variance accounted for by an interitem correlation, by definition, is uncorrelated with the factor, so that its presence will not tend to produce scores that are systematically too high or too low with respect to the factor. Further, though the presence of unwanted interitem correlations implies that a scale is not a perfectly pure measure of an underlying factor, it does not imply a problematic ratio of signal to noise. Social and behavioral scientists routinely tolerate some noise, as long as the signal remains dominant and the form of the noise does not imply biased estimates of the construct of interest. Consider α, the standard measure of reliability. A value of 0.80, which is widely regarded as good, implies a ratio of reliable to unreliable variance (or signal:noise), of 4 to 1 $[0.80/(1.0 - 0.80) = 4/1]$. A value of 0.70, widely regarded as acceptable, yields a ratio of 2.33 to 1 $[0.70/(1.0 - 0.70) = 7/3 = 2.33/1]$.

The problem of how to evaluate reliability when scales are not precisely unifactorial was assessed by Rogers, Schmitt, and Mullins (2002) who concluded that on "the practical issue of when multidimensionality actually makes a difference empirically, . . . a CFI value above .80 is always associated with a difference in reliability indices less than .03. Hence, this CFI value may be used as an indication that alpha would adequately represent the reliability of a measure" (pp. 194–195). None of our CFI values fell below the suggested criterion of .80. Cronbach's α reliability coefficients are presented in Appendix C for all scales used at the Grades 3, 6, and 9 follow-up assessments.

Statistical Analyses

Because cases were clustered within BBBF and comparison sites, and sites were chosen nonrandomly, standard errors had to be computed with due allowance for clustering, and on the understanding that inferences should not be drawn beyond the set of sites from which data were available. STATA (Stata Corporation, 2005) was used to obtain appropriate standard errors for the influence of covariates. Covariate-adjusted residuals were then used to compare BBBF and comparison sites. Tests for differences between each BBBF site

44

and its comparison site, and then between the combined BBBF and combined comparison sites, were conducted through bootstrapping, again in STATA. Two-tailed tests of significance ($p < .05$) were employed for all analyses.

For all dependent variables, a standard set of covariates was tested, including birth year and gender of the interview respondent (typically the mother), gender of child, number of siblings, marital status, single parent status, respondents' education, employment status, family income, cultural category (Anglophone or Francophone), and immigrant status. Before testing for differences in outcomes, the data were weighted to remove mean differences in covariates between the BBBF and comparison cohorts, through a procedure developed by Friedman (2001) and incorporated within Ridgeway, McCaffrey, and Morral's (2006) R package *twang*. This procedure, *generalized boosted regression*, provides a robust estimate of the probability that a given case lies in one group or the other, given its scores on a set of variables which predict group membership. These probabilities are created from the regression coefficients of many bootstrapped samples, in this work 30,000 samples, which are used to create a final set of regression weights for the predictors. Based on these and a subject's scores on the predictors, each case in the comparison group is assigned a weight. When applied, these weights will produce a comparison sample closely resembling the BBBF group. The unweighted and weighted sociodemographic characteristics of the BBBF and comparison cohorts, when youth were in Grade 9, are found in Table 9.

We were interested in examining patterns of outcome results that were common to all three BBBF sites (cross-site patterns) and patterns of outcomes that were specific to each of the three BBBF sites (within-site patterns). The purpose of the cross-site analyses was to examine outcomes across all three BBBF sites relative to the comparison sites. These analyses were designed to determine the extent to which the BBBF program model was associated with similar effects across all three project communities. On the other hand, the within-site analyses were designed to examine whether different patterns of outcomes existed among the three BBBF sites relative to their respective comparison site. Details of both types of analyses are described below.

Cross-Site Patterns

To distinguish combined BBBF site effects (which we refer to as *cross-site* effects) from site-specific effects, we used a strategy outlined in Peters, Petrunka, and Arnold (2003). We developed this strategy because, due to the limited number of sites, a standard sign-test would have had low statistical power.

First, we performed an all-site analysis on each of the outcome measures. This involved pooling data from the three BBBF sites and comparing

TABLE 9

SOCIODEMOGRAPHIC CHARACTERISTICS OF FAMILIES IN LONGITUDINAL COHORT WHEN
YOUTH WERE IN GRADE 9

	Unweighted			Weighted[a]		
Family Characteristic	BBBF Sites $(n = 431)$	C Sites $(n = 223)$	p	BBBF Sites $(n = 431)$	C Sites $(n = 223)$	p
Respondent's birth year	1962	1961	.001	1962	1962	.824
Gender of respondent (0 = male, 1 = female)	0.93	0.93	.824	0.93	0.93	.926
Gender of child (0 = male, 1 = female)	0.51	0.43	.052	0.51	0.50	.889
Number of siblings	0.88	0.88	.850	0.88	0.88	.896
Marital status						
Ever married (%)	0.84	0.85	.799	0.84	0.85	.676
Respondent in common-law relationship (%)	0.07	0.05	.238	0.07	0.07	.848
Single parent status (%)	0.30	0.29	.790	0.30	0.27	.542
Respondent's education (number of years)	13.89	14.32	.015	13.89	13.89	.973
Employed full time (%)	0.58	0.62	.309	0.58	0.63	.310
Employed part time (%)	0.14	0.18	.249	0.14	0.14	.984
Monthly household income	$3,535	$3,865	.089	$3,535	$3,535	.999
Cultural category						
Anglophone (%)	0.36	0.19	.000	0.36	0.35	.789
Francophone (%)	0.28	0.36	.029	0.28	0.31	.384
Immigrant status (%)	0.34	0.52	.000	0.34	0.37	.404

Note.—BBBF = Better Beginnings, Better Futures; C = comparison sites.
[a]All subjects in the BBBF sites were assigned a weight of 1, and comparison subjects were assigned weights higher or lower than 1 to produce a final set of weights that balanced the covariates in a multivariate manner between the BBBF sites and comparison sites.

with pooled data from the two comparison sites. *Cross-site patterns* were identified by first selecting measures that were significant in the all-site analysis. Second, if the overall cross-site pattern was statistically significant, we examined each of the BBBF sites individually, and compared each with its corresponding comparison site. This enabled us to determine whether the pattern of individual site results was consistent with the overall all-site result. Third, as described in Peters et al. (2003), scores were assigned to the individual site test results: 2 points for a significant result in the same direction as the all-site effect and 1 point for a nonsignificant result in the same direction. A result in the opposite direction was treated as ruling out a general cross-site pattern. These scores were then summed for each measure. A summed score of 4 or greater was required to identify a significant cross-site pattern. The sum of scores assigned can be referred to a table of critical values, ensuring that each cross-site pattern reported is significant at $p < .05$. For example, for three tests (one for each project site), a score of 2 for a significant result and two scores of 1 for results in the same direction sum to 4, which yields $p < .05$. Given the scoring system, a significant cross-site effect required three criteria to be met: (a) the "all-site" result for pooled data from three project sites was significantly different from pooled data from comparison sites, (b) the result for at least one individual site was significantly different from its matched comparison site, and (c) no site showed results in the opposite direction.

Within-Site Patterns

With programs set up to meet local needs, results may well differ among sites. Within each domain (e.g., parent's ratings of child's social functioning or parent's ratings of child's emotional and behavioral problems), we examined the results to determine if the within-site results were consistent. As described above, scores were assigned to results according to the following formula: 2 points for a significant result, 1 point for a nonsignificant result in the same direction, and -1 for a nonsignificant result in the opposite direction. No within-site pattern could be identified if one of the results was significant in the opposite direction. Within each domain and within each site, these scores were then summed. The sum of scores assigned can be referred to a table of critical values, ensuring that each within-site pattern reported is significant at .05. For example, with a topic domain of four measures, a summed score of 5 or higher is required for the within-site pattern to be significant at $p < .05$.

Effect Sizes

For nondichotomous variables effect sizes were calculated by subtracting the BBBF site score from the comparison site score, and then dividing by the standard deviation (SD) for the full sample. For dichotomous variables, where changes in percentages are of interest, they were transformed by the formula $\phi = 2$ arcsine p^5, wherein p is the percentage of interest. The transformation was used to provide a straightforward linkage between effect size and statistical power. Although Cohen (1977) emphasized that labeling an effect large or small is arbitrary, the conventions he suggested are widely used. Accordingly, an effect size of .20 is referred to as small, .50 as moderate, and .80 as large. In program outcome research, effect sizes are typically small (Hundert et al., 1999; McCartney & Rosenthal, 2000). All effect sizes reported in this monograph are d statistics.

A question often asked of intervention projects is whether the intervention worked more effectively for certain subgroups of participants than for others. Of particular interest is whether or not an intervention has greater or lesser impact on high-risk groups, and if so, what are the particular risk variables that moderate effectiveness. Answers to these questions are central to the issue of whether certain interventions should be targeted or universal (Offord, 1996; Offord et al., 1998). Most model longitudinal intervention projects in the early childhood literature have been carried out only on very high-risk samples where the analysis of moderating variables has not been particularly salient (e.g., the High/Scope Perry Preschool Project, Schweinhart et al., 1993; the Abecedarian Project, Ramey & Campbell, 1984; the Montreal Prevention Experiment, Tremblay et al., 1996; and the Chicago Child–Parent Centers, Reynolds, 2000). When everyone is at high risk, there is no way to compare the effects of high-risk samples to low-risk samples because the low-risk samples are absent. A notable exception is the Elmira (New York) Nurse Home Visitation Project (Olds, 1997). In this project, that included an intervention group of 97 first-time mothers from a high-risk community, it was demonstrated that most of the positive long-term outcome effects were limited to a particularly high-risk subgroup of 38 unmarried, low socioeconomic mothers and their children (Olds et al., 1997, 1998).

Because the BBBF project is a universal intervention in high-risk neighborhoods, it is possible to examine whether the outcome effects, both positive and negative, were limited to particular subgroups of participants (i.e., outcomes were moderated by particular characteristics or risk factors). The RCU examined the effects of five potential moderator variables when the youth were in Grades 6 and 9. At Grade 6, the RCU analyzed 23 outcome variables for the moderational analyses (those outcome variables that were part of a significant cross-site pattern as well as the four types of child emotional and behavioral problems as rated separately by parents, teachers, and children because these are considered key outcome variables in the goals of the BBBF project). At Grade 9, all 61 variables were included in the moderational analyses. The five potential moderator variables were selected because they have been identified as important risk factors in many studies of child and family development, including analyses of the NLSCY (Willms, 2002). Of the five potential moderators, three—parent's education, monthly household income, and the high-risk index[1]—are continuous variables, whereas gender of child and single parent status are dichotomous variables. The continuous variables were converted into standardized scores in the analysis to avoid multicollinearity (Frazier, Tix, & Barron, 2004). The BBBF versus comparison site variable was employed as the predictor variable in all of the moderational analyses. Results for the Grade 6 analyses indicated that only two of the 115 analyses yielded a significant ($p < .05$) interaction between the predictor and moderator variables; however, with a p value of .05, one would expect 6 of the 115 analyses to be significant due to chance. At Grade 9, only 5 of the 305 analyses yielded a significant ($p < .05$) interaction between the predictor and moderator variables; however, with a p value of .05, one would expect 15 of the 305 analyses to be significant due to chance.

Therefore, as a general conclusion, the selected risk factors did not moderate the direction or strength of the relationship between the BBBF project and the Grades 6 and 9 outcome measures at a magnitude that our sample size allowed us to discover. Is there evidence that the BBBF programs are having a greater impact on particular subgroups of children or families? The answer, based on the Grades 6 and 9 outcomes, is no. Similar results of moderational analyses have recently been reported from the Fast Track project in the United States (McMahon & Conduct Problems Prevention Research Group, 2004). The Fast Track project involved a number of intervention components with a sample of high-risk children with conduct problems in Grades 1 and 2. The intervention components included social skills training groups, parent training groups, home visiting, and tutoring reading skills. Analyses of follow-up data collected when the children were in Grade 4 examined the possible moderating effects of a number of variables, including child's gender, race, family socioeconomic status, single-parent status, and parent's education. There was no indication of a significant moderating effect of any of these variables on children's outcome in Grade 4. It was concluded that these results are positive in that they indicate that the Fast Track program effects were generalizable across a wide variety of child and family characteristics. A similar conclusion seems warranted for the program effects from the BBBF project.

Economic Analysis

We estimated the direct costs to government of investing in the BBBF programs through the development of a cost formula to evaluate the financial investment per child per intervention site. These costs were compared with the savings or monetizable benefits associated with participation in BBBF programs (based on utilization of resources in health care and social services, schools, social assistance, and the justice system) up to Grade 9. Results of the economic analysis are described in chapter V.

NOTE

1. The high-risk index was created by combining nine risk indicators pertaining to the parents. These included single parent status, parent unemployment status, low parent education, low family income, high stressful life events, high parental depression, high hostile-ineffective parenting, low social support, and low family functioning. Each of the nondichotomous variables was converted into a dichotomous variable based on the 90th percentile cut-off score from the NLSCY normative sample if available (hostile–ineffective parenting, low social support, low family functioning) or 1 SD above the mean for the combined samples from the BBBF and comparison sites (stressful life events, parental depression).

III. CHILD OUTCOMES AT GRADES 3, 6, AND 9

In this chapter, we examine the first study question discussed in chapter I: What are the long-term effects of the Better Beginnings, Better Futures (BBBF) project participation on social, emotional, behavioral, cognitive, and physical development of children and youth? The theoretical framework of this study is Bronfenbrenner's (1979) ecological model, which emphasizes that children's development in different domains is connected (see chapter I). That is, social, emotional, cognitive, and physical development are linked—change in one area almost always leads to change in another. For example, research shows that children's development in the social and emotional domains is strongly related to school adjustment and performance, such as secondary school academic success and high school completion (Boisjoli et al., 2007). Further, within an ecological framework, development is influenced not only by characteristics of the child but also by characteristics of the family, school, and the broader social environment (Bronfenbrenner, 1979). In examining the project effects on children's functioning, we explore some of the microsystematic and mesosystematic changes associated with the BBBF project. The microsystems are the immediate settings surrounding the child, including home and school, whereas the mesosystems are the interconnections between these settings, such as the child's relationships with friends.

This study offers a novel contribution to the literature in several ways. First, we examine effects at several key developmental periods: We report effects associated with BBBF at Grade 3, 1 year after the end of BBBF programs; at Grade 6 when children are entering puberty and early adolescence; and at Grade 9 when youth have reached middle adolescence. Early developmental opportunities can establish a critical foundation for children's academic success, health, and general well-being; thus, it is essential to examine if preventive interventions are associated with improvements in protective skills and competencies later in childhood and into adolescence (Anderson et al., 2003). As noted in chapter I, although there are several notable exceptions, few early childhood programs to date have long-term follow-up that spans critical developmental periods. In this chapter, we examine effects associated with BBBF from Grades 3 to 9 across four developmental domains that are described in detail below. Although previously published reports have documented the success of BBBF up to Grade 3 (e.g., Peters et al., 2003), we have included the Grade 3 results here to provide a more complete picture of the effects of BBBF programming over 6 years of follow-up.

Second, BBBF employed an ecological approach to programming, with a broad range of child-, parent-, family-, and community-focused programs offered in each of the project sites. Programs targeted microsystems in the children's environment, such as family, school, peer, and community systems. Programs were also designed to improve the connections and interrelations among the microsystems (such as the connections between family and school).

Many preventive interventions for young children to date have concentrated on either cognitive or social-emotional development (Durlak et al., 2007; Karoly et al., 2005; Nelson et al., 2003). In contrast, BBBF emphasized a comprehensive and ecological view of children's development. BBBF programs were designed to effect change in four key developmental domains, including social functioning, emotional and behavioral problems, school functioning, and health. Figure 1, presented in chapter I, illustrates the pathways through which BBBF was hypothesized to positively impact these domains of child development. In the following section, we describe the developmental importance of each of the four domains in the context of BBBF.

THE CHILD: DEVELOPMENT IN DIFFERENT DOMAINS

Prosocial behaviors and social skills are important protective factors in preventing behavioral and emotional problems in early school-aged children (Eisenberg & Fabes, 1998). Healthy social functioning continues to be important as children move into adolescence, when there is greater participation in social contexts outside the home, such as peer groups (Dupere, Lacourse, Willms, Leventhal, & Tremblay, 2008). Further, teachers identify social skills as key behaviors important for school success. Positive behaviors include interacting effectively with peers and developing and maintaining friendships (Fad & Ryser, 1993). In middle childhood (Grade 3), BBBF measures in the social functioning domain focused on parent and teacher ratings of the children's social behaviors and self-control. As the children entered adolescence, we continued to gather information from parents and teachers. At these follow-ups (Grades 6 and 9), we also asked youth to reflect on their relationships with friends. Thus, the outcomes are developmentally relevant.

Children's emotional and behavior problems, such as anxiety, depression, aggression, and hyperactivity are important to monitor because these problems are associated with poorer social and school functioning and can have deleterious effects into adolescence and early adulthood. Childhood anxiety, for example, may lead to children's avoidance of important socializing and developmental activities, including child classroom participation, peer involvement, and autonomous functioning (Albano, Chorpita, & Barlow, 1996; Kendall et al., 1992). Childhood depression has been associated with later poor psychosocial and academic outcomes, and increased risk for substance abuse (Birmaher et al., 1996). Behavioral problems such as aggressive, oppositional/defiant, or hyperactive behaviors impose a substantial burden on parents and teachers, cause rejection by peers, and are the most frequent basis for childhood referrals for mental health treatment. Often these problems lead to a lifetime of serious difficulties involving the law (Hinshaw & Lee, 2003). We anticipated that BBBF may be associated with reductions in children's emotional and behavior problems, in line with results from reviews of early childhood prevention programs (e.g., Karoly et al., 2005; Webster-Stratton & Taylor, 2001). Because the BBBF longitudinal study included several developmental periods, our assessment of emotional and behavioral problems needed to be comprehensive and developmentally appropriate. Measures of emotional and behavioral problems in BBBF in Grade 3 focused on parents' and teachers' ratings of problems such as anxiety, aggressive and oppositional behaviors, and hyperactivity–inattention. When youth reached Grades 6 and 9, we also assessed youth self-reports of each emotional and behavioral problem to gain a more comprehensive perspective of the effects in this domain. In Grade 9, we added measures of problems that can emerge in early adolescence, including delinquent behaviors and arrests.

It is essential to measure children's school functioning and academic achievement across developmental periods of mid-late childhood and into adolescence because success in these areas of development is related to long-term well-being. Research indicates that dropping out of high school is a long-term process that can begin before the child starts high school. Analyses of the Canadian National Longitudinal Survey of Children and Youth (NLSCY) data indicate that grade retention and poor performance in school at ages 10 and 11 are related to dropping out of school at age 16 or 17 (see Bushnik, Barr-Telford, & Bussiere, 2004). Throughout the BBBF follow-up period, we assessed a range of school functioning measures, with the focus changing as children moved through different developmental stages. In Grade 3, we focused on academic achievement and use of special education. As children entered the transition into adolescence, we added developmentally appropriate measures that assessed how effectively the children were functioning in school. Measures added at Grades 6 and 9 included

53

school preparedness, school attendance, suspensions, and behavioral incidents in school records, and later career aspirations. To assess the quality of the family–school mesosystem, we assessed parent involvement with school.

In the BBBF project model, the promotion of optimal development also incorporated physical health, health risk behaviors, nutrition, and health service utilization. Few early childhood interventions report any physical health–related outcomes (Karoly et al., 2005; Russell, 2002). Some studies with long-term follow-up report data for program effects on health risk behaviors; however, results are uneven and the range of behaviors measured is sometimes rather narrow. For example, the Montreal Prevention Experiment had a positive effect on boys' alcohol and drug use at age 15 but had no effect on rates of sexual intercourse (Tremblay et al., 1996). The Chicago Child–Parent Centers program had no long-term effects on adolescent substance or tobacco use (Reynolds et al., 2007). A novel contribution of this study is that we have collected information from childhood into adolescence on a broader range of developmentally appropriate health measures including physical health, nutrition, and health risk behaviors. At early follow-up (Grade 3), we focused on normative health indicators such as general health ratings, chronic conditions, and body mass index (BMI). Once children reached early adolescence, we added measures of health risk behaviors, including alcohol, smoking, marijuana use, injuries, and sexual activity, because these risky behaviors tend to emerge during this developmental period. Details of each measure are described below. A summary of the reliability coefficients for each scale at each time-point is presented in Appendix C.

MEASURES

Social Functioning

To assess youth social behaviors, ratings on the 10-item Prosocial Scale from the NLSCY (Statistics Canada, 1995) were collected from parents when the youth were in Grades 6 and 9. Items were rated from 0 = *never* to 2 = *often*. Examples of items include "shows sympathy for a child who has made a mistake" and "will invite others to join in a game." Total scores ranged from 0 to 20, with high scores indicating frequent prosocial behaviors. Child *social support* was measured with an item from the NLSCY; parents were asked how many adults or teenagers have an important relationship with their child at Grades 3, 6, and 9. Child–parent conflict resolution skills were measured with the eight-item NLSCY Conflict Resolution Scale, which parents completed when youth were in Grade 9. Response categories ranged from 0 = *not at all* to 4 = *almost all of the time*.

Examples of items include "when we argue we stay angry for a very long time" and "when we disagree, I refuse to talk to [child's name]." Total scores ranged from 8 to 32, with higher scores indicating poorer conflict resolution skills.

Self-esteem was measured at Grades 6 and 9 with the four-item NLSCY General Self-Esteem Scale. Youth responded on a 5-point scale where 1 = *false*, 3 = *sometimes false/sometimes true*, and 5 = *true*. Examples of items include "in general, I like the way I am" and "a lot of things about me are good." Total scores ranged from 4 to 20, with higher scores indicating higher self-esteem. A set of questions from the NLSCY were combined to create an index that focused on *children's extracurricular activities*. In Grades 6 and 9, youth reported how often they had engaged in several leisure activities (e.g., "sports with a coach," "dance/gymnastics/karate," and "music, drama, or arts group").

Children's ability to handle conflict situations was measured with the six-item Conflict Management subscale of the Social Skills Rating Scale (Gresham & Elliott, 1990), which teachers completed at Grades 3, 6, and 9. Teachers responded on a 3-point scale from 0 = *never* to 2 = *very often* (e.g., "controls temper in conflict situations with peers" and "receives criticism well"). Total scores ranged from 0 to 12, with higher scores indicating greater self-control and conflict management skills.

Emotional and Behavioral Problems

We measured child behavior problems using several subscales from the NLSCY at Grades 3, 6, and 9. For all subscales (with the exception of Delinquency) parents, teachers, and youth responded on a 3-point scale from 0 = *never or not true* to 2 = *often or very true* as to how well items described the child. Each subscale had between 5 and 10 items, depending on the respondent. Examples of items on the Emotional-Anxiety Disorder subscale include "is nervous, high strung or tense" and "is not as happy as other children." Total scores ranged from 0 to 16 (eight items) for the parent ratings, 0 to 10 (five items) for the teacher ratings, and 0 to 14 (seven items) for the youth ratings. Examples of items on the Physical Aggression subscale include "when someone accidentally hurts him/her, [child's name] reacts with anger and fighting" and "physically attacks people." Total scores ranged from 0 to 12 and for both parent and youth ratings. Examples of items on the Indirect Aggression subscale include "when mad at someone, [child's name] becomes friends with another as revenge" and "when mad at someone, says to others: let's not be with him/her." Total scores ranged from 0 to 10 for both parent and youth ratings. Examples of items on the Hyperactivity–Inattention subscale include "can't sit still or is restless," and "can't concentrate or pay attention for long." Total scores ranged from

0 to16 (eight items) for the parent ratings, 0 to 14 (seven items) for the teacher ratings, and 0 to 12 (six items) for the youth ratings. For the Delinquency Scale, parents provided ratings on 6 items and youth provided ratings on 10 items. Parents responded on a 3-point scale from 0 = *never or not true* to 2 = *often or very true* as to how well items described the child. Examples of parent-rated items include "steals at home" and "vandalizes." For 9 of the 10 youth-rated items, youth responded on a 4-point scale from 0 = *never* to 3 = *5 or more times*. The remaining youth item was dichotomous; youth responded either 0 = *no, I wasn't a part of gang* or 1 = *yes, I was a part of gang*. Examples of youth-rated items include "stayed out all night without permission" and "stole something." Total scores ranged from 0 to 12 for the parent scale and 0 to 28 for the youth scale, with higher scores indicating more frequent delinquent behaviors. At Grade 9, youth were also asked if they had *ever been arrested*.

Parent ratings of oppositional–defiant symptoms at Grades 3, 6, and 9 were assessed with the eight-item Oppositional–Defiant subscale from the Child Behavior Problems subscales of the Revised Ontario Child Health Study (Boyle et al., 1993). Parents responded on a 3-point scale from 0 = *never or not true* to 2 = *often or very true* as to whether their child, for example, "argues a lot with adults" or "blames others for own mistakes." Total scores ranged from 0 to 16, with higher scores indicating higher levels of oppositional–defiant behavior. Parent ratings of child depressive symptoms at Grades 3, 6, and 9 were assessed with the three-item Depression subscale from the Child Behavior Problems subscales of the Revised Ontario Child Health Study (Boyle et al., 1993). Parents responded on a 3-point scale from 0 = *never or not true* to 2 = *often or very true* as to whether their child "feels worthless or inferior" and "has difficulty making decisions." Total scores ranged from 0 to 6, with higher scores indicating higher levels of depression.

At Grade 9, youth provided ratings on a nine-item Delinquent Friends Scale, which was created by BBBF researchers based on items from the NLSCY. Youth responded on a 4-point scale from 0 = *none* to 3 = *all* to how many of their close friends "smoke cigarettes," "drink alcohol," "break the law," "have been suspended from school," and "have dropped out of school for more than a week." Total scores ranged from 0 to 27 with higher scores indicating higher levels of delinquency among friends.

School Functioning

To measure school functioning, parents indicated whether or not the youth had ever repeated a grade. Also, teachers provided ratings for each research child on the four-item NLSCY Student Preparedness Scale at Grades 6 and 9 using a 5-point scale from 1 = *never* to 5 = *always*. Teachers indicated how often since the beginning of school the previous fall the child had arrived at school "without materials needed for school work," "too tired to do school work," "without homework completed," "late," or "hungry." Total scores ranged from 4 to 20, with higher scores indicating the child was less prepared for school. For the four-item Adaptive Functioning Scale (Achenbach, McConaughy, & Howell, 1987), teachers rated each child at Grades 3, 6, and 9 on a 7-point scale from 1 = *much less* to 7 = *much more* in reference to typical students of the same age. Items included "how hard is s/he working" and "how appropriate is his/her behavior." Total scores ranged from 4 to 28, with higher scores indicating more adaptive functioning. Also, teachers provided information at Grades 6 and 9 on *suspensions* and *how far they hoped the child would go in school/education* (responses to this question could range from 1 = *complete some secondary or high school* to 5 = *obtain a university degree*).

To assess *academic achievement*, at Grade 9 teachers reported the level of the youth's current academic achievement on a 5-point scale from the NLSCY, with responses ranging from 1 = *near the top of the class* to 5 = *near the bottom of the class*. Additionally, we obtained data from the Canadian Education Quality and Accountability Office (EQAO) for standardized provincial mathematics achievement test results at Grades 3, 6, and 9. To assess the use of special education at Grades 3, 6, and 9, teachers indicated whether the student had received special education services or individual education plans. At Grades 6 and 9, teachers also indicated whether the child was limited by a learning disability.

Health and Health Risk Behaviors

Children's *general physical health* was assessed at Grades 3, 6, and 9, by asking parents to rate their child's health on a 5-point scale from 1 = *excellent* to 5 = *poor*. *Chronic health conditions* were also assessed with items from the NLSCY. In Grades 3–9, parents were asked to indicate which (if any) chronic conditions their child experienced, from a list of 14 conditions including food allergies, bronchitis, epilepsy, and kidney disease. At Grades 3, 6, and 9, parents were asked whether their child had a physical or mental condition or health problem that limited their activities at home or school. Parents were also asked how many hours per week their children were *exposed to second-hand smoke* in Grades 6 and 9. *Height* and *weight* were measured in Grades 3, 6, and 9 by trained research assistants, according to established guidelines (Lohman, Roche, & Martorell, 1988). Height was measured twice to the nearest 0.1 cm using a modified tape measure (Microtoise, CMS Weighing Equipment, London, U.K.) and weight was measured twice to the nearest 0.2 kg with a strain-gauge digital scale (Wonderscale, Health-o-meter Inc., Bridgeview, IL). BMI was calculated as weight (kg) divided by height (m) squared.

In Grades 6 and 9, youth answered questions designed to assess their *eating behaviors*. The questions had been validated for use with school-aged children (Evers, Taylor, Manske, & Midgett, 2001). The first question, "how often do you have something for breakfast," allowed for five responses: *every day, some days, rarely, weekends only*, and *never*. Daily breakfast consumption was determined by combining the latter four categories to identify the proportion of students who did not consume breakfast every day. The second question, "how often have you eaten any of these foods in the last seven days," was followed by a list of 25 foods and food groups with five possible responses, including *at least twice daily, once a day, 4–6 times per week, 1–3 times per week*, and *never*. The frequencies of intake were converted to number of servings per day ($2 = $ *at least twice a day*, $1 = $ *once a day*, $.71 = $ *4–6 times per week*, and $.29 = $ *1–3 times per week*) and were subsequently collapsed into the four food groups of Canada's Food Guide ("vegetables and fruit," "grain products," "milk and alternatives," and "meat and alternatives") plus an "other foods" (high fat/low nutrient density) group. The number of servings was then compared with Canada's Food Guide recommendations (Health Canada, 2007).

In Grades 6 and 9, youth answered questions from the NLSCY on their *alcohol and smoking experience*. In Grade 6, youth were asked "have you ever had a drink of alcohol" (responses were $0 = $ *no* or $1 = $ *yes*); in Grade 9, youth described their experiences with alcohol on a 9-point scale from $1 = $ *I have never had a drink of alcohol* to $9 = $ *I drink 6–7 times per week*. At Grades 6 and 9, youth described their experiences with smoking cigarettes. Responses were coded as $1 = $ *never smoked*, $2 = $ *only a few puffs*, or $3 = $ *more than a few puffs*. At Grade 9, a single item assessed *use of marijuana* during the past 12 months. Response categories ranged from $0 = $ *I have never done it* to $6 = $ *I have used it about 6–7 days a week*.

Grade 9 youth provided ratings on a Stress Index from the NLSCY, which included events such as painful breakup with boy/girlfriend, serious problem at school, pregnancy or abortion, and divorce or separation of parents. Responses for each item were $0 = $ *no* or $1 = $ *yes*. The index had total scores ranging from 0 to 6, where a higher value indicated more stressors. Grade 9 youth were asked the number of times they had been *injured* and required treatment from a doctor or nurse in the past 12 months; response categories were $1 = $ *I have not been treated for an injury* to $5 = $ *4 or more times*. *Consensual sexual activity* was assessed at Grade 9 with the question "Have you ever had consensual sexual intercourse?" Responses were $0 = $ *no* or $1 = $ *yes*.

RESULTS

As outlined in chapter II, we were interested in examining patterns of outcome results that were common to all three BBBF sites (cross-site patterns) and patterns of outcomes that were specific to each of the three BBBF sites (within-site patterns). In the following sections we describe significant cross-site patterns on measures in each of the four child development domains (social functioning, emotional and behavioral problems, school functioning, and health/health risk behaviors). Then we describe significant within-site patterns in each of the four domains. Tables in this chapter summarize the direction of differences for each individual measure with a "+" indicating an outcome difference favorable to BBBF and a "−" indicating an outcome favorable to comparison sites. Statistically significant patterns of results are shaded in the table. The effect size (ES) is presented for each measure involved in a significant pattern. In Appendix D, means and standard deviations are listed for all measures.

Cross-Site Patterns

Social Functioning

Table 10 summarizes the cross-site patterns and ES for social functioning.

Although there was no evidence of enhanced social functioning among BBBF children at Grade 3, 3 years later, in Grade 6, parents from the BBBF sites rated their children significantly higher in prosocial behavior than did parents from the control sites ($p < .01$; ES $= .32$), and BBBF parents identified a greater number of people who have an important relationship with their child than did parents from the comparison sites ($p < .01$; ES $= .33$). Also, teachers from the BBBF sites rated youth more highly in terms of self-control in social conflict situations than did teachers from the comparison sites ($p < .01$; ES $= .34$).

At Grade 9, parents from the BBBF sites continued to identify a greater number of people who have an important relationship with their child than did parents from the comparison sites ($p < .01$; ES $= .26$) and also provided higher ratings on the NLSCY Conflict Resolution Scale ($p < .05$; ES $= .18$). At the same time, however, BBBF youth themselves provided lower ratings on the Self-Esteem Scale than youth at comparison sites ($p < .01$; ES $= -.29$).

Emotional and Behavioral Problems

The results for the analyses of children's emotional and behavioral problems are presented in Table 11.

In Grades 3, 6, and 9, teachers rated children from the BBBF communities as displaying fewer hyperactivity and inattention behavior problems than children from comparison sites ($p < .01$ at all Grades; ES $= .23$ at Grade 3; .29 at Grade 6; and .33 at Grade 9). At Grades 3 and 9, BBBF teachers also reported lower scores on the Emotional-Anxiety Disorder

59

TABLE 10

EFFECT SIZES AND CROSS-SITE PATTERNS FOR CHILD SOCIAL FUNCTIONING

Measures	Grade 3 Effects				Grade 6 Effects				Grade 9 Effects			
	Cornwall Versus Comparison Site	Sudbury Versus Comparison Site	Highfield Versus Comparison Site	BBBF Sites Combined Versus Comparison Sites	Cornwall Versus Comparison Site	Sudbury Versus Comparison Site	Highfield Versus Comparison Site	BBBF Sites Combined Versus Comparison Sites	Cornwall Versus Comparison Site	Sudbury Versus Comparison Site	Highfield Versus Comparison Site	BBBF Sites Combined Versus Comparison Sites
Child social functioning												
Parent-rated												
Prosocial Behavior Scale					+ .12	+ .06	+** .62	+** .32	−	−	−	−
Number of people important to child	+	+	−**	+	+** .74	+** .39	− .02	+** .33ª	+* .38	+** .33	+ .06	+** .26
Conflict Resolution Scale									+* .28	+** .32	− .04	+* .18ª
Child-rated												
Self-Esteem Scale					−	−	−	−	−* .30	− .24	−** .35	−** .29
Extracurricular Activities Index	+	−	+	+	+	+	+	+	+	+	−	−
Teacher-rated												
Self-Control/Conflict Management Scale	+			+	+** .34	+** .46	+* .25	+** .34	+*	+*	+	+

Note.—BBBF = Better Beginnings, Better Futures; + = favorable effect of the BBBF project; − = undesirable negative effect of the BBBF project. A blank space indicates that data on that measure were not collected at that time-point.

In this table, dark shading is used to indicate a significant cross-site pattern nonbeneficial for BBBF. Light shading is used to indicate a significant cross-site pattern in favor of BBBF. A significant cross-site effect required three criteria to be met, including (a) the result for overall BBBF sites versus comparison sites was significant; (b) the result for at least one individual site was significantly different from its matched comparison site; and (c) no individual site showed results in the opposite direction.

[a]In Tables 10–13 and Table 18, there are seven cross-site patterns where criterion (c) was not met. In these seven exceptional cases, results for two of the three BBBF sites were statistically significant in the same direction; the result for the third site was in the opposite direction but the effect size was close to zero (ES < .10). Therefore, we deemed these seven cases to merit consideration.

*p < .05, **p < .01.

TABLE 11
Effect Sizes and Cross-Site Patterns for Child Emotional and Behavioral Problems

Measures	Grade 3 Effects				Grade 6 Effects				Grade 9 Effects			
	Cornwall Versus Comparison Site	Sudbury Versus Comparison Site	Highfield Versus Comparison Site	BBBF Sites Combined Versus Comparison Sites	Cornwall Versus Comparison Site	Sudbury Versus Comparison Site	Highfield Versus Comparison Site	BBBF Sites Combined Versus Comparison Sites	Cornwall Versus Comparison Site	Sudbury Versus Comparison Site	Highfield Versus Comparison Site	BBBF Sites Combined Versus Comparison Sites
Child emotional and behavioral problems												
Parent-rated												
Emotional–Anxiety Disorder Scale	−	−	−	−	+	−	−**	−*	+	+	−	−
Physical Aggression Scale	+	−	+	+	−* .25	−* .25	.14	.21	+	+	−*	+*
Indirect Aggression Scale	+	−	+	−	−* .22	−* .11	−* .23	−** .20	+	+	−*	+**
Hyperactivity–Inattention Scale	+	+	−	−	+	+	−	−	+*	+	−*	−
Delinquency Scale	+	+	+	+	+	+	+	+	+	+	−	+
Oppositional–Defiant Scale	+	+	+	−	−	+	−** .23	−	+	+	−	−
Depression Scale	−	−	+	−	− .14	.20	−** .23	.21	−	−	−**	−
Teacher-rated												
Emotional–Anxiety Disorder Scale	+** .61	+** .36	− .04	+** .26[a]	+* .34	+** .35	+ .21	+** .29	+ .23	+ .38	+ .05	+* .22
Hyperactivity–Inattention Scale	+* .32	+ .16	+* .24	+** .23	+* .34	+** .35	+ .21	+** .29	+** .45	+** .48	+ .18	+** .33

TABLE 11 (Contd.)

Measures	Grade 3 Effects				Grade 6 Effects				Grade 9 Effects			
	Cornwall Versus Comparison Site	Sudbury Versus Comparison Site	Highfield Versus Comparison Site	BBBF Sites Combined Versus Comparison Sites	Cornwall Versus Comparison Site	Sudbury Versus Comparison Site	Highfield Versus Comparison Site	BBBF Sites Combined Versus Comparison Sites	Cornwall Versus Comparison Site	Sudbury Versus Comparison Site	Highfield Versus Comparison Site	BBBF Sites Combined Versus Comparison Sites
Child-rated												
Emotional-Anxiety Disorder Scale					–	–	+	–	–** .43	–** .37	– .12	–** .26
Physical Aggression Scale					–** .36	–* .24	+ .01	–* .16[a]	–	–	–	–
Indirect Aggression Scale					–	–	+	+	+	+	+	+
Hyperactivity-Inattention Scale					–**	–	+	+	–	+	+	–
Delinquency Scale					–**	–	+	–	+	–	+	+
Ever arrested/taken to police station									+	+	+	+
Delinquent Friends Scale									–	–**	+	–

Note.—See Table 10.

62

Scale among BBBF children (Grade 3: $p < .01$, ES = .26; Grade 9: $p < .05$, ES = .22).

The ratings provided by parents and youth showed different patterns. In fact at Grade 6, BBBF parents rated their children as displaying more behaviors linked to physical aggression ($p < .01$; ES = $-.21$), indirect aggression ($p < .01$; ES = $-.20$), and depression ($p < .01$; ES = $-.21$) than did parents from the comparison sites, although these differences were not present at Grade 9. Youth self-ratings indicated that BBBF youth displayed more physical aggression at Grade 6 ($p < .05$; ES = $-.16$) and more emotional-anxious behaviors at Grade 9 than those from comparison sites ($p < .01$; ES = $-.26$).

School Functioning

The results for the analyses of children's school functioning are presented in Table 12.

At Grade 3, there was no evidence of enhanced academic achievement or school functioning in BBBF children compared with comparison site children. Later follow-up assessments, however, indicated that youth from BBBF sites had experienced a range of improvements in school functioning and academic achievement, relative to the youth from comparison sites. BBBF youth performed significantly better on the EQAO mathematics test at Grade 6 ($p < .05$; ES = .21). Results of this test indicated that 52% of youth from the BBBF sites reached Level 3 or 4, indicating that they were at or above grade level, which is the standard of comparison used by EQAO, whereas only 40% of children in the comparison sites attained this level of achievement. Also in Grade 6, teachers reported that fewer youth from BBBF sites had been suspended in that school year ($p < .05$; ES = .21). Further, teachers' ratings at Grade 6 indicated that youth from BBBF sites required fewer special education services than youth from comparison sites (22% vs. 32% for BBBF and comparison sites, respectively, $p < .05$; ES = .22).

At Grade 9, positive effects on school functioning were again evident. Results indicated that BBBF youth again required significantly fewer special education services (19% vs. 27%, for BBBF and comparison sites, respectively; $p < .05$; ES = .20). A lower proportion of BBBF youth had repeated an academic year (10% vs. 17%; $p < .01$; ES = .22). Teachers rated youth in BBBF communities more highly on the Adaptive Functioning Scale ($p < .05$; ES = .22) and indicated that they were more prepared for school ($p < .05$; ES = .25) than youth in comparison sites. Teachers also indicated that youth at the BBBF sites had the potential to complete more education than youth at the comparison sites ($p < .01$; ES = .27). Teacher ratings of

TABLE 12
EFFECT SIZES AND CROSS-SITE PATTERNS FOR SCHOOL FUNCTIONING

Measures	Grade 3 Effects				Grade 6 Effects				Grade 9 Effects			
	Cornwall Versus Comparison Site	Sudbury Versus Comparison Site	Highfield Versus Comparison Site	BBBF Sites Combined Versus Comparison Sites	Cornwall Versus Comparison Site	Sudbury Versus Comparison Site	Highfield Versus Comparison Site	BBBF Sites Combined Versus Comparison Sites	Cornwall Versus Comparison Site	Sudbury Versus Comparison Site	Highfield Versus Comparison Site	BBBF Sites Combined Versus Comparison Sites
School functioning												
Parent-rated												
Child repeated a grade					+	+	−	+	+** .43	+* .32	+ .06	+** .22
Teacher-rated												
Student Preparedness Scale		+**			+	+	+	+*	+ .27	+* .33	+ .20	+* .25
Adaptive Functioning Scale	+		−	−	+	+	+	+	+* .37	+* .30	+ .12	+* .22
Child suspended since last fall					+ .09	+ .18	+* .26	+* .21	+	+	+	—
How far hope child will go in school					−	+	+	+	+* .38	+* .37	+* .12	+ .27
Child's current academic achievement												
Standardized mathematics test	−	+**	−	+	+* .31	+* .47	+* .00	+* .21	+	+	+	+
Child received special education/services	+		+	+	+* .39	+** .67	− .08	+** .22[a]	+ .15	+ .30	+ .15	+* .20
Child limitations due to learning disability					+	+	+	+*	+	+	+*	+

Note.—See Table 10.

64

children's disability and current academic achievement were consistently positive for children from the BBBF sites, although these results did not constitute a statistically significant pattern.

Health and Health Risk Behaviors

Table 13 lists cross-site patterns and ES for physical health, nutrition, and health risk behaviors.

In Grades 3, 6, and 9, parents from BBBF sites reported that their children had a significantly higher number of chronic conditions, such as asthma, than did parents from comparison sites. The effects sizes were $-.22$ in Grade 3 ($p < .01$), $-.19$ in Grade 6 ($p < .01$), and $-.18$ in Grade 9 ($p < .05$). Specifically, the proportion of children with chronic conditions was 43.8% in BBBF sites versus 33.7% in comparison sites at Grade 3; 48.0% versus 34.5% at Grade 6; and 47.4% versus 36.5% at Grade 9. The most prevalent chronic conditions in Grade 9 were allergies (36% in BBBF vs. 21.1% in comparison sites), and asthma (22.5% in BBBF vs. 15.3% in comparison sites). At Grade 6, BBBF parents provided significantly lower general health ratings for their children's health than did parents in comparison sites ($p < .05$; ES $= -.18$). The pattern of significantly different general health ratings was not observed at Grade 3 or 9. At Grade 3, children from BBBF sites had significantly higher BMI than those from comparison sites (18.1 vs. 17.4 kg/m^2, respectively; $p < .01$, ES $= -.21$). The significant difference in BMI was not maintained at either the Grade 6 or 9 follow-up assessments.

Within-Site Patterns

Social Functioning

Table 14 summarizes the within-site patterns and ES for children's social functioning. We analyzed the data for within-site patterns separately for measures that were collected from parents, teachers, and the children themselves.

As shown in Table 14, there was a significant positive pattern for the two measures of social functioning collected from parents in both Cornwall and Sudbury when their children were in Grade 6. The one measure of social functioning collected from teachers was consistently positive in all three sites at Grades 6 and 9 although it was not possible to analyze within-site patterns on a single measure. At Grade 9, a significant negative pattern appeared in Highfield resulting from poorer ratings by Highfield youth on the two measures of self-esteem and extracurricular activities.

TABLE 13

EFFECT SIZES AND CROSS-SITE PATTERNS FOR CHILD HEALTH AND HEALTH RISK BEHAVIORS

Measures	Grade 3 Effects				Grade 6 Effects				Grade 9 Effects			
	Cornwall Versus Comparison Site	Sudbury Versus Comparison Site	Highfield Versus Comparison Site	BBBF Sites Combined Versus Comparison Sites	Cornwall Versus Comparison Site	Sudbury Versus Comparison Site	Highfield Versus Comparison Site	BBBF Sites Combined Versus Comparison Sites	Cornwall Versus Comparison Site	Sudbury Versus Comparison Site	Highfield Versus Comparison Site	BBBF Sites Combined Versus Comparison Sites
Child health and health risk behaviors												
Parent-rated												
General health rating	+	−	−	−	−* .15	−* .26	−* .15	−* .18	+	−	+	+
Number of chronic conditions	−** .30	−** .33	− .06	−** .22	.15	−* .28	.14	−** .19	.11	.14	−** .20	−* .18
Child limited by health problems	−	−	+	−	+*	+*	−	+	+	+	+	+
Child's exposure to second-hand smoke					+*		+	+	+	+	+	+
Child-rated												
Body mass index	−* .29	− .17	− .20	−** .21	+	−	+	+	+	+	+	−
Breakfast consumption					+	+	+	+	−	−	+	−
Meets all four food groups recommendation					+	−	+**	+**	+*	+	−	−
Alcohol consumption					+	−	+	+	−	+	+	−
Smoking experience					+	−	+	−	−	−	+	−
Number of times injured in past 12 months					+	+	+	+	−	−	+	−*
Experience with marijuana					+	−	+	+	+	−	+	−*
Stress Index					+	+	+	+	+	−*	+	−
Ever had consensual sex					+	+	+	+	+	−	−	+

Note.—See Table 10.

TABLE 14

EFFECT SIZES AND WITHIN-SITE PATTERNS FOR CHILD SOCIAL FUNCTIONING

Measures	Grade 3 Effects			Grade 6 Effects			Grade 9 Effects		
	Cornwall Versus Comparison Site	Sudbury Versus Comparison Site	Highfield Versus Comparison Site	Cornwall Versus Comparison Site	Sudbury Versus Comparison Site	Highfield Versus Comparison Site	Cornwall Versus Comparison Site	Sudbury Versus Comparison Site	Highfield Versus Comparison Site
Child social functioning									
Parent-rated									
Prosocial Behavior Scale	+			+ .12	+ .06	+**	−	−	−
Number of people important to child		+	−**	+*** .74	+** .39	−	+*	+**	+
Conflict Resolution Scale						−	+*	+**	−
Child-rated									
Self-Esteem Scale				−	−	−	−*	−	−** −.35
Extracurricular Activities Index				+	+	+	+	+	− −.26
Teacher-rated									
Self Control/Conflict Management Scale	+	−	+	+**	+**	+*	+*	+*	+

Note.—BBBF = Better Beginnings, Better Futures; + = favorable effect of the BBBF project; − = undesirable negative effect of the BBBF project.
A blank space indicates that data on that measure were not collected at that time-point.
In this table, dark shading is used to indicate a significant within-site pattern in favor of BBBF. Light shading is used to indicate a significant within-site pattern non-beneficial for BBBF. Within each domain (e.g., parent's ratings of child's social functioning), we examined the results to determine if the within-site results were consistent. Scores were assigned to results according to the following formula: 2 points for a significant result, 1 point for a nonsignificant result in the same direction, and − 1 for a nonsignificant result in the opposite direction. No within-site pattern could be identified if one of the results was significant in the opposite direction. Within each domain and within each site, these scores were then summed. The sum of scores assigned can be referred to a table of critical values, ensuring that each within-site pattern reported is significant at .05.
*p < .05, **p < .01.

Emotional and Behavioral Problems

The results of the analyses of within-site patterns of children's emotional and behavioral problems are summarized in Table 15.

At Grade 6, parents from the BBBF sites in Sudbury and Highfield consistently rated their children as showing higher levels of emotional and behavioral problems than parents from the comparison sites on six of the seven measures. This negative pattern continued at Grade 9 for Highfield but not Sudbury. However, at Grade 9, parents from Cornwall showed consistently lower ratings on all seven measures of their child's emotional and behavioral problems than those from the comparison site in Ottawa-Vanier.

The within-site analyses of teacher ratings of children's emotional and behavioral problems yielded results strikingly different from parent ratings. As shown in Table 15, teachers rated children from the Cornwall BBBF site as showing fewer problems than those from the comparison site at all three grade levels, with a similar pattern of results for teacher ratings of children from Sudbury at Grades 3 and 9. Self-ratings by youth of their emotional and behavioral problems showed a negative pattern at Grade 6 in Sudbury and Cornwall relative to their comparison site. It is interesting to note that the within-site patterns of emotional and behavioral problems were generally more negative by both parents and youth from the BBBF sites and generally more positive for teachers.

School Functioning

The results of the within-site analyses of measures of the child's school functioning are presented in Table 16. Although there were no significant within-site patterns on measures collected at Grade 3, positive patterns on measures emerged for ratings within the Cornwall and Sudbury BBBF site at Grade 6 and for ratings within all three BBBF sites at Grade 9.

These results indicate that the positive cross-site patterns of school functioning in Grades 6 and 9, reported in Table 12, were present in all three BBBF sites with stronger effects in the Cornwall and Sudbury sites than in Highfield.

It is important to note that these positive BBBF outcomes for school functioning are consistent with the positive outcomes on teacher reports of better social functioning and fewer emotional and behavioral problems for BBBF children reported earlier, again with the results somewhat stronger for the Cornwall and Sudbury sites than for Highfield.

Health and Health Risk Behaviors

The results of the analyses of within-site patterns for measures in the domain of child health and health risk are presented in Table 17. No

68

TABLE 15
EFFECT SIZES AND WITHIN-SITE PATTERNS FOR CHILD EMOTIONAL AND BEHAVIORAL PROBLEMS

Measures	Grade 3 Effects			Grade 6 Effects			Grade 9 Effects	
	Cornwall Versus Comparison Site	Sudbury Versus Comparison Site	Highfield Versus Comparison Site	Cornwall Versus Comparison Site	Sudbury Versus Comparison Site	Highfield Versus Comparison Site	Sudbury Versus Comparison Site	Highfield Versus Comparison Site
Child emotional and behavioral problems								
Parent-rated								
Emotional-Anxiety Disorder Scale	−	−	−	+.19	−.14	−.26**	+	−.12
Physical Aggression Scale	+	−	+	+.09	−.25*	−.14	+	−.17*
Indirect Aggression Scale	+	−	+	+.13	−.11	−.23*	+	−.17*
Hyperactivity–Inattention Scale	+	+	−	+.25	−.03	.10	−	−.14
Delinquency Scale	+	+	+	+.17	+.08	+.05	+	−.14*
Oppositional Defiant Scale	+	−	+	+.17	.02	.08	+	.13
Depression Scale	−	−	−	+.23	−.20	−.23**	−	−.14
Teacher-rated								
Emotional-Anxiety Disorder Scale	+** .61	+** .36	−	+.03	−	−	+** .38	+

TABLE 15 (Contd.)

Measures	Grade 3 Effects			Grade 6 Effects			Grade 9 Effects		
	Cornwall Versus Comparison Site	Sudbury Versus Comparison Site	Highfield Versus Comparison Site	Cornwall Versus Comparison Site	Sudbury Versus Comparison Site	Highfield Versus Comparison Site	Cornwall Versus Comparison Site	Sudbury Versus Comparison Site	Highfield Versus Comparison Site
Hyperactivity–Inattention Scale	+** .32	+ .16	+*	+* .34	+**	+	+** .45	+** .48	+
Child-rated									
Emotional-Anxiety Disorder Scale				– .12	– .08	+	–**	–**	–
Physical Aggression Scale				–** .36	–* .24	+	–	–	–
Indirect Aggression Scale				– .22	– .11	+	+	+	+
Hyperactivity–Inattention Scale				–** .11	– .02	+	–	–	+
Delinquency Scale				–** .34	– .15	+	–	–	+
Ever Arrested/Taken to police station							+	+	+
Delinquent Friends Scale							–	–**	+

Note.—See Table 14.

70

TABLE 16
EFFECT SIZES AND WITHIN-SITE PATTERNS FOR SCHOOL FUNCTIONING

Measures	Grade 3 Effects			Grade 6 Effects			Grade 9 Effects		
	Cornwall Versus Comparison Site	Sudbury Versus Comparison Site	Highfield Versus Comparison Site	Cornwall Versus Comparison Site	Sudbury Versus Comparison Site	Highfield Versus Comparison Site	Cornwall Versus Comparison Site	Sudbury Versus Comparison Site	Highfield Versus Comparison Site
School functioning									
Parent-rated									
Child repeated a grade				+	+	+	+**	+*	+
Teacher-rated									
Student Preparedness Scale	+			+ .22	+ .15	+	+* .27	+* .33	+ .20
Adaptive Functioning Scale	+	−		+ .18	+ .17	−	+* .37	+* .30	+ .12
Child suspended since last fall			+*	+ .09	+ .18	+*	+ .03	+ .02	− .03
How far hope child will go in school				+	+ .25	+	+* .38	+* .37	+ .12
Child's current academic achievement	−			− .05	+	+	+* .33	+* .34	+ .01
Standardized mathematics test	−	+**	+	+* .31	+* .47	+	− .20	+ .26	+ .07
Child received special education/services	+	−	+	+* .39	+** .67	−	+ .15	+* .30	+ .15
Child limitations due to learning disability				.21	.32	+	+ .13	+ .08	+* .29

Note.—See Table 14.

TABLE 17

EFFECT SIZES AND WITHIN-SITE PATTERNS FOR CHILD HEALTH AND HEALTH RISK BEHAVIORS

Measures	Grade 3 Effects			Grade 6 Effects			Grade 9 Effects		
	Cornwall Versus Comparison Site	Sudbury Versus Comparison Site	Highfield Versus Comparison Site	Cornwall Versus Comparison Site	Sudbury Versus Comparison Site	Highfield Versus Comparison Site	Cornwall Versus Comparison Site	Sudbury Versus Comparison Site	Highfield Versus Comparison Site
Child health and health risk behaviors									
Parent-rated									
General health rating	+	.00	—	—	—*	—	+	—	+
Number of chronic conditions	—**	—**	—	—	—*	—	—	—	—**
Child limited by health problems	—	—	+	+*	+*	—	+	+	—
Child's exposure to second-hand smoke	+*			+*	+*	—	+	+	+
Child-rated									
Body mass index	—*	—	—	+ .19	—	+ .04	+	— .23	+
Breakfast consumption				+ .06	+	.00	—	— .15	+
Meets all four food groups recommendations				+ .20	—	+** .38	+*	+ .05	—
Alcohol consumption				+ .22	—	+ .11	—	— .16	+
Smoking experience				+ .08	—	+ .02	—	— .19	+
Number of times injured in past 12 months				+ .07	+	+ .16	—	— .16	—
Experience with marijuana							+	— .14	+
Stress Index							+	—* .28	—
Ever had consensual sex							+	.00	—

Note.—See Table 14.

within-site patterns based on parent ratings of the children's health existed at either Grades 3, 6, or 9.

Several measures of health and health risk based on children's self-report were collected starting at Grade 6. For these measures, positive within-site patterns resulted in Cornwall and Highfield. These patterns were not present at Grade 9. However, for the Sudbury site, a negative pattern of within-site youth reported measures of health and health risk was present at Grade 9.

DISCUSSION

The BBBF mandate was to develop programs that would positively impact all areas of children's development, not to focus exclusively on one developmental domain, such as cognitive or academic functioning. Our findings reflect this ecological approach, as positive effects were evident in both social and school functioning domains, and there was evidence of fewer emotional and behavioral problems at school.

Improvements in social functioning among children from BBBF sites were most evident at the Grade 6 follow-up, when children were entering early adolescence. The effect sizes we observed for measures of social functioning were similar in magnitude to those reported by Nelson et al. (2003) in a meta-analysis of 34 preschool prevention programs. It is possible that the improvements we observed in the social domain at Grade 6 (including more prosocial behaviors, greater number of people in social network, greater self-control, and better conflict management at school) contributed to the pronounced effects on school functioning that we observed at Grade 9, when youth had reached mid adolescence. Indeed, a large body of research suggests that children's social and emotional functioning are intimately linked with cognitive development, school adjustment, and academic performance (Bursuck & Asher, 1986; Gresham, 1992; O'Neil, Welsh, Parke, Wang, & Strand, 1997; Zins, Blodworth, Weissberg, & Walberg, 2004). The improvements in school functioning associated with all three BBBF sites at Grade 9 included fewer special education services, less grade repetition, better adaptive functioning/behavior at school, better preparedness to learn in the classroom, and potential to go further in school according to teachers. At Grade 6 we also observed higher academic achievement in mathematics and fewer suspensions from school among BBBF youth. Previous evaluations have demonstrated positive effects of similar magnitude on educational progress and school functioning into adolescence, with the most pronounced effects on grade retention and special education (Karoly et al., 2005; Nelson et al., 2003).

In order to assess children's functioning across diverse situations (home, school, neighborhood), we obtained ratings from multiple informants at each follow-up assessment. At Grade 3, parents and teachers provided ratings; at Grades 6 and 9 we added children's self-reports for most measures. We observed some discrepancies among teacher, parent, and child self-ratings for measures in the emotional and behavioral domains. Specifically, teacher ratings indicated significant reductions/improvements in emotional and behavioral problems in school (less hyperactivity–inattention at Grades 3, 6, and 9 and less emotional anxiety at Grades 3 and 9). Parent and youth ratings, however, indicated that some measures of emotional and behavioral problems were worse among BBBF youth. Parent ratings at Grade 6 indicated more aggressive behavior and depression; youth ratings at Grade 9 indicated lower self-esteem and higher emotional anxiety. These discrepancies among informants, however, should not necessarily cast doubt on the validity or reliability of one or more informants. Rather, according to Achenbach et al. (1987), variations in reports by different informants confirm that these informants should not be substituted for one another because each sees the child in different contexts and may interact differently with the child. Achenbach et al. (1987) noted larger differences among different informants during adolescence; our results seem to match that trend.

Related to the importance of multiple informants, research by Bramlett, Scott, and Rowell (2000) indicates that parent ratings may have limited utility in predicting actual school success. Bramlett and colleagues evaluated children who participated in the Head Start early childhood program in the United States and reported that teacher ratings of children's temperamental characteristics were better predictors of later school success and classroom behavior than were parent ratings (Bramlett et al., 2000). This finding may help to explain why BBBF youth demonstrated such significant improvements in school functioning at Grade 9, despite somewhat disappointing parent ratings for emotional and behavioral problems at Grade 6.

In terms of emotional anxiety, at Grade 9, teachers rated BBBF children lower on this scale, whereas BBBF youth themselves provided higher ratings than youth in comparison sites. It is possible that the youth self-reports of increased anxiety and decreased self-esteem at Grade 9 were related to their improved school functioning. At least one other study has reported that emotional problems in adolescence are associated with academic success. Analyses of NLSCY data illustrated that the prevalence of self-rated anxiety problems at age 15 was higher among youth who had strong reading skills in preadolescence (Beswick & Willms, 2008). Thus, a possible explanation for the higher levels of anxiety and lower self-esteem among BBBF youth at Grade 9 is that the improvements in their school and academic functioning were associated with increased concerns and anxiety about doing well at school. The BBBF programs between JK and Grade 2 emphasized the importance of doing well academically. Although this academic focus may have translated into better school and academic functioning in adolescence, it may also have increased the youths' critical evaluation of themselves, leading to higher self-rated emotional problems and lower self-esteem.

In the academic domain, despite the lower use of special education services at Grade 9, we did not observe a continuation of the better academic performance in mathematics noted in Grade 6. It is possible that the tests used to evaluate academic performance did not enable us to identify the variations in students' performance, or that the BBBF classroom-based programming was not intensive enough to produce an effect strong enough to endure for 6 years. Although previous studies have reported significant positive effects on long-term academic functioning into adolescence (e.g., Reynolds, 2000; Schweinhart et al., 1993), those preventive interventions provided students with specific and intensive interventions that targeted intellectual and academic development. While BBBF classroom-based and before- and after-school programs emphasized the importance of doing well in school, the goal of the project was not to target specifically the cognitive/academic domain; rather, the intention of BBBF was to develop holistic programs that had the potential to positively impact all areas of children's development.

We were somewhat surprised to observe few positive effects in the health domain, despite BBBF's ecological, comprehensive approach. Reviews of adolescent health promotion programs, however, have indicated that attempts at healthy behavior change among adolescents often have limited effectiveness (Lister-Sharp, Chapman, Stewart-Brown, & Sowden, 1999; Thomas, Micucci, Ciliska, & Mirza, 2005; Wandersman & Florin, 2003). The effective school health promotion programs focus not only on students but also on schoolwide changes and community involvement (Thomas et al., 2005). For example, those schools that have implemented comprehensive healthy eating programs (e.g., a combination of food service changes, classroom curriculum, physical activity programs, and family involvement) have reported lower rates of overweight, healthier diets, and higher levels of physical activity than schools without these programs (Veugelers & Fitzgerald, 2005). Although BBBF was comprehensive and involved a variety of programs with the potential to positively impact children's health, even comprehensive interventions are unlikely to have a lifelong impact because they are offered at one point in a child's development (Tremblay et al., 1996). Perhaps BBBF could have offered "booster" sessions at strategic points in development (e.g., during transition to high school). These follow-up sessions would have targeted age-specific developmental challenges, such as alcohol between the ages of 10 and 12, or drugs and sexual intercourse between the ages of 12 and 14. Parents may also have benefitted from booster workshops during their children's developmental transitions (Tremblay et al., 1996).

The purpose of the cross-site analyses was to examine outcomes across all three BBBF sites relative to the comparison sites. These were the primary analyses, designed to determine the extent to which the general BBBF model was associated with similar effects across all three project communities. On the other hand, the within-site analyses were designed to examine whether different patterns of outcomes existed among the three BBBF sites relative to their respective comparison site. The analyses of patterns of outcomes within each of the BBBF sites for the four child development domains yielded the most positive outcomes for children from the Cornwall BBBF site relative to its comparison site. Teacher ratings resulted in a significant pattern of fewer emotional and behavioral problems in children from Cornwall than from their comparison site for measures collected at Grades 3, 6, and 9 and rated the children from Cornwall more positively on a measure of social functioning at Grades 6 and 9. Parents from Cornwall rated their children as showing better social functioning at Grade 6 and fewer emotional/behavioral problems at Grade 9, and they reported that their child had repeated fewer grades by Grade 9 than children from their comparison site. The youth self-reports from the Cornwall BBBF site showed a positive pattern across the measures of health and health risk behaviors at Grade 6 but also a negative pattern of more emotional and behavioral problems at Grade 6 relative to the comparison site. In summary, out of the total number of 20 possible within-site patterns analyzed, there were 8 positive patterns and 1 negative pattern within the Cornwall site measures.

The within-site analyses of the measures comparing the Sudbury BBBF site to its comparison site yielded positive patterns for teacher ratings of fewer emotional and behavioral problems at Grades 3 and 9, positive patterns for school functioning at Grades 6 and 9, and positive ratings on the single measure of social functioning at Grades 6 and 9. For parents, there was also a positive pattern of social functioning at Grade 6. These five positive patterns are very similar to those from Cornwall described above, as is the negative pattern of children reporting more emotional and behavioral problems in both sites at Grade 6. However, at Grade 6, parents from Sudbury rated the children as showing more emotional and behavioral problems and youth self-ratings also showed the same negative pattern. Also, at Grade 9, youth from Sudbury indicated a pattern of higher levels of health risk behaviors relative to youth from the comparison site. Thus, for Sudbury, the within-site analyses yielded generally positive results based on teacher measures, as was the case in Cornwall, but parents reports yielded one positive and one negative pattern for social functioning and children's emotional and behavioral problems, and the ratings by the children themselves resulted in two negative patterns, emotional and behavioral problems in Grade 6 and health risk behaviors in Grade 9.

For the Highfield BBBF site, there were five significant within-site patterns. Two patterns were positive, namely teacher ratings of better school functioning at Grade 9, similar to those from Cornwall and Sudbury, and children's reports of fewer health risk behaviors at Grade 6, a result mirroring that from Cornwall. However, on two occasions, Grades 6 and 9, Highfield parents rated their children as having more emotional and behavioral problems, a negative pattern similar to that observed in Sudbury parent ratings in Grade 6. Finally, at Grade 9, Highfield children rated themselves as having lower self-esteem and less engagement in extracurricular activities than children from the comparison site.

Although the positive patterns of school functioning applied to all three BBBF sites, there was some indication that the within-site effects in the other domains of child outcome measures were less consistent in the Highfield site. A possible reason for this may have been the highly multicultural makeup of the Highfield community, which is, in fact, one of the most multicultural communities in Canada. Over 40 languages are spoken in the Highfield community, and 60% of the Highfield parents who participated in the longitudinal research reported in the monograph were born outside of Canada (see chapter II). Consequently, the multicultural nature of Highfield may have posed substantially greater challenges than Cornwall or Sudbury for providing effective BBBF child-focused prevention programs.

SUMMARY

The cross-site analyses of the outcome results for the four child developmental domains indicated that positive outcomes favoring children from the three BBBF sites occurred in social functioning at Grades 6 and 9 and better school functioning and fewer emotional and behavioral problems as rated by teachers in Grades 3, 6, and 9. On the other hand, parent ratings of children's emotional and behavioral problems were significantly higher for children from the BBBF sites for the measures of physical and indirect aggression and depression at Grade 6. BBBF children's self-ratings of physical aggression were also higher at Grade 6. Measures from the domain of physical health and health risk over the three time periods suggested that the health of the BBBF children was generally poorer than that of the comparison site children.

The ratio of positive to negative cross-site patterns increased substantially from Grades 6 (seven positive, six negative) to 9 (nine positive, three negative). Measures of parent and teacher ratings of social functioning, fewer hyperactive–inattention behaviors and emotional anxiety problems at school, and better school performance accounted for the positive cross-site patterns favoring BBBF children at Grade 9, while parents' ratings of more chronic health conditions in their children and youth rating themselves as lower in self-esteem and experiencing more emotional anxiety problems accounted for the negative pattern for BBBF youth in Grade 9.

The analyses of child outcomes within each of the three BBBF sites relative to their comparison sites resulted in positive outcomes in Cornwall and Sudbury for parent ratings of social functioning, teacher ratings of school functioning, and fewer emotional and behavioral problems. Teacher ratings of school functioning yielded a positive BBBF pattern in Highfield only in Grade 9. Why did the most consistently positive BBBF outcomes occur on measures of school functioning? Many of the child-focused programs in all three BBBF sites were organized around the local schools. In Highfield and Cornwall, many of those programs were delivered in the child's classroom, while in Sudbury, the child-focused programs occurred predominantly immediately before and after school. This may have accounted for the findings that the most consistent positive effects involved ratings of children's functioning in the school environment.[1]

Findings reported in this chapter demonstrate that substantial long-term impacts on children's social and school functioning can be achieved with an ecological approach and community involvement. In the following chapter, we examine the effects of the BBBF project on parent, family, and community outcomes.

NOTE

1. We should mention here that at Grades 3, 6, and 9, we analyzed ratings by teachers of children still residing in the BBBF neighborhood versus those residing elsewhere. No significant differences resulted from the analyses, suggesting that the generally positive teacher ratings of children from the BBBF sites were not influenced by teacher knowledge of children's program participation.

IV. PARENT, FAMILY, AND COMMUNITY OUTCOMES AT GRADES 3, 6, AND 9

The previous chapter investigated effects of Better Beginnings, Better Futures (BBBF) on several developmental domains, including children's social functioning, emotional and behavioral problems, school functioning, and health. In this chapter, we examine the second major study question that was outlined in chapter I: To what extent does BBBF participation positively affect parent health, parenting behaviors, family functioning, and community involvement? We examine results in these domains for parent, family, and community data that were collected when children were in Grades 3, 6, and 9.

THE IMPORTANCE OF PARENTS, FAMILIES, AND COMMUNITIES FOR THE WELL-BEING OF CHILDREN AND ADOLESCENTS

Bronfenbrenner's (1979) ecological theory has had an important influence in conceptualizing child development, and it is now recognized that important levels of analysis for understanding the child are the parents, family (Bronfenbrenner, 1986b), and neighborhood (Leventhal & Brooks-Gunn, 2000). Indeed, parents, families, and communities provide a critical context in which adolescents live, work, and play, and have a profound impact on their well-being.

Although there is some controversy over the extent to which parents and families influence their adolescent children's behavior (Harris, 1998), there is a considerable body of evidence that links early parenting practices to a range of adolescent outcomes. Most of this research focuses on three dimensions of parents' behavior: (a) parents' support for and responsiveness to their children, (b) their behavioral control of their children's behavior through firm and consistent disciplinary practices, and (c) psychological control of their children's behavior through practices such as withdrawal of love. Parental support has been linked to better academic performance (Herman, Dornbusch, Herron, & Herting, 1997), higher levels of social skill (Gray & Steinberg, 1999), enhanced feelings of adolescent well-being (Gray & Steinberg, 1999), lower levels of depression (Garber, Robinson, & Valentiner, 1997), and fewer internalizing or externalizing problems (Fauber, Forehand, Thomas, & Wierson, 1990). Moderate levels of behavioral control have been linked to lower levels of delinquency, antisocial behavior, and substance abuse in adolescence (Buehler, 2006; Galambos, Barker, & Almeida, 2003; Pettit, Laird, Dodge, Bates, & Criss, 2001).

Family characteristics, at a more general level, also influence the well-being of adolescents who are a part of those families. Families in which members provide one another with emotional support ("connection") but at the same time allow members to express their individuality ("individuation") tend to promote healthy personality development in adolescents (Grotevant & Cooper, 1986). Indeed, longitudinal research suggests that individuals who, during adolescence, experience healthy families in which members support one another but encourage independence, show the benefits up to 25 years later (Bell & Bell, 2005).

The community context in which adolescents live also has important effects on health and development (Leventhal & Brooks-Gunn, 2000). Communities vary widely in terms of the kinds of problems that young people within those communities experience. In a survey of more than 33,000 youth in Grades 9–12 in 112 different communities in the United States (Blyth & Roehlkepartain, 1993), wide variations in at-risk behaviors such as alcohol and drug use, sexual activity, and antisocial behavior were found. Much of the variation in these risk behaviors can be attributed to the level of socioeconomic disadvantage present in the neighborhood (Aneshensel & Sucoff, 1996; Schneiders et al., 2003). Another key community characteristic associated with the well-being of young people has to do with the kinds of opportunities that young people have to participate in community life through structured activities such as sports, music, and work with religious or cultural organizations in their neighborhoods (Blyth & Leffert, 1995; Blyth & Roehlkepartain, 1993). Among demographically and socioeconomically similar communities, those which experienced fewer problem behaviors in their young people were the communities that had more activities available for their youth (Blyth & Leffert, 1995). Participation in community activities allows adolescents to come into contact with caring adults, which is also a significant factor in promoting adolescent well-being (Catalano, Berglund, Ryan, Lonczak, & Hawkins, 2002).

EFFECTIVE PREVENTION PROGRAMS FOR THE PROMOTION OF PARENT, FAMILY, AND COMMUNITY WELL-BEING

As examined in earlier chapters, preventive interventions have been shown to be effective in reducing social and emotional problems for children and promoting the long-term well-being of children and families (Durlak et al., 2007; Weisz, Sandler, Durlak, & Anton, 2005). Some prevention programs have provided family support such as home visitation and parenting skills programs, and are designed to strengthen parent and family well-being, which can indirectly enhance children's well-being (Kumpfer & Alvarado, 2003; Nelson, Laurendeau, Chamberland, & Peirson, 2001). Meta-analytic reviews of family support programs have consistently shown positive impacts on parents' functioning, family well-being, parenting, and parent-child relationships (Durlak et al., 2007; Geeraert, Van den Noortgate, Grietans, & Onghena, 2004; Lundahl, Nimer, & Parsons, 2006; MacLeod & Nelson, 2000; Nelson et al., 2003).

Some community-based prevention projects have taken a community development approach that involves engaging residents in the community development process, building community capacity, coalitions, and partnerships, and striving to improve community conditions (e.g., safety) and residents' sense of community. As described in chapter I, there has been considerably less research that examines community outcomes of these community-driven approaches to prevention. In a review of 526 studies, Durlak et al. (2007) identified only two programs that examined community outcomes and these were limited to measures of how much children bonded with adults other than parents or teachers in the community.

Despite the growing belief that optimal program development should include the meaningful input of key stakeholders, including members of the families who will be participating in these programs, few programs to date have granted community members a significant role in program development or implementation. In addition, few prevention programs have adopted the kind of comprehensive, ecological, holistic approach that is now advocated by policy makers. The BBBF Project, by contrast, was a multisite, comprehensive, universal, community-based program that was designed to influence a wide range of child, family, and community outcomes. As Durlak et al. (2007) noted in their recent review of universal, competence promotion programs for children and adolescent, BBBF was unique as a large-scale community-based intervention that used participatory research methods to target families, schools, and community-based organizations. One of the key goals guiding BBBF from its inception was to strengthen parents, families, and the neighborhood in responding to the needs of young children. As previously described in chapter I, Figure 1 illustrates the pathways through which BBBF was hypothesized to positively impact these systems. The research reported here describes the effects of BBBF on parents, families, and communities, at the Grades 3, 6, and 9 follow-up assessments.

MEASURES

Details of each measure are described below. A summary of the reliability coefficients for each scale at each time-point is presented in Appendix C.

Parent Health and Health Risk Behaviors

Parent health and parent risk behaviors were assessed with a range of measures at Grades 3, 6, and 9. Parents answered the question, "in general, would you say your health is: excellent, very good, good, or fair or poor?" Parents also reported their current *weight* and *height*. Body mass index was calculated by weight (kg) divided by height (m) squared. We collected data on *smoking*, wherein parents were asked the number of cigarettes smoked each day, with answers ranging from: $0 = none$ to $2 = more\ than\ half\ a\ pack$. At Grades 3, 6, and 9, two questions in the parent interview were combined to form a Problems with Professional Services Index, including "was there ever a time during the past 12 months when you wanted to see a professional for your child but did not" and "did you ever feel you were not getting as good service as other people?" Responses to each item were $0 = no$ or $1 = yes$. The index had a range of 0–2, with higher values indicating more problems with professional service.

Parent/Family Functioning

Parents' perceived social support was assessed when their children were in Grades 3, 6, and 9 with a six-item version of the Social Provisions Scale (Cutrona & Russell, 1987). Items (e.g., "I have family and friends who help me feel safe, secure, and happy" and "if something went wrong, no one would help me") were rated on a 4-point scale from $1 = strongly\ disagree$ to $4 = strongly\ agree$. Total scores ranged from a low of 6 to 24, with high scores indicating more social support. As well, parental depressive symptoms were assessed with 12 items from the Center for Epidemiological Studies Depression Scale (Radloff, 1977). Items were rated on a 4-point scale from $1 = rarely\ or\ none\ of\ the\ time$ to $4 = most\ or\ all\ of\ the\ time$. Total scores ranged from 12 to 48, with higher scores indicating greater prevalence of depressive symptoms. *Marital satisfaction* was assessed on one item from the Quality of Life Survey (Institute for Social Research, 1981), where 0 indicated *complete dissatisfaction* with the relationship and 10 indicated *complete satisfaction*.

82

Three measures were used to assess family functioning and family stress when children were in Grades 3, 6, and 9. Seven items from the General Functioning Scale of the Family Assessment Device (FAD) provided a global assessment of the quality of family functioning (Epstein, Baldwin, & Bishop, 1983). Parents rated how strongly they agree or disagree with the seven statements on a 4-point scale (1 = *strongly disagree* to 4 = *strongly agree*). Sample items included "in times of crisis we can turn to each other for support" and "we express feelings to each other." Total scores ranged from a low of 7 indicating very poor family functioning to a high of 28 indicating excellent family functioning. Parents were asked whether a set of 13 potentially *stressful events* (e.g., losing a job, separation from a spouse or partner) had occurred in the past year (Institute for Social Research, 1981). Total scores ranged from 0 to 13, with higher scores indicating more stress. In addition, three questions examined the degree of *financial stress* being experienced by the family as indicated by the use of food banks, and not having enough money for daily living expenses and for paying monthly bills. Responses were rated from 0 = *false* or 1 = *true*, and the three items were summed into one index (total score ranged from 0 to 3).

Parenting was assessed using a scale from the Canadian National Longitudinal Survey of Children and Youth (NLSCY), the Hostile-Ineffective Parenting Scale, when their children were in Grades 3, 6, and 9. Parents were asked to indicate how often they engage in seven behaviors (e.g., "how often do you think that the kind of punishment you give your child depends on your mood?") toward their child, which were rated from 0 = *never* to 4 = *many times a day*. Total scores ranged from 0 to 28, with high scores indicating more frequent hostile-ineffective parenting. In addition, Grade 9 youth were also asked three questions from the NLSCY about how often their *parents monitored their activities*. The questions (e.g., "parents want to know exactly where I am and what I am doing") were rated on a 4-point scale from 0 = *never* to 4 = *always*. The total scores ranged from 0 to 12, with high scores indicating a high level of monitoring.

Community Involvement and Neighborhood Quality

We assessed parents' neighborhood activities and individual social activities when their children were in Grades 3, 6, and 9. *Parents' neighborhood activities* over the past year were measured with a six-item scale developed by BBBF researchers. Parents indicated how often they participated in neighborhood activities using a 3-point rating scale from 0 = *not at all* to 2 = *frequently*. Total scores ranged from 0 to 12, with higher scores indicating higher levels of neighborhood activity. Examples of items included "attended a recreational event" and "attended neighborhood events." *Parents' individual social activities* were assessed with an index created by combining responses to three questions regarding how often in the last month parents got together with friends, got together with other families in the community, and attended spiritual or religious services.

Parents' *sense of community involvement* was assessed using five items selected from a scale designed to measure neighborhood cohesion (Buckner, 1988). Items included, for example, "I feel like I belong to this neighborhood" and "I feel I am important to this neighborhood." Parents responded on a 4-point scale from 1 = *strongly agree* to 4 = *strongly disagree*. Total scores ranged from 5 to 20.

The measure of *neighborhood satisfaction* was developed by the Quality of Urban Life Surveys (Institute for Social Research, 1981). This measure consisted of five items. Parents were asked to rate neighborhood quality in terms of condition of buildings, streets, neighbors, safety and crime, as well as conduciveness to raising children. The rating scale ranged from 1 = *poor* to 5 = *excellent*, with total scores ranging from 4 to 30.

The Health Care and Social Service Utilization Index, created by BBBF researchers, assessed parents' use of health care and social services *for their child* in the past year. At Grades 3, 6, and 9, parents indicated whether or not they had seen or talked on the telephone with a family physician, other medical doctor, specialist, public health nurse, psychologist/psychiatrist, dentist/orthodontist, child welfare worker, or any other person trained to provide treatment and counsel (e.g., speech therapist or social worker); and whether they had attended an emergency room, after-hours clinic or parent resource center for their child. Responses to each item were 0 = *no* or 1 = *yes*. The index had a total score of 0–7, with higher values indicating higher health and social service utilization.

RESULTS

Cross-Site Patterns

In the sections below, we report *p* values, effect sizes (ES), and pattern direction (+ or −) for statistically significant patterns of results across the three BBBF Project sites relative to the comparison sites (see Table 18). As in chapter III, a "+" pattern indicates an outcome favorable to BBBF and a "−" pattern is favorable to the comparison sites. In Appendix D, means and standard deviations are listed for all outcome measures presented in this chapter.

Parent Health and Health Risk Behaviors

Despite observing no significant difference in parent-rated health at Grade 3, at the Grade 6 follow-up, there was a significant negative pattern

TABLE 18
Effect Sizes and Cross-Site Patterns for Parent, Family, and Community Outcomes

Measures	Grade 3 Effects				Grade 6 Effects				Grade 9 Effects			
	Cornwall Versus Comparison Site	Sudbury Versus Comparison Site	Highfield Versus Comparison Site	BBBF Sites Combined Versus Comparison Sites	Cornwall Versus Comparison Site	Sudbury Versus Comparison Site	Highfield Versus Comparison Site	BBBF Sites Combined Versus Comparison Sites	Cornwall Versus Comparison Site	Sudbury Versus Comparison Site	Highfield Versus Comparison Site	BBBF Sites Combined Versus Comparison Sites
Parent health and health risk behaviors												
Parent-rated												
Self-rated health	+	−	−	−	− .16	− .14	−** .27	−** .20	+	+	−	+
Body mass index	+	+	+	+	+	+	−	−	+	+	+	+
Smoking	+	+	+	−	+	+	−	+	−	−	+	+
Problems with Professional Service Index	−*	−	+	−	+	−	+	+	+	+	+	+
Parent/family functioning												
Parent-rated												
Social Support Scale	+	−	−	−	+** .75	+** .38	+ .11	+** .38	+** .45	+** .44	+** .35	+** .40
Depression Scale	+*	−	−**	−	+	−	+	−	+	+	+	+
Marital satisfaction	+*	+	−	+	+	+	+	+	+* .41	+* .30	+ .12	+* .26
Family Functioning Scale	− .05	−** .54	− .01	−** .23	+** .58	+ .09	+** .27	+** .31	+ .38	+** .36	+ .14	+** .28

TABLE 18 (Contd.)

Measures	Grade 3 Effects				Grade 6 Effects				Grade 9 Effects			
	Cornwall Versus Comparison Site	Sudbury Versus Comparison Site	Highfield Versus Comparison Site	BBBF Sites Combined Versus Comparison Sites	Cornwall Versus Comparison Site	Sudbury Versus Comparison Site	Highfield Versus Comparison Site	BBBF Sites Combined Versus Comparison Sites	Cornwall Versus Comparison Site	Sudbury Versus Comparison Site	Highfield Versus Comparison Site	BBBF Sites Combined Versus Comparison Sites
Stressful life events	+	−	+	+	−** .31	−** .40	−* .17	−** .29	+	−	−	−
Financial stress	−	+	+	+	−	−*	+	+	+**	+*	−	+
Hostile-Ineffective Parenting Scale	−	+	+	+	−* .20	−* .22	−** .26	−** .24	+*	+*	−	+*
Child-rated												
Parent Monitoring Scale									−** .39	−* .25	−** .38	−** .33
Community involvement and neighborhood quality												
Parent-rated												
Neighborhood Activities Scale	+* .23	+	+	+	+* .21	+* .36	+ .03	+* .19	+	+	+	+
Parent's Social Activities Index	+	+* .27	− .03	+* .15[a]	+	+	−	−	+	+	−	+
Sense of Community Involvement Scale	+	+	+	+	+** .43	+ .08	+** .32	+** .30	+	+	+	+*
Neighborhood Satisfaction Scale	+*	−*	−	−*	+** .67	− .09	+* .28	+* .35[a]	+** .62	+ .02	+* .39	+** .41

Health Care and Social Services Utilization Index											
+** .60	+* .18	+ .07	+** .25	+** .45	+ .12	+ .06	+** .20	—	—	+	—

Note.—BBBF = Better Beginnings, Better Futures; + = favorable effect of the BBBF project; – = undesirable or negative effect of the BBBF project.

A blank space indicates that data on that measure were not collected at that time-point.

In this table, dark shading is used to indicate a significant cross-site pattern in favor of BBBF. Light shading is used to indicate a significant cross-site pattern nonbeneficial for BBBF. A significant cross-site effect required three criteria to be met, including (a) the result for overall BBBF sites versus comparison sites was significant; (b) the result for at least one individual site was significantly different from its matched comparison site; and (c) no individual site showed results in the opposite direction.

[a] In Tables 10–13 and 18, there are seven cross-site patterns where criterion (c) was not met. In these seven exceptional cases, results for two of the three BBBF sites were statistically significant in the same direction; the result for the third site was in the opposite direction but the effect size was close to zero (ES < .10). Therefore, we deemed these seven cases to merit consideration.

*p < .05, **p < .01.

on parent-rated health with parents in BBBF communities having significantly worse self-rated health ($p<.01$; ES $= -.20$). By Grade 9, however, this effect was no longer evident. There were no other significant health differences between parents from BBBF sites and from comparison sites at any time point.

Parent/Family Functioning

At both Grades 6 and 9, there were significant positive outcomes associated with BBBF program participation on parents' social support. The cross-site patterns were significant at both time periods ($p<.01$; ES $= .38$ at Grade 6 and .40 at Grade 9). There was also a significant positive pattern for BBBF parents' self-reported marital satisfaction at Grade 9 ($p<.05$; ES $= .26$), but not at Grades 3 or 6. Although we observed a negative pattern associated with scores on the general functioning scale of the FAD for BBBF families at Grade 3 ($p<.01$; ES $= -.23$), there were significant positive patterns on the measure of family functioning at both Grades 6 ($p<.01$; ES $= .31$) and 9 ($p<.01$; ES $= .28$) across the three BBBF sites. When the children were in Grade 6, there was a significant negative pattern indicating that parents from the BBBF sites reported higher levels of stressful life events than those from the comparison sites on the stressful life events measure ($p<.01$; ES $= -.29$). However, this negative effect was no longer apparent at Grade 9. Likewise, there was a significant negative pattern on the Hostile-Ineffective Parenting Scale at Grade 6 ($p<.01$; ES $= -.24$), possibly influenced by the greater perceived stress by the BBBF parents. At Grade 9, however, the direction of findings for this scale favored BBBF. Finally, Grade 9 youth from the BBBF sites reported less monitoring by their parents than youth from the comparison sites ($p<.01$; ES $= -.33$).

Parent Community Involvement and Neighborhood Quality

Findings at both Grades 3 and 6 indicated that parents who participated in BBBF were more active in the community. At Grade 3, parents from the BBBF sites reported more social activities ($p<.05$; ES $= .15$) and in Grade 6, they reported more neighborhood activities ($p<.05$; ES $= .19$) than parents from comparison sites. Also, when children were in Grade 6, parents living in the BBBF sites indicated that they had a greater sense of community involvement ($p<.01$; ES $= .30$) than parents living in comparison sites. At Grades 6 and 9, results suggested that parents living in the BBBF sites were more satisfied with their neighborhoods ($p<.01$; ES $= .35$ and .41 for Grades 6 and 9, respectively). Also, in Grades 3 and 6, BBBF parents reported using health care and social services for their child more frequently than parents at comparison sites ($p < .01$; ES = .25 at Grade 3 and .20 at Grade 6); this difference, however, was not observed in Grade 9.

Within-Site Patterns

The results from the analyses of within-site patterns are presented in Table 19; the within-site analyses were designed to examine whether different patterns of outcomes existed across all measures within each of the domains of parent health, parent/family functioning, and also community involvement and quality among the three BBBF sites relative to their respective comparison site.

Parent Health and Health Risk Behaviors

No significant within-site patterns resulted from these analyses.

Parent/Family Functioning

At Grade 9, significant within-site patterns favoring the two BBBF sites in Cornwall and Sudbury resulted. These patterns resulted from parent perceptions of greater social support, less personal depression, greater marital satisfaction, more positive general family functioning, less perceived stress and less hostile ineffective parenting for parents from Cornwall and Sudbury relative to their comparison sites. In Highfield, parents also reported positive outcomes relative to the comparison site on measures of social support, depression, marital satisfaction, and family functioning at Grade 9. However, nonsignificant negative outcomes on the two measures of stress and hostile parenting for Highfield prevented the positive pattern across all these measures that existed in Cornwall and Sudbury. Because parental monitoring was the only child report measure in this domain no within-site pattern was possible.

Parent Community Involvement and Neighborhood Quality

The analyses yielded two positive within-site patterns, both for parents from the Cornwall site when the children were in Grade 3 and again when they were in Grade 6. Although ratings on those measures remained predominantly positive for Cornwall parents at Grade 9, the pattern was not statistically significant. It is interesting to note, however, that analyses of the 45 outcomes reported in Table 18 were predominantly in the positive

TABLE 19

EFFECT SIZES AND WITHIN-SITE PATTERNS FOR PARENT, FAMILY, AND COMMUNITY OUTCOMES

Measures	Grade 3 Effects Cornwall Versus Comparison Site	Grade 3 Effects Sudbury Versus Comparison Site	Grade 3 Effects Highfield Versus Comparison Site	Grade 6 Effects Cornwall Versus Comparison Site	Grade 6 Effects Sudbury Versus Comparison Site	Grade 6 Effects Highfield Versus Comparison Site	Grade 9 Effects Cornwall Versus Comparison Site	Grade 9 Effects Sudbury Versus Comparison Site	Grade 9 Effects Highfield Versus Comparison Site
Parent health and health risk behaviors									
Parent-rated									
Self-rated health	+	−	−	−	−	−**	+	+	+
Body mass index	+	+	−	+	−	−	+	+	+
Smoking	+	+	+	+	+	−	+	−	+
Problems with Professional Service Index	−*	−	+	+	−	+	+	+	+
Parent/family functioning									
Parent-rated									
Social Support Scale	+	−	−	+**	+**	+	+** .45	+** .44	+**
Depression Scale	+	−	−**	−	−	+	+ .16	+ .09	+
Marital satisfaction	+*	+	−	+	+	+	+** .41	+* .30	+
Family Functioning Scale	−	−**	+	+**	+	+**	+** .38	+** .36	+
Stressful life events	+	−	+	−**	−**	−*	+ .24	− .08	−
Financial stress	−	−	+	−	−	+	+** .32	+* .27	−

Measure									
Hostile-Ineffective Parenting Scale									
Child-rated	—	+	—	+	—	—*	—*	+* .26	—
Parent Monitoring Scale	—**			—**		—*	—**	+* .28	—**
Community involvement and neighborhood quality									
Parent-rated									
Neighborhood Activities Scale	.07 +*	+	+ .21	+*	+	+	+	+	+
Parent's Social Activities Index	.23 +	+*	— .05 +**	+	—	+	+	+	—
Sense of Community Involvement Scale	.10 +*	+	+ .43 +**	+**	+	+**	+	+	+
Neighborhood Satisfaction Scale	.28 +**a	—**	— .67 +**a	+*	—	+**	+**	+	+*
Health Care and Social Services Utilization Index	.60 +***a	+*	.45 +**a	+	+	+	+	—	+

Note.—BBBF = Better Beginnings, Better Futures; + = favorable effect of the BBBF project; — = undesirable or negative effect of the BBBF project.
A blank space indicates that data on that measure were not collected at that time-point.
In this table, dark shading is used to indicate a significant within-site pattern in favor of BBBF. Light shading is used to indicate a significant within-site pattern nonbeneficial for BBBF. Within each domain (e.g., parent's ratings of family functioning), we examined the results to determine if the within-site results were consistent. Scores were assigned to results according to the following formula: 2 points for a significant result, 1 point for a nonsignificant result in the same direction, and − 1 for a nonsignificant result in the opposite direction. No within-site pattern could be identified if one of the results was significant in the opposite direction. Within each domain and within each site, these scores were then summed. The sum of scores assigned can be referred to a table of critical values, ensuring that each within-site pattern reported is significant at .05.
*p < .05, **p < .01.

direction, favoring the BBBF sites. It was these results that yielded the many positive cross-site patterns on the measures of community involvement and neighborhood quality described earlier.

DISCUSSION

In line with Bronfenbrenner's (1979, 1986a) ecological theory, and its subsequent development to include issues relating to resilience in children (Luthar, Sawyer, & Brown, 2006; Sandler, 2001), there have been increasing calls for comprehensive, community-driven, prevention initiatives for young children and families. There have yet to be rigorous controlled evaluations of such initiatives (Durlak et al., 2007). Our aim in this monograph was to begin to fill that gap by evaluating the effects of the BBBF Project in terms of changes in the microsystems and mesosystems that are important to the prevention of developmental problems and the enhancement of the well-being of children. In this chapter, we examined the effects associated with BBBF at parent, family, and community levels, and observed some significant findings for each group of outcome measures.

Parent Outcomes

There was a positive pattern favoring parents from the BBBF sites on social support at both Grades 6 and 9. The finding of enhanced social support is consistent with qualitative data that we have gathered, which showed that many parents reported making friends and feeling less isolated as a function of their participation in BBBF (Nelson, Pancer, Hayward, & Peters, 2005). The strong expectation for parent participation in BBBF and the many socially oriented activities and programs offered by the sites brought parents into contact with other community members, thus potentially creating several different avenues for increased social support. Another positive BBBF pattern observed at the Grade 9 follow-up was for marital satisfaction, despite no significant impact on this measure at Grade 3 or 6.

Previous evaluations of family support programs have demonstrated positive impacts on parents. Two meta-analytic reviews have reported positive impacts on parent functioning, with ES ranging from .25 to .58 (Geeraert et al., 2004; Lundahl et al., 2006). The ES we observed for measures of parent functioning were similar in magnitude to those reported in these two reviews. One of the premises of a comprehensive, ecological approach to prevention is that in order for parents to be effective change agents for their children, they must be functioning well themselves. The findings of increased social support and enhanced marital satisfaction when the children were in Grade 9 suggest that BBBF programs had positive effects on parents' social and emotional well-being.

Family and Parenting Outcomes

Whereas there was a negative effect on the measure of family functioning at the short-term follow-up (Grade 3), we found a clear and consistent improvement in family functioning at both the Grades 6 and 9 follow-up periods. The observed ES of .31 and .28 on family functioning are similar in magnitude to those reported in meta-analytic reviews (Durlak et al., 2007; Geeraert et al., 2004; Lundahl et al., 2006; MacLeod & Nelson, 2000; Nelson et al., 2003). The importance of overall family climate for the well-being of adolescents has been documented in previous research (Gorman-Smith, Tolan, Loeber, & Henry, 1998; Grotevant & Cooper, 1986). For example, Bell and Bell (2005) found that family climate during adolescence predicted participants' psychological well-being at midlife, more than 25 years later. Thus, family climate appears to be an important protective factor that can be enhanced through community-based interventions such as BBBF.

Other family and parenting outcomes were not positively impacted by BBBF. In fact, on some of these outcomes, BBBF families fared worse than those in the comparison sites. When the children were in Grade 6, BBBF parents reported significantly more stressful life events than those in the comparison sites. Closer inspection of the results revealed that out of the 13 items on the stressful life events index, 33% of the parents from the BBBF sites indicated three or more events had occurred in the past year, whereas only 18% of the comparison site parents identified three or more events. The largest differences between BBBF and comparison sites occurred on the following items: "lost job or was unemployed" (26% of BBBF parents compared with 11% of comparison site parents), "serious illness of someone dear" (32% vs. 16%), and "death of someone dear" (27% vs. 16%). It is not apparent how the BBBF programs would have impacted these stressful life events. No comparable differences in stressful events occurred at either Grade 3 or 9, so these seem to have been a series of events at Grade 6 that substantially increased the stress of BBBF families relative to the comparison site families.

The finding of higher levels of hostile-ineffective parent behavior at Grade 6 in the BBBF sites was unexpected because improved parenting was an explicit and important goal of BBBF and each of the three sites had programs to support parents and to improve their parenting skills. Meta-analytic reviews of family support and prevention programs have consistently reported improved parenting resulting from such programs (Durlak et al., 2007; Geeraert et al., 2004; Lundahl et al., 2006; MacLeod & Nelson,

2000; Nelson et al., 2003), although most of these programs have been implemented with parents of very aggressive children ages 3–6.

It may have been that the hostile-ineffective parenting outcome at Grade 6 reflected the pattern of increased stress in the BBBF families because punitive parenting is often based on parents' mood rather than a conscious disciplinary strategy (Greenwald, Bank, Reid, & Knutson, 1998). It is also possible that the sites did not select the most effective parenting programs based on available research because none of the three sites employed an evidence-based parenting program but rather relied on more general parent support activities for parents. Recent reviews (e.g., Eyberg, Nelson, & Boggs, 2008; Piquero, Farrington, Welsh, Tremblay, & Jennings, 2008) have identified several parent training programs as effective in demonstrating improved parenting skills and decreased severe behavioral problems in preschool and primary-aged children (e.g., Positive Parenting Program [Triple-P], Sanders, Markie-Dodds, Turner, & Ralph, 2004); Incredible Years (IY, Webster-Stratton, Reid, & Hammond, 2001). These parent training programs aim to teach parents how to avoid the negative reciprocal interactions with aggressive and oppositional children. Had this type of parent training been provided, BBBF parents may have been better equipped to deal effectively with their children's aggressive behaviors and may not have resorted to hostile-ineffective interactions. Clearly, this is one important area that needs to be examined more thoroughly and strengthened in the BBBF Project.

The one parenting effect at Grade 9 that was considered in our analyses to be negative was that BBBF children reported that their parents monitored their whereabouts significantly less than parents in the comparison communities. Again, the need for age-appropriate and evidence-based approaches to parent training is underscored by this finding. As children reach adolescence, they can stray into relationships with deviant peers or develop behavioral or other problems unless their parents play an active role in monitoring their relationships and behavior. It is also possible, however, that the BBBF parents monitored their children less because they viewed their neighborhoods as safer and less likely to pose a threat to their children (as evidenced by the significant positive neighborhood satisfaction at Grades 6 and 9).

The generally positive outcomes for the three BBBF sites on measures of family and parent functioning, most strongly apparent in Cornwall and Sudbury, reflect the significant positive cross-site patterns on the measures of social support and family functioning at Grades 6 and 9 and marital satisfaction at Grade 9. Thus, it appears that there have been increasingly positive outcomes for BBBF sites in the general area of parent and family functioning in Grade 6 and 9, and that those positive outcomes were stronger for the Cornwall and Sudbury sites.

At Grade 9, positive impacts were found for the Cornwall and Sudbury sites, but not for the Highfield site, on parent ratings of parent/family functioning. This is a surprising finding because Highfield devoted more of its budget (33%) to parent/family-focused programs than either Cornwall (15%) or Sudbury (18%) and Highfield had a much higher percentage of parents participating 40 or more times in BBBF programs (62%) than either Cornwall (15%) or Sudbury (16%). The possible reasons for more positive findings for Cornwall and Sudbury relative to Highfield that we made in chapter III regarding child outcomes may apply to these findings as well. The vast multicultural makeup of the Highfield community may have made it a more challenging environment in which to provide parent/family services that are effective. The fact that parents speak more than 40 different languages in Highfield, whereas the Cornwall and Sudbury communities are relatively more homogenous in terms of language and culture, suggests differential challenges in the ability of the sites to be sensitive to issues of language and culture.

Community Outcomes

Among prevention programs for children and families, BBBF is one of the few initiatives that had an explicit focus on community participation and community change. Thus, positive effects were expected for community outcomes as well as for parent, family, and parenting outcomes. At Grade 3, the BBBF families showed significantly more involvement in social activities and greater use of health and social services. At Grade 6, the BBBF families showed significantly higher levels of parental involvement in neighborhood activities, a greater sense of community involvement, greater neighborhood satisfaction, and more use of health and social services than parents from comparison sites. At Grade 9, significantly higher levels of neighborhood satisfaction continued in BBBF neighborhoods. Also, analyses of within-site effects yielded a positive pattern across all five measures of community involvement and neighborhood quality only for the Cornwall site in Grades 3 and 6.

These findings suggest that the positive community impact of the BBBF programs may have crested when children were in Grade 6. This trend may reflect age- and school-related changes. As young adolescents move into high school, the level of homework and school-based extracurricular activities leaves many students and their parents with little time to pursue other community activities. Thus, families with children in high school often lead highly scheduled, busy lives.

Parent ratings of community involvement and neighborhood quality were significantly more positive for only the Cornwall site at Grades 6 and 9. Cornwall did allocate more of its budget to community development programs (26%) than Sudbury (16%), which may help to explain why Cornwall outperformed Sudbury on this set of outcomes. However, compared with Cornwall, Highfield devoted a comparable amount of its budget (29%) to community development activities. In spite of this comparability of resource allocation, the challenges of focusing on community activities to celebrate and enhance the Francophone culture in Cornwall seem far less than that for Highfield, with its diverse cultural makeup. In short, Highfield may have been more a difficult community in which to provide effective community-focused programs.

These findings confirmed the expectation that BBBF participatory mechanisms and activities would increase community involvement and positive feelings toward the neighborhood in which the parents and their children live. At the BBBF sites, staff worked intensively with parents, providing home visits, parent support, and information about programs and resources in the local community. This active involvement with and provision of information to parents may have facilitated parents' ability to locate and use available community resources. The three BBBF Projects became a focus for community pride and solidarity among families and agencies and contributed to the capacity of local service organizations in a variety of ways. In addition, the BBBF Projects created new community resources that may also have enhanced parents' satisfaction with their neighborhoods. For example, the Cornwall BBBF Project was instrumental in the creation of the incorporated Community Action Group that helped to create prevention initiatives beyond the BBBF mandate such as a youth center for teens, a municipal skate park for teens, and the development of a disposal of toxic waste education program.

Recently, researchers evaluating the comprehensive, community-based Sure Start Local Programmes (SSLP) for young children in the United Kingdom have reported cross-sectional outcome measures of families with 3-year-old children living in SSLP neighborhoods compared with families living elsewhere in the United Kingdom (Belsky et al., 2006; Melhuish, Barnes, Leyland, Romaniuk, & the National Evaluation of Sure Start Research Team et al., 2008; see also comments by Rutter, 2006).

Outcomes results on two community measures similar to our measures of health and social service utilization and neighborhood satisfaction have been reported: the family's use of local support services, and the mother's ratings of the neighborhood as a "place to live and raise children." In the first analysis of these results, Belsky et al. (2006) reported that the SSLPs did not seem to affect mothers' reports of service use and mothers of 3-year-old children rated their local neighborhood as a significantly less desirable place to live and raise children. Melhuish et al. (2008), using a different comparison group than that employed by Belsky et al. (2006), reported mothers from the SSLP neighborhoods reported greater family use of services than the comparison group but no significant differences in ratings of neighborhood quality.

We are not aware of any other evaluations of prevention programs for young children and their families that have rigorously examined and found positive community outcomes on measures of community involvement and satisfaction. Although there is some evidence that community-driven interventions can improve community capacity and partnerships (Beauvais & Jenson, 2003; Bouchard, 2005), most of that research has not employed comparison groups to enable an adequate examination of cause and effects of the community interventions, nor has it examined a broad range of potential outcomes (Barnes et al., 2006; Wandersman & Florin, 2003). This is a novel contribution of the BBBF initiative and this research. A comprehensive review by Leventhal and Brooks-Gunn (2000) has shown that children who grow up in neighborhoods that are safe and secure and where community members feel connected to one another and actively participate in the community show more positive outcomes as they reach adolescence compared with children who live in violent, unsafe places, characterized by isolation and suspicion and fear of neighbors. Therefore, it is important to strive to improve communities to make them better places to live and raise children.

SUMMARY

As with the child outcome analyses reported in chapter III, we examined the parent, family, and community outcomes for patterns of consistent results across the three sites for each of the three outcomes measures and within each of the three sites for patterns of consistent results across the various measures in each outcome domain. The cross-site analyses of measures of parent and family functioning indicated a trend of more positive outcomes associated with the BBBF sites over time, with the most positive outcomes at Grade 9. Also, significant within-site patterns across the various parent and family measures occurred in both Cornwall and Sudbury at Grade 9. For the measures of community involvement and neighborhood quality, there were consistently positive outcomes favoring the BBBF sites, with strongest effects occurring across the three sites at Grade 6, and most consistently in the Cornwall site in Grades 3 and 6.

Three general observations are evident from these findings. First, the results regarding parent, family, parenting, and community outcomes of BBBF are mixed. For each group of outcomes, there were some positive findings, but there were also several outcomes on which the BBBF and comparison communities did not differ, and some outcomes on which the comparison communities outperformed BBBF. Comprehensive initiatives like BBBF are rather ambitious in that they strive to change a broad range of child, family, school, and community outcomes. Realistically, not all such outcomes will be achieved in these communitywide, community-driven initiatives. More narrowly focused prevention programs should have a better chance of changing the small number of outcomes that they target. Perhaps in the future there could be a better integration of a platform of comprehensive community initiatives, carried out in conjunction with more narrowly focused prevention programs to achieve the best results. For example, given that no positive cross-site patterns of parenting behavior were observed, comprehensive community initiatives might be better served by adopting more systematic, evidence-based parenting programs to suit their particular contexts. Further research is needed to determine whether such parenting programs are effective when carried out in the context of a universal, comprehensive community-based platform such as BBBF than when implemented on their own without community support and with highly targeted samples of parents with very aggressive children.

Second, at the short-term follow-up when the children were in Grade 3, the BBBF Project appeared to have relatively few positive associations with parent, family, and community outcome measures. In contrast, at the Grades 6 and 9 follow-up assessments, a range of positive project effects were evident. These observations suggest that some positive impacts of early prevention programs may not become apparent until later follow-up periods. This phenomenon also been reported in evaluations of more narrowly focused prevention programs (Nelson et al., 2003). It is, therefore, essential to gather longitudinal follow-up data on early intervention programs. Currently, we are following up the BBBF participants at age 18 after they are scheduled to complete high school to determine even longer term effects of the intervention.

Third, consistency in several positive outcomes across the three BBBF sites was achieved despite varied community contexts and programs. Although all of the communities were characterized by overall low-income levels, they differed in terms of location and demographic composition. The Cornwall site was in a medium-sized city and was geared to the Francophone population; the Highfield site in the Toronto area was home to a large immigrant population, primarily from South Asia and the Caribbean; whereas the Sudbury site was in a medium-sized northern city in Ontario and included Anglophone, Francophone, and Aboriginal people in the community. Moreover, unlike more prescriptive prevention programs with a specific curriculum outlined in a manual and based on previous research, BBBF programs were developed at the local level by residents and service providers. Although each site was mandated to have child-focused, parent- and family-focused, and community-focused programs, each site chose which programs would be developed within these rather broad parameters.

There were many programs in common across the sites, but they were implemented in different ways and some programs were site-specific. In spite of differences across sites in terms of programs offered, all three sites offered programs that were designed to achieve positive child, parent/family, and community outcomes. Hawe et al. (2004) have made an important distinction between the form and function of programs in complex community interventions that is relevant here. By function, they are referring to the broad purpose of a program, whereas form is the more specific programmatic expression of the form. An example is that all BBBF sites pursued the goal of engaging community residents in decision making and local community development activities (the function of a community-level intervention), whereas the forms that this took varied by site (activities to enhance French language and culture in Cornwall, culturally relevant community development activities for Aboriginal people in Sudbury, and multicultural celebrations in Highfield).

In conclusion, findings presented in this chapter provide evidence that some positive parent, family, parenting, and community outcomes of the BBBF Project may persist to the point when children reach adolescence. These, in turn, have the potential to positively impact the long-term development and well-being of children from the BBBF Project into later adolescence and beyond. In the next chapter, we examine the economic costs and benefits to government associated with the BBBF Project.

V. ECONOMIC ANALYSIS

The previous two chapters investigated the effects of Better Beginnings, Better Futures (BBBF) on child, parent, family, and community outcomes at Grades 3, 6, and 9. In this chapter, we present results for the economic analysis of BBBF, the first economic analysis of a Canadian early childhood prevention study. Given that funding for prevention and intervention programs is scarce, economic evaluation provides a useful tool for informing policy makers whether a prevention program is a good use of society's limited resources.

As described in chapter I, much evidence exists that early childhood interventions have beneficial effects on children's cognitive and behavioral outcomes and school competence (e.g., Brooks-Gunn, 2003; Karoly et al., 2005; Webster-Stratton & Taylor, 2001). It is also clear that early childhood prevention programs can have lasting positive impacts through adolescence and into adulthood on important societal outcomes including educational attainment, criminal activity, employment, earnings, and use of social services (Boisjoli et al., 2007; Reynolds et al., 2007; Schweinhart et al., 2005). Despite mounting evidence that early childhood interventions are effective, few studies of programs for children and youth in the United States and none in Canada have included an economic analysis (Crooks & Peters, 2002; Foster & Jones, 2005; Karoly et al., 1998, 2005; Mrazek & Brown, 2002; Waddell et al., 2007). Four notable exceptions are the Elmira Prenatal/Early Infancy Project (PEIP; Karoly et al., 1998); the Carolina Abecedarian Project (Barnett & Masse, 2007; Masse & Barnett, 2002); the Chicago Child–Parent Centers (CPC) program (Reynolds, Temple, Robertson, & Mann, 2002); and the High/Scope Perry Preschool Project (PPP; Barnett, 1996; Nores, Belfield, Barnett, & Schweinhart, 2005). All four of these early childhood intervention studies have reported economic analyses based on follow-up data for children, and in some cases their parents, to the child's age of 15 (PEIP), 21 (Abecedarian and CPC), and 40 (PPP). The programs differed in terms of program focus, intensity, and ages of children served; however, all showed strong positive returns on government investments.

Economic analyses results from these four studies have been frequently cited as a rationale by policymakers for investing in early childhood interventions (Bruner, 2004). Indeed, policymakers want to know, "Does prevention pay? Can an ounce of prevention avoid (at least) an ounce of cure? More specifically for public policy purposes, is there credible scientific evidence that for each dollar a legislature spends on 'research-based' prevention or early intervention programs for youth, more than a dollar's worth of benefits will be generated? If so, what are the policy options that offer taxpayers the best return on their dollar?" (Aos et al., 2004, p. 1).

In the next section, we review the findings from these four seminal early childhood intervention studies that have reported economic analyses.

ECONOMIC ANALYSES IN EARLY CHILDHOOD INTERVENTIONS

Elmira PEIP

The Elmira PEIP provided home visits prenatally and monthly for a maximum of 2 years postnatal by highly trained registered nurses to a group of 116 families. As described by Karoly et al. (1998), the PEIP helped young children and their mothers by providing parent education, social support, and referrals to social services. Using follow-up data on children up to age 15, Karoly and colleagues calculated costs and savings to government in both a higher risk and lower risk sample on four monetizable outcomes: use of health services, maternal employment, welfare use, and criminal justice system costs. For children, the criminal justice system costs were based on their projected lifetime criminal justice system involvement; for mothers, costs were based on the period of time up to when their children turned 15 years of age. Karoly and colleagues reported a net savings to government of $18,611 in the higher risk sample; 57% of this savings was attributable to less welfare use by mothers. For the lower risk group, the project yielded $3,775 in benefits, which did not cover the program costs of the PEIP ($6,083); thus, there was a net cost to government of $2,307 per child.

Carolina Abecedarian Project

The Carolina Abecedarian Project (Barnett & Masse, 2007; Masse & Barnett, 2002) provided a small group of 57 children living in poverty with year-round, full-day, high-quality, center-based care from infancy to school entry at age 5. Staff from the center also carried out home visits every 2 weeks for 4 years. Highly trained staff provided an individualized curriculum designed to promote cognitive and motor development, social skills, and language in the participating children. Barnett and Masse (2007)

101

reported a cost-benefit analysis of the Abecedarian program on a group of children up to age 21 and their mothers. Benefits were estimated for the following monetizable outcomes: projected lifetime earnings and fringe benefits of participants and their mothers, program effect on gross earnings of future generations, use of special education, postsecondary school costs, smoking, and welfare use. Despite the high cost of this intensive center-based program, the Abecedarian Project resulted in a net savings of $94,802 per child. Approximately 81% of the net savings of the program was attributable to the projected lifetime earnings of the participants and their mothers.

Chicago CPC

Reynolds et al. (2002) also reported substantial economic benefits of the Chicago CPC program when the children were 21 years of age. They examined the economic benefits of the three CPC programs (preschool for ages 3–5, school-age for Grades 1–3, and extended programs for ages 3–9) from the perspective of the program participants, taxpayers/crime victims, and society. The CPC mainly served African American children from high-poverty neighborhoods and was a large-scale, preschool program ($n = 989$). The preschool program provided a structured half-day program during the 9-month school year for 3- and 4-year-olds and was designed as an early education program to prepare children for school through promotion of language and reading skills. The program was expanded to continue programs and services for children through third grade, including full-day (6 hr) kindergarten. The primary grades program provided reduced class sizes, parental involvement activities, and instructional coordination. All three CPC programs yielded economic benefits that exceeded their program costs. Economic benefits were measured either by age 21 or projected through adulthood (e.g., projected lifetime earnings, projected costs of an adult criminal career). The preschool program yielded the highest economic benefits to society ($41,067 net benefit per child) and the school-age program yielded the lowest net benefit to society ($1,963 net benefit per child). For the preschool program, Reynolds et al. (2002) reported that the largest benefit was from program participants' increased projected lifetime earnings resulting from greater educational attainment (represents 43% of benefits). Other significant preschool program economic effects included reduced criminal justice costs in adolescence and projected through adulthood (15% of benefits) and increased taxes on earnings projected from educational attainment (15% of benefits).

PPP

The PPP (Schweinhart et al., 1993) began in Ypsilanti Michigan in 1962 and was designed to improve the personal and economic opportunities for a small group of 3- and 4-year-old children ($n = 58$) with low IQ (<85) from very low socioeconomic status families. The intervention involved 1 or 2 years of preschool and weekly home visits during the school year. The preschool intervention consisted of daily 150-min center-based classes by certified public school teachers and weekly 90-min home visits. The most recent analyses of the economic impacts of the PPP examined outcome data on participants as they reached the age of 40 and, when applicable, projected forward to age 65 (Nores et al., 2005). Examples of economic benefits that were examined include participants' earnings, tax contributions associated with increased earnings, criminal activity (including judicial system costs and crime victim costs), and welfare reliance. Nores and colleagues found that the net benefit to society (which includes both participant benefits and benefits to public/taxpayers) of the PPP was $229,645 per participant. Approximately 70% of this benefit can be attributed to crime savings.

It is interesting to note that these four early childhood studies vary as to which economic impacts are important. For the PEIP, a net savings to government was only found in the higher risk sample, with most of the savings attributable to less welfare use by mothers. For both the Abecedarian and CPC preschool projects, the projected lifetime earnings of participants based on educational attainment resulted in the highest economic benefit. For the PPP, crime effects were the strongest economic benefit. The four programs also differed in total program investment per child; for example, the CPC school-age program had the lowest investment per child at $2,981 (1998 U.S. dollars), and the Abecedarian had the highest at $35,864 (2002 U.S. dollars). Despite the differences in program focus and intensity, and the broad array of economic outcomes reported, these four studies collectively offer strong evidence that early childhood intervention programs can generate benefits that outweigh program costs (Karoly et al., 2005). Also, these studies highlight the importance of long-term follow-up of study participants because most of the economic returns did not begin to occur until participating children reached adulthood (Bruner, 2004).

QUANTIFYING THE COSTS AND SAVINGS OF THE BBBF PROJECT

As in the case of these four exemplary economic analyses of early childhood education programs described above, economic benefits are typically divided into three categories: benefits to program participants (e.g., increased income from improved education), benefits to nonprogram participants (e.g., reduced costs to crime victims), and benefits to government/taxpayers (e.g., decreased remedial education costs, decreased costs to the justice system). The costing perspective of the BBBF economic analysis was the Canadian government/taxpayers. We refer to this analysis as *cost-savings analysis* (Karoly et al., 1998), to differentiate it from the more traditional cost-benefit analysis. The overall objective of this chapter was to explore whether government expenditures on the BBBF program represent a sound social investment. Our cost-savings analysis includes 12 monetizable benefits (based on utilization of resources in health care and social services, schools, social assistance, and in the justice system) up to age 15.

We consider the results of our cost-savings analysis to be a conservative estimate for three reasons. First, we restricted the benefits to those that can be monetized. Other potentially important project outcome effects on children or families such as increased social support or more prosocial behavior are not included in our cost-savings analysis because their monetary value is not available, and thereby our analyses likely underestimate the total impact of the BBBF programs. Also, we chose to exclude any *projected* savings to government, such as the potential savings of averting a youth in our research sample from a life of crime or the projected lifetime savings of reduction in welfare costs. Third, by examining the cost savings to government in young children (from ages 4 to 15), we may be less likely to demonstrate that the BBBF programs are saving the government money as most of the above-mentioned studies were not able to show positive economic benefits until the children were in late adolescence and early adulthood. Being able to demonstrate, however, that BBBF is "on track" using our conservative cost-savings analysis is important in order to assure government that their use of tax revenues can be justified.

ECONOMIC METHODS

The goal of our economic analysis was to determine whether monetary benefits (i.e., government savings) for children in the BBBF programs were greater than those for children in the comparison sites as of age 15 and, if so, whether these differences offset the costs to the government of providing the BBBF program. A cost-savings analysis was conducted using average program costs for each child for up to 4 years of BBBF programs from 1993 to 1997 and 12 monetizable outcome measures when the children were in Junior Kindergarten (JK) to Grade 9. Costs of the BBBF programs were the values of the resources used to implement and operate the programs in each of the three BBBF sites. The 12 monetizable benefits were based on utilization of government resources in health care (Canada has a government-funded health care system) and social services, remedial education, the criminal justice system, and welfare/disability programs. The present value of BBBF program costs was subtracted from the present value of program benefits to obtain the net present value of BBBF. All dollar figures that we report were discounted at a rate of 3%. This discount rate falls within the range of rates commonly used and recommended in public-policy analysis (e.g., Karoly et al., 1998, 2005; Moore, Boardman, Vining, Weimer, & Greenberg, 2004; Reynolds et al., 2002). Sensitivity analyses were conducted using a range of discount rates (0%–10%) to test the robustness of the cost-savings analysis.

We focused solely on the costing perspective of the government because in elementary grades and early adolescence there are very few monetizable outcome measures available that yield economic benefits to program participants. Data for outcomes such as increased high school graduation rates and decreased use of tobacco, alcohol, and illicit drugs will only become available as the children develop through adolescence into early adulthood.

Costs of the BBBF Project

Costs represent the value of the resources used to deliver the BBBF programs in the three communities in Ontario. Costs of the programs consist of the direct government expenditures necessary to run the programs. The key elements in early childhood interventions are labor (of varying levels of skill and expertise), facilities, equipment, materials, and any other items that were necessary to the successful implementation of the interventions.

Complete direct government costs were available for the three BBBF sites for the years of 1995/1996 and 1996/1997. These 2 years best represent the costs of the BBBF project for several reasons. All site programs had been operating at full funding levels for 2 years (1993/1994 and 1994/1995). Programs had been fine-tuned, staff was experienced in their positions, and the programs were well-known in the local neighborhoods and beyond. Thus, the likely annualized costs for operating the local BBBF programs are accurately reflected in the 1995/1996 and 1996/1997 budget figures presented in this chapter.

Direct Government Costs

In the three BBBF sites, programs funded directly by the Ontario government were implemented and operated under three major categories: child-focused, family/parent-focused, and community development. Approximately $1.7 million was spent on these programs by the three sites combined each year; specifically, program costs in Cornwall were $580,938, in Highfield $512,166, and in Sudbury $657,942. The average program cost based on 1996/1997 data was $583,682 per site per year. As mentioned in chapter II, the distribution of expenditures across the three major program categories did vary among the three sites: In Cornwall and Sudbury, child-focused programs received most of the budget allocation (59% in Cornwall and 66% in Sudbury), whereas in Highfield, resources were more evenly distributed among the three program types.

Average Annual Direct Costs Per Child

The BBBF programs were available to and potentially accessed by all children in the respective site locations. Thus, the cost of the programs has been related to the *total* number of children in each of these areas; that is, we have calculated a "cost per capita" based on an "intent-to-treat" analysis. School records were used to obtain estimates of the number of children between 4 and 8 years old who were attending schools served by BBBF programs. Census data were not appropriate for use because data were only reported for the age group 5–14 years. In Highfield and Cornwall, many programs were school based so that *all* children attending school would have access to the programs. The Sudbury site provided program participation data on 3 of the 18 programs; these data revealed that over 80% of the cohort participated in programs, and it is very likely that almost all of the remaining children would have been involved in one of their classroom-based programs. Therefore, we are confident that using the school records to estimate the number of children in the sites between 4 and 8 years old provided us with a realistic estimate of program participation. Table 20 reveals that the average annual cost per child in the three sites combined for 1996/1997 was CDN$1,130 and ranged from $991 in Highfield to $1,308 in Sudbury.

Direct Government Costs Per Child for Up to 4 Years of Programming

The BBBF program was offered to each child for the 4-year period between JK and Grade 2. The cost of each child's program involvement was

TABLE 20

TOTAL NUMBER OF CHILDREN IN THE BETTER BEGINNINGS, BETTER FUTURES (BBBF) SITES AND DIRECT COST PER CHILD IN 1996/1997

Sites	Direct Costs 1996/1997	Number of Children[a]	Cost/Child/Year
Cornwall	$580,938	529	$1,098
Highfield	$512,166	517	$991
Sudbury	$657,942	503	$1,308
All sites	$1,751,046	1,549	$1,130

[a]Based on the school records for areas served by BBBF for children in Junior Kindergarten to Grade 2 in 1996/1997.

106

therefore calculated by combining the program costs from JK (1993/1994), Senior Kindergarten (SK; 1994/1995), Grade 1 (1995/1996), and Grade 2 (1996/1997). The BBBF program costs were in 1996 dollars and were discounted at 3% per annum. Direct costs to government of providing the full 4 years of BBBF programming per child was $4,594 in Cornwall, $4,146 in Sudbury, and $5,472 in Highfield.

Many of the BBBF children, however, moved out of the project sites before they received all 48 months of programs. Therefore, in order to capture the *actual* costs associated with a child's exposure to the program, we determined the number of months each child in our longitudinal research sample had lived in the BBBF site and then calculated program costs for each child by multiplying the length of residence in the BBBF site (up to 48 months or Grade 2) with the monthly average cost per child. On average, research children had lived in a BBBF site for approximately 30 months. For research children from the BBBF sites, the average government allocation per child over the years of program exposure (discounted from 1996 costs) was $2,964; program costs for research children from the comparison sites were estimated to be $0 because the government did not invest BBBF project funds in these sites.

Of course, there were many other types of government funds invested in both the BBBF sites and comparison sites. There is no indication, however, of differential government investment in BBBF versus comparison sites in these other types of government funds, so program costs presented in Table 20 can be used to calculate incremental cost differences.

Monetizable Outcomes for Youth and Their Families

Twelve outcome measures collected from youth and their parents from the BBBF sites and comparison sites were monetized. These monetizable outcomes were based on utilization of government resources in health care and social services, remedial education, the criminal justice system, and social assistance. Our approach to analyzing an outcome measure was to find all past data points that were available for that variable from JK to Grade 9 and then to obtain adjusted scores by running each of them through a regression procedure to eliminate the effects of covariates; we used the same set of covariates and analytic approach to obtain adjusted means of an outcome as described in the statistical analyses section of the methodology chapter described earlier in this monograph. All missing values, including the values of the missing grades (such as Grades 4, 5, 7, and 8 when no data collection took place), were replaced by interpolated values, given that there were at least 60% data points present. Inverse distance weighting method, also known as Shepard's method (Shepard, 1968), was used in the calculation of interpolated values. A 3% discount rate was applied for all cost data.

Visit to a Family Physician

Each parent was asked if his/her child had visited a family physician in the last year. An answer of *yes* was scored as 1 and *no* as 0. This question was asked at five data collection periods, when children were in Grades 1, 2, 3, 6, and 9. Five separate logistic regression analyses were conducted to obtain the adjusted scores. The cost to the provincial government of a visit to a family physician was $29.44 per visit in 2001 (Browne, Gafni, & Roberts, 2002), and we applied a 3% discount rate to calculate the present value of family physician for other years, such as 2000 ($30.32), 2003 ($27.75), and so on.

Hospital Emergency Room Use

Each parent was asked if his/her child had gone to the emergency room at a hospital in the last year. An answer of *yes* was scored as 1 and *no* as 0. This question was asked at all seven data collection periods, when children were in Grades JK, SK, 1, 2, 3, 6, and 9. The cost to the provincial government of a visit to an emergency room was $195.76 in 2001 (Browne et al., 2002).

Number of Serious Child Injuries

When children were in JK to Grade 6, parents were asked if their child had been injured in the past year (either seriously enough to limit normal activities or seriously enough to require medical attention) and, if *yes*, how many times. At Grade 9, the youth reported such injuries instead of the parent; youth indicated number of times they were seriously injured using response categories from 0 = *never injured* to 4 = *injured 4 or more times*. We estimated the cost of each injury to the health care system to be $4,000 in 1996. We based this figure on Angus et al. (1998) calculations of the total 1996 cost of unintentional injuries to adults and children in Canada including direct and indirect costs for hospitalized and nonhospitalized cases. Angus and colleagues concluded that a reduction of 650,000 injuries would save the government $2.6 billion; therefore, we divided $2.6 billion by 650,000 injuries to come up with a figure of $4,000 per injury.

Number of Overnight Stays in Hospital

When children were in JK to Grade 6, parents were asked if their children had stayed overnight in a hospital in the past year and, if so, how many times. At Grade 9, the youth provided this information instead of the parent. The cost to the provincial government of an overnight stay in a hospital was $816.35 in 2001 in Ontario (Browne et al., 2002).

Visit to a Nurse Practitioner

Each parent was asked if his or her child had seen a public health nurse or nurse practitioner in the past year. An answer of *yes* was scored as 1 and *no* as 0. This question was asked when children were in Grades 1, 2, 3, 6, and 9. The cost to the provincial government of a visit to a nurse practitioner was $19.00 in 2001 (Browne et al., 2002).

Visit by a Children's Aid Worker

Each parent was asked if his or her child had been visited by a child welfare worker or children's aid worker in the past year. An answer of *yes* was scored as 1 and a *no* as 0. This question was asked when children were in Grades 1, 2, 3, 6, and 9. The cost to the provincial government of a visit by a children's aid worker was $60.00 per visit in 2001 (Browne et al., 2002).

Elementary School Grade Repetition

Both teachers and parents were asked if the child had repeated a grade and, if so, which grade(s). A table was created from these data indicating which grades the child had repeated and in which calendar year. Each occurrence of a repeated grade was assigned a value of 1. The discount rate was based on a cost to government of $6,151 for the 2002/2003 school year in Ontario.

Use of Special Education Services

Grade 9 teachers were asked if each research child had an Individualized Education Plan; had been identified by an "identification, placement and revision committee"; or had used any additional support services (speech therapist, social worker, behavior therapist, child psychiatrist, special education teacher, or an education or teacher assistant). Any affirmative answer was coded as 1 (*the child had received special education services*); other responses were coded as 0 (*did not receive special education services*). Teachers also provided information on the use of special education services when children were in Grades 1, 2, 3, and 6. The cost to government of special education was $6,794 in the 2001/2002 school year based on the average special education costs of three school boards in Ontario (Limestone District School Board, Kingston; Ottawa-Carleton School Board; and Toronto District School Board).

Number of Arrests

This outcome measure was collected for the first time when youth were in Grade 9. Each youth was asked if he or she had ever been arrested and, if so, how many times, with response categories ranging from 0 = *never arrested* to 5 = *arrested 5 or more times*. The average cost per police investigation in 1998 was $500 (Hepworth, 2000).

Number of Court Appearances

This outcome measure was collected for the first time when youth were in Grade 9. Each youth was asked if he or she had ever been to a court for a crime. An answer of *yes* was coded as 1 and *no* as 0. The average cost per court trial in 1998 was $1,250 (Hepworth, 2000).

Social Welfare Assistance

When parents were interviewed in 2003, they were asked if they were currently receiving any government social assistance or Ontario Works Payments and, if so, how much. We verified the reported social assistance payments by comparing the amounts to guidelines from the National Council on Welfare (2004). For example, if a parent reported having received social assistance, we determined that the minimum payment the parent should receive was $1,160 per month. Reported monthly payments ranged from $1,160 to $1,800; an annual figure based on 12 months of payments was then calculated.

Ontario Disability Support Program

When parents were interviewed in 2003, they were asked if they were currently receiving any payments from Ontario Disability Support and the value of these payments. We verified the reported disability payments by comparing the reported amounts to guidelines from the Ontario Disability Support Program (Ontario Ministry of Community and Social Services, 2007). For example, a single parent with one child received a monthly disability payment of $829 and two parents with one child received $940. Reported monthly payments ranged from $829 to $1,621; an annual figure based on 12 months of payments was then calculated.

ECONOMIC ANALYSIS

A cost-savings analysis was conducted using all program costs for up to 4 years of BBBF programs from 1993 to 1997 and program benefits based on

12 monetizable outcome measures when the children were in JK to Grade 9. Equation (1) was used to calculate the average government cost for each of the 12 monetizable outcome measures (adjusted for covariate effects) for BBBF and comparison sites separately.

$$\bar{C}_d = \sum_{k=\text{JK}}^{\text{Gr9}} \sum_{j=1}^{12} \sum_{i=1}^{n_{jk}^d} v_{ijk}^d o_{ijk}^d / n_{jk}^d \quad \text{and} \quad \bar{C}_c = \sum_{k=\text{JK}}^{\text{Gr9}} \sum_{j=1}^{12} \sum_{i=1}^{n_{jk}^c} v_{ijk}^c o_{ijk}^c / n_{jk}^c \quad (1)$$

where $\bar{C}_d$ is the total average costs to government of the 12 monetizable outcomes in the BBBF demonstration sites; $\bar{C}_c$ the total average costs to government of the 12 monetizable outcomes in the comparison sites; d the BBBF demonstration sites; c the comparison sites; k the index of grades QJ;(JK, SK, . . ., Gr9); j the index of monetizable outcomes (1, . . ., 12); i the index of children (1, . . ., n_{jk}); v the value of monetizable outcomes (\$); o the occurrences of the monetizable outcome (adjusted for covariates); and n the sample size.

We then calculated the present value of the BBBF program savings/benefits to government by comparing the total utilization of government resources for services in the BBBF sites versus the comparison sites using the following equation:

$$\Delta B = \bar{C}_c - \bar{C}_d \quad (2)$$

Next, the present value of BBBF program costs was subtracted from the present value of the BBBF program savings/benefits to obtain the final net present value of BBBF. All monetary benefits and program costs were converted to 2003 Canadian dollar figures. A positive result would indicate that the BBBF program resulted in a cost savings to government.

RESULTS

Overall, participation in the BBBF program was associated with economic benefits/savings to government; as shown in Table 21, the present value of program benefits to government was \$3,876 per child. As described earlier, the average BBBF program cost per child was \$2,964. To calculate the net present value of the BBBF project, the present value of BBBF program costs (\$2,964) was subtracted from the present value of the BBBF program benefits (\$3,876); thus, the net present value of BBBF was \$912 per child by Grade 9. In other words, the savings gained in the 12 public/government agencies more than covers the cost per child amount for BBBF programs by the time children reach age 15.

TABLE 21

PRESENT VALUE OF BETTER BEGINNINGS, BETTER FUTURES (BBBF) PROGRAM BENEFITS PER PARTICIPANT SPANNING THE TIME PERIOD FROM WHEN CHILDREN WERE IN JUNIOR KINDERGARTEN TO GRADE 9

Monetizable Outcome Measures[a]	$\bar{C}_d$ $ Cost to Government of Providing Service in BBBF Sites[b]	$\bar{C}_c$ $ Cost to Government of Providing Service in Comparison Sites[b]	$\Delta B = \bar{C}_c - \bar{C}_d$ $ Present Value of Program Benefits to Government
Health care and social services			
Visits to a family physician	219	217	− 2
Hospital emergency room use	519	362	− 157
Number of serious injuries	13,448	12,958	− 490
Number of overnight stays in hospital	863	551	− 312
Visits with a nurse practitioner	25	12	− 13
Family involvement with Children's Aid Society	87	79	− 8
Subtotal			− 982
Remedial education			
Grade repetition	921	1,264	343
Use of special education services	15,211	19,246	4,035
Subtotal			4,378
Criminal justice system			
Arrests	113	136	23
Court appearances	61	35	− 26
Subtotal			− 3
Welfare/disability programs			
Social welfare assistance	1,370	1,646	276
Ontario Disability Support Program	725	932	207
Subtotal			483
Total			3,876

Note.— All dollars are present value in 2003 Canadian dollars discounted at 3%.
[a]Outcomes adjusted for birth year and gender of the interview respondent, gender of child, number of siblings, marital status, single parent status, respondents' education, employment status, family income, cultural category (Anglophone or Francophone), and immigrant status.
[b]The cost values are based on the value of each outcome as outlined in chapter V (e.g., $29.44 for a visit to a family physician), multiplied by frequency of occurrence of that outcome for each child in our longitudinal sample for that year (e.g., 0 = *no family physician visit* or 1 = *yes, visited family physician*). Mean values are then summed over time from Junior Kindergarten to Grade 9. The specific values for each time period are provided in Appendix E.

There were higher per child costs to government in the BBBF sites relative to the comparison sites for 7 of the 12 outcome measures: visits with a family physician, hospital emergency room use, serious child injuries, overnight stay in hospital, visits with nurse practitioner, family involvement with Children's Aid Society, and number of court appearances. Of these, serious child injuries resulted in the highest cost difference between the BBBF sites versus the comparison sites (a difference of $490).

There were, however, savings to government in the BBBF sites in five of the outcomes: children's grade repetition and use of special education services, arrests, and amount parents received from social assistance and disability support programs. Of these, reduced use of special education services resulted in the highest cost savings to the government between the BBBF sites versus the comparison sites (a savings of $4,035). For the four main categories of government resources (health care and social services, remedial education, criminal justice system, and social assistance), the largest savings were found in remedial education ($4,378). There were virtually no differences between the BBBF sites and comparison sites for government expenditures in the area of criminal justice system as of Grade 9.

Appendix E provides a detailed summary of the cost calculations (with 95% confidence intervals) for all monetizable outcomes in each year from JK to Grade 9.

Sensitivity Analysis

Because benefit estimates vary as a function of the discount rate, we estimated the benefits of the BBBF program using discount rates from 0% to 10% to determine the extent to which our conclusions were significantly altered by the discount rate employed. As shown in Figure 3, benefits to government exceeded program costs under all of the discount rates. Specifically, benefits to government ranged from $3,473 using a 0% discount to $4,831 at a 10% discount. Using the customary discount rate of 3% in public-policy analysis, the average child incremental net benefit to government of providing the BBBF program was $3,876.

Benefit-Cost Ratio

We also calculated BBBF monetary return to government as a ratio of benefits to costs. This was calculated as:

$$\text{benefit-cost ratio} = \text{benefits}/\text{costs}$$

A ratio >1 implied that benefits outweigh costs and the project is economically desirable. In our calculation, benefits were represented as the net benefit to government of the BBBF program ($3,876). Costs were represented as the cost to government of providing the BBBF program for up to 4 years per child ($2,964). We calculated the benefit to cost ratio to be 1.31:1. Thus, for every dollar invested by the government, a return of $1.31 per child was received.

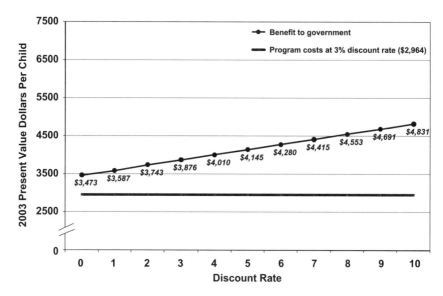

FIGURE 3.—Sensitivity analysis for government benefits and costs in the Better Beginnings, Better Futures Project.

DISCUSSION

This cohort of the BBBF project has already paid for itself. The Province of Ontario is currently reaping dividends from its investment made in the community interventions. As the first economic analysis of an early childhood prevention project in Canada, the results of the analyses of the BBBF project are instructive. On average, the government allocation per child over the years of BBBF program exposure was CDN$2,964 (in 2003 U.S. dollar figures this translates to $2,115). With these government funds, the BBBF communities funded a range of programs, including home visiting, parent support programs, child-focused play groups, and school and classroom programs. In comparison with program costs of the four early childhood intervention studies described in this chapter (e.g., converting all costs to 2003 U.S. dollar figures, the PEIP at $7,134; the CPC preschool program at $7,554; the PPP at $16,205; and the Abecedarian at $36,497), it appears that the annual costs of operating the BBBF projects are extremely modest. The BBBF program costs seem particularly reasonable when one considers that many of the BBBF programs were new to the neighborhoods and also that the programs were ecological. That is, BBBF programs focused on children, parents, and the local neighborhood; were integrated with other local services; and were developed in collaboration with local residents.

114

Results from the cost-savings analysis indicated that by Grade 9 the average per child/family costs to government were approximately $912 lower for BBBF sites than the comparison sites. In other words, the savings gained in the lower use of government-funded services more than covered the cost per child amount for BBBF programs by the time children reached age 15. For the four main categories of government resources examined (health care and social services, remedial education, criminal justice system, and social assistance), the largest savings to government were found in remedial education. There were virtually no differences between the BBBF sites and comparison sites for government expenditures in the area of the criminal justice system by the time the children were in Grade 9.

Contributions to Knowledge

Because the focus of the BBBF economic analysis was on identifying outcomes that have the potential to produce cost savings to the government/taxpayers, we thought it would be informative to compare findings from BBBF with other early childhood prevention projects. As shown in Table 22, the PPP yielded the highest return to government; for every dollar invested, the government yielded a return of $12.90. In contrast, the lowest return to government occurred in the PEIP analyses of lower risk families, which revealed that for every dollar invested, the government only realized a return of 62¢; thus, the government actually lost money. Masse and Barnett (2002) also reported that the estimated benefits to government/taxpayers fell short of program costs. Results from the BBBF analyses demonstrated a modest return of investment to government of $1.31 per dollar invested. This finding is similar to the CPC school-age program, which showed a return of $1.42. In both the BBBF and CPC projects, most of the savings to government was due to reductions in remedial education.

Being able to demonstrate that a prevention or early intervention program yields cost savings to government or taxpayers is a challenge for most studies. In a recent comprehensive review, Aos et al. (2004) carried out cost-benefit analyses on 61 types of programs designed to prevent serious social problems in adolescence and young adulthood. Of these, 19 programs involved preschool or early school-aged children. The other 42 types of programs involved adolescents and included youth development, mentoring, substance abuse prevention, teen pregnancy prevention, and juvenile offender programs. Of the 19 childhood programs analyzed by Aos and colleagues, 10 resulted in long-term monetary benefits that offset program costs. Of these 10, however, only 3 yielded economic benefits to government/taxpayers, and the value of these benefits relative to program costs was very small. Thus, in this context of other economic analyses of

115

TABLE 22

COMPARISON OF BENEFITS TO GENERAL PUBLIC/TAXPAYERS/GOVERNMENT OF FIVE EARLY CHILDHOOD PREVENTION PROJECTS

Program	Age of Children	Total Investment Per Child	Net Current Value for Taxpayers/ Government[a]	Benefit:Cost Ratio	Key Areas of Savings
Carolina Abecedarian Project (age 21)[b]	Infancy to age 5	$36,497	Masse and Barnett (2002) reported that estimates of benefits to taxpayers and government fell short of program costs at discount rate of 3% (specific figures were not provided)	Less than $1.00	NA
Chicago Child-Parent Centers Program (age 21)[c]	Preschool program (ages 3–4)	$7,554	$21,537 for preschool program	$3.85	Juvenile crime and crime victims: 31% Projected taxes on lifetime earnings: 28% Remedial education: 19%
	School-age program (ages 5–6)	$3,365	$1,397 for school-age program	$1.42	Remedial education: 79%
	Extended program (ages 3–9 years)	$4,580	$11,895 for extended program	$3.60	Remedial education: 31% Juvenile crime and crime victims: 29% Projected taxes on lifetime earnings: 21%
Elmira Prenatal/ Early Infancy Project (age 15)[d]	Ages prenatal to 2	$7,134	$2,705 for lower risk families $21,826 for higher risk families	$0.62 $4.06	NA Welfare use 57% Taxes from increased employment 23% Criminal justice 19%

High/Scope Perry Preschool Project (age 40)[e]	Ages 3 and 4	$16,205	$192,821		$12.90	Crime costs 88%
Better Beginnings, Better Futures (age 15)[f]	Ages 4–8	$2,115	$651		$1.31	Remedial education 99%

[a]Discount rate of 3% used except for Elmira Prenatal/Early Infancy Project which used 4% discount rate.
[b]2002 U.S. dollars converted to 2003 U.S. dollars using average annual Consumer Price Index.
[c]1998 U.S. dollars converted to 2003 U.S. dollars using average annual Consumer Price Index.
[d]1996 U.S. dollars converted to 2003 U.S. dollars using average annual Consumer Price Index.
[e]2000 U.S. dollars converted to 2003 U.S. dollars using average annual Consumer Price Index.
[f]2003 Canadian dollars converted to 2003 U.S. dollars using .7135 conversion rate (which was the average annual exchange in 2003 based on tallying monthly Bank of Canada exchange rates in 2003).

117

prevention/intervention projects, the modest return on investment of the Grade 9 BBBF analyses is encouraging.

Limitations and Qualifications

Findings from our cost-savings analysis should be interpreted within the context of three qualifications. First, our economic analysis, and those reported in this chapter, do not include all project outcomes, only those that can be monetized. Other potentially important project outcome effects on children or families such as increased social support or more prosocial behavior are not included in cost-benefit or cost-savings analyses because their monetary value is not known. Therefore, the economic analyses may underestimate the total impact of the intervention/prevention program being examined.

Second, our findings are likely to be a conservative estimate of the economic benefits of the BBBF program for several reasons. We only examined benefits from the perspective of the government/taxpayers. Other studies also included benefits to program participants (e.g., increased income from improved education) and benefits to nonprogram participants (e.g., reduced costs to crime victims). Had we included these additional perspectives, our overall benefits would likely have been much higher. Also, we did not include any projected savings to government, such as the potential savings of averting a youth from a life of crime, in our research sample or the projected lifetime savings of reduction in welfare costs. Because the youth in our study were only 15, we were not confident that the data would yield robust projections. We plan to include these types of benefits when youth reach age 18 and older. Finally, we are reporting results at a much earlier age compared with most of the above-mentioned studies. Usually, the more positive economic benefits do not appear until children are into adulthood.

Third, volunteer time and space, often referred to as "services in kind," have not been included as a program cost in our economic analysis. These service contributions may be important to consider, particularly for community-based interventions such as BBBF. This limitation may also apply to the other studies reviewed in this chapter if the programs relied on volunteers or donated space. The decision maker who is paying for part of the overall cost of implementing the intervention is not likely to be interested in the costs of volunteers or donated space. Yet if the more successful interventions include significant contributions that are "paid" for by organizations and people external to that decision maker, policymakers should be aware of these cost distributions. Otherwise, decisions about which interventions to replicate or implement on a larger scale might be based on an erroneous foundation. Therefore, it is important to consider these "services in kind" costs because, even if government did not have to pay for this time, it does represent a cost to someone. For example, staff at the BBBF program sites recorded the number of volunteer hours provided at each of their sites for 3 years, 1994–1997. Details with respect to how these volunteer hours were converted to dollar figures were discussed in a technical report (Peters et al., 2000). Results indicated that, on average, $175,000 of unpaid volunteer hours was provided each year at each of the BBBF sites. We did not include this in-kind program cost in our economic analysis because our cost-savings analysis was solely focusing on costs and savings from a government/tax payer perspective. Further, we did not gather the corresponding services-in-kind data in the comparison sites. It could be that there is even more volunteer time required in a community without program resources like BBBF to help provide support for disadvantaged families. There are important longer term questions concerning the relationship between direct funding and provision of valuable services in kind. For example, how much difference (if any) do the extent and variation in services in kind make to the impacts of programs? Is there a "best practices" combination of paid and unpaid resources that would serve as a benchmark and that could be used for the replication and dissemination of similar programs in the future? What are the measurable benefits to volunteers of volunteering their time? These issues deserve further investigation.

Policy Implications

In 1990, the BBBF longitudinal study was planned by the Ontario government as a 25-year study to follow program and comparison children through adolescence into early adulthood in order to allow for an analysis of these cost-savings outcomes (Government of Ontario, 1990). It was to be the first of its kind in Canada to determine whether the long-term monetary benefits or government savings for an early childhood prevention project would offset program costs. We now have evidence that investing in early childhood prevention programs in Canada can be a worthwhile endeavor.

Preliminary findings from our cost-savings analysis suggest that BBBF has the potential to save the Canadian government millions of dollars. For example, approximately 1,500 children have been served by the three BBBF programs site each year, and the project has been in existence for 15 years. If we estimate the savings to government of each child in the BBBF program at $912 savings per child over the 15 years the program has been operating, this yields approximately $20 million savings to government ($912/child × 1,500 children × 15 years). We have some evidence to suggest that the effects we found with the longitudinal cohort would continue for children who entered the BBBF program after 1994. Our research team obtained teacher ratings of children living in the BBBF and comparison sites in the spring of 2003. This group of children was born 5 years later than the longitudinal sample described in this monograph. The results generally indicated more positive child outcomes from schools in the BBBF neighborhoods than from schools in the comparison communities. Also, the size of these differences was generally greater in 2003 than they had been 5 years earlier. These findings support the view that the BBBF programs not only continued to have positive impacts on children's social, emotional, behavioral, and academic functioning but also these impacts strengthened over this 5-year period (for more details, see report by Nelson et al., 2005).

Conclusion

There are few cost-benefit analyses of early intervention and prevention projects reported in the literature, yet these analyses are essential for the ultimate formulation of policy and adoption and dissemination of intervention programs. More complete and detailed evaluation of interventions is needed and must be built into programs when they are designed, as was the case for BBBF. The emerging cost-savings results of the BBBF project when youth were age 15 bodes well for further potential economic benefits through high school and beyond. Being able to demonstrate that BBBF is "on track" using our conservative cost-savings analysis is important in order to assure government that their use of tax revenues can be justified in economic terms as well as in other positive outcomes for the children and their families that are difficult to monetize. It is likely that, if our longitudinal research is continued through late adolescence and early adulthood, the evidence for cost savings will become more robust. In order for this to occur, however, long-term, longitudinal follow-up is essential. Such cost-benefit analyses will likely make important contributions to social policy formulation in the future.

VI. DISCUSSION

In this monograph, we reported the medium- and long-term effects of Better Beginnings, Better Futures (BBBF), a universal, ecological, community-based prevention project for young children and their families living in disadvantaged neighborhoods. The ecological perspective underlined all aspects of the BBBF project, including design, implementation, program evaluation, and longitudinal analysis of medium- and long-term effects. A strength of this perspective is the ability to view families, schools, and communities as social systems that are capable of evolution and transformation, rather than systems that are eternally fixed or unalterable (Bronfenbrenner, 1977). The BBBF programs were available to all children ages 4–8 years old and their families living in three economically disadvantaged communities in Ontario, Canada. The overall objectives were to mobilize change in multiple settings, promote healthy child and family development in the long term, and enhance the abilities of disadvantaged communities to provide for young children and their families.

In this monograph, we addressed three main questions.

1. What were the medium- and long-term outcomes associated with project participation on children's social, emotional, behavioral, cognitive, and physical development?

2. To what extent was project participation associated with positive outcomes on parent health, parenting behaviors, family functioning, and community involvement?

3. Did the economic benefits of participation, up to Grade 9, outweigh the project costs?

In the sections below, we examine each of these questions in turn.

Child Outcomes

The BBBF mandate was to develop programs that would positively affect all areas of child's development, not focus exclusively on one devel-

121

opmental domain, such as cognitive or academic functioning. Our findings reflect this ecological approach, with positive effects evident in social and school functioning domains as well as evidence of fewer emotional and behavioral problems in school.

Improvements in social functioning among children from BBBF sites were most evident at the Grade 6 follow-up, when children had reached early adolescence. It is possible that improvements in this domain (more prosocial behaviors, greater number of people in their social network, greater self-control and conflict management at school) contributed to the pronounced effects on school functioning that we observed when youth reached midadolescence (Grade 9). Indeed, a large body of research suggests that children's social and emotional functioning are intimately linked with cognitive development, school adjustment, and academic performance (Bursuck & Asher, 1986; Gresham, 1992; O'Neil et al., 1997; Zins et al., 2004).

There was clear evidence of long-term positive outcomes in children's school functioning associated with the BBBF project at the end of Grade 9, 7 years after the programming ended. Five positive effects were observed in the school functioning domain at Grade 9: Youth who had participated in the BBBF project were better prepared and more adapted to school, less likely to repeat a grade, and required fewer special education services such as special classes or specialized services offered by psychologists or social workers. They also had the potential to pursue their education for longer than students from the comparison sites, according to their teachers. Some of these effects had been evident at Grade 6 (such as special education placement), but most emerged at Grade 9, further underlining the importance of long-term follow-up.

Because children may behave differently in different environmental settings, such as home, school, and other social situations, it is important to collect information about children's functioning from parents, teachers, and, when old enough, children themselves (Achenbach et al., 1987; Bramlett et al., 2000). In this study, we observed some discrepancies among teacher, parent, and child ratings for measures in the emotional and behavioral domains. Whereas teacher ratings indicated significantly fewer behavioral and emotional problems, parent ratings (especially at Grade 6) conveyed evidence of greater emotional and behavioral problems among youth from the BBBF sites. These differences suggest that the youth were in fact behaving quite differently in the home and school environments.

Surprisingly, despite their apparent success in various aspects of school functioning, including fewer teacher-rated emotional and behavioral problems, youth from the BBBF sites rated themselves as having lower self-esteem and more emotional/anxiety problems in Grade 9 than youth from the comparison sites. This somewhat paradoxical result suggests that better school functioning at Grade 9 may be associated with increased feelings of anxiety and lower self-esteem. Although there is little research on this topic, results from a recent analysis of longitudinal data from the Canadian National Longitudinal Survey of Children and Youth (NLSCY) data have indicated that the prevalence of self-rated anxiety problems at age 15 was higher among youth who had stronger reading skills in preadolescence (Beswick & Willms, 2008). As Beswick and Willms noted, "high-achieving children may have greater fears about success in school and in social situations" (p. 30). Thus, a possible explanation for the higher levels of anxiety and lower self-esteem among BBBF youth at Grade 9 is that the improvements in their school and academic functioning were associated with greater fears or anxiety about doing well at school. The BBBF programs between Junior Kindergarten (JK) and Grade 2 emphasized the importance of doing well academically. Although this academic focus may have translated into better school and academic functioning in adolescence, it may also have increased the youths' critical evaluation of themselves, leading to higher self-rated emotional problems and lower self-esteem. Further research on this topic is needed.

For health-related outcomes in children, there was little indication of positive project effects. At each follow-up assessment it was apparent that children in BBBF sites experienced a greater number of chronic health conditions. It was somewhat surprising to find few positive effects in the health domain, despite BBBF's ecological, comprehensive approach. Reviews of adolescent health promotion programs, however, have indicated that attempts at healthy behavior change among youth often have limited effectiveness (Lister-Sharp et al., 1999; Thomas et al., 2005; Wandersman & Florin, 2003). Although BBBF was comprehensive and involved a variety of programs with the potential to positively affect children's health, there were no comprehensive school health programs offered in the BBBF sites that had the intensity to positively affect the health behaviors of children.

Although the positive patterns of school functioning applied to all three BBBF sites, there was some indication that the within-site effects in the other domains of child outcome measures were less consistent in the Highfield site. A possible reason for this may have been the highly multicultural makeup of the Highfield community. As described in Chapter II, more than 40 languages were spoken in the Highfield community, and 60% of the Highfield parents who participated in the longitudinal research were born outside of Canada. Consequently, the multicultural nature of Highfield may have posed substantially greater challenges than Cornwall or Sudbury for providing effective BBBF child-focused prevention programs.

In summary, there was a range of child/youth-related effects associated with BBBF participation with findings centered on the social and school functioning domains. Developmentally, it seems plausible that the enhanced prosocial behaviors, relationships with others, and self-control evident among BBBF children in early adolescence may have been related to the improvements in school functioning that had emerged by midadolescence.

Parent and Family Outcomes

Regarding measures of parent and family functioning, parents from BBBF sites reported greater feelings of social support and more positive ratings of marital satisfaction and general family functioning. Although these differences were also present when their children were in Grades 6, there were more consistently positive effects at Grade 9. At Grade 6, BBBF parents reported more stressful life events, poorer physical health, and higher levels of hostile-ineffective parenting behaviors than parents from the comparison sites. None of these negative BBBF effects was statistically significant in the parents' ratings at either Grade 3 or Grade 9. In fact, at Grade 9, three of the four measures changed in the direction of more positive outcomes for BBBF parents.

The apparently higher levels of stress and more hostile interactions with their children reported by BBBF parents at Grade 6, along with the finding that these parents also rated their children as having more emotional and behavioral problems, suggests that the transition to adolescence may have been particularly difficult one for the BBBF families. Whatever support programs that BBBF parents participated in were not adequate to prevent emotional and behavioral problems in their children, nor were programs able to prevent parents from using more hostile-ineffective parenting techniques relative to parents from the comparison sites.

At the same time, BBBF parents were reporting greater feelings of social support and general family functioning. The findings that these feelings of positive support and family functioning continued when their children were in Grade 9, and that the parent stress, hostile parenting, and child behavior problems had subsided by this follow-up, suggest that the parents successfully overcame the earlier conflicts during the 3-year period when their children moved from Grade 6 to Grade 9.

At Grade 9, positive impacts were found for the Cornwall and Sudbury sites, but not for the Highfield site, on parent ratings of parent/family functioning. The possible reasons for more positive findings for Cornwall and Sudbury relative to Highfield regarding child outcomes may apply to these findings as well. The vast multicultural makeup of the Highfield community may have made it a more challenging environment in which to provide parent/family services that are effective. The fact that parents speak more than 40 different languages in Highfield, whereas the Cornwall and Sudbury communities are relatively more homogenous in terms of language and culture, suggests differential challenges in the ability of the sites to be sensitive to issues of language and culture.

Neighborhood/Community Outcomes

An array of positive neighborhood-level effects was evident at the Grade 6 follow-up. At this time, parents from the BBBF sites reported more involvement in neighborhood activities, a greater sense of community involvement, and greater satisfaction with the quality of their neighborhoods and more frequent use of health and social services than those from the comparison sites. These findings confirm the expectation that BBBF participatory mechanisms and activities would increase positive feelings toward the neighborhoods in which parents and children lived. These more positive neighborhood connections and perceptions may also have contributed to the support necessary to successfully adjust to the stress and conflict with their young adolescent children at home.

It is interesting that the only negative BBBF finding at Grade 9 in the measures of parent, family, and neighborhood functioning was the perception by the youth from the project sites that their parents monitored them less closely than youth from the comparison sites, for example their behavior with friends and adherence to curfews. One possible explanation for this finding is that the decreased monitoring may have resulted from the BBBF parents having more trust and confidence in their child's safety.

Within the domain of community involvement and neighborhood quality, parent ratings were significantly more positive for only the Cornwall site at Grades 6 and 9. As noted earlier, Cornwall did allocate more of its budget to community development programs (26%) than did Sudbury (16%), which may help to explain why Cornwall outperformed Sudbury on this set of outcomes. However, compared with Cornwall, Highfield devoted a comparable amount of its budget (29%) to community development activities. In spite of this comparability of resource allocation, the challenges of focusing on community activities to celebrate and enhance the Francophone culture in Cornwall seem far less than that for Highfield, with its diverse cultural makeup. In short, Highfield may have been more a difficult community to provide effective community-focused programs.

Economic Benefits

The third major research question examined whether the long-term economic benefits of BBBF participation outweighed the project costs? As described in Chapter V, by the time youth had reached Grade 9, BBBF participation was associated with savings to government of US$912 per child. These savings were obtained through the lower use of government-funded services among BBBF families and more than covered the cost per child of the program (which was US$2,964). The largest savings to government were found in remedial education. Given that approximately 1,500 children continue to be served by the three BBBF program sites each year, the US$912 savings per child over the 15 years that the program has been operating means that the total cost savings to the Ontario government has been over US$20 million to date (1,500 children × 20 years × US$912).

It is encouraging to find this substantial economic benefit to government despite our rather conservative estimates of financial benefits in comparison with many other economic analyses (e.g., we did not utilize any *projected* savings to government such as the potential savings of averting a youth from a life of crime or the projected lifetime savings of reduction in welfare costs that are common in economic analyses). Further, results from the economic analysis at age 15 are also encouraging because most previous studies have not been able to show positive economic benefits that offset program costs until children are young adults. Being able to demonstrate that BBBF is "on track" using such a conservative cost-savings analysis is important in order to assure government funders that their use of tax revenues can be justified in economic terms as well as in other positive outcomes for children and their families that are difficult to monetize.

METHODOLOGICAL CONSIDERATIONS

In this section, we discuss several limitations that may affect the interpretability of findings; we also examine some of the methodological strengths of this monograph.

Research Design

We utilized a quasi-experimental design. The process that the Ontario government funders used to select the three BBBF project sites precluded the use of a cluster randomized controlled trial design (i.e., to randomly assign potential sites to either a "BBBF project site condition" or a "control or comparison site condition"). Rather, the three project sites were selected by the government through a competitive request for proposals procedure. The Research Coordination Unit (RCU) was then charged with the task of identifying sociodemographically, culturally, and linguistically similar communities to the three selected project sites to function as comparison or control sites. Randomized controlled trial designs are generally considered to be more rigorous designs than the matched control group design used here. However, as observed by McCall and Green (2004), "random assignment can produce cause and effect conclusions, but public services are never randomly assigned and their effectiveness may well depend on participants' motivation or belief in the services" (p. 1). McCall and Green suggest incorporating alternative, quasi-experimental research methods that emphasize external validity—that is, that match real-life circumstances. Such was the quasi-experimental matched group design used in the present research. Our analyses have confirmed that the BBBF and comparison cohorts were well matched on several family factors that may be confounded with program effects. These included parent cultural group, single parent status, parental education, father's employment status, and monthly income. Also, our statistical analyses took into account other potential sources of bias including sample selection bias, as described in Chapter II.

Program Implementation

The wide variety (range) of programs developed and implemented by each BBBF site were not, with the exception of the *Lions–Quest Skills for Growing* program (Quest International, 1990) in Highfield, attempts at faithful replications of "best-practice" or "empirically validated" programs for children or parents. For example, all three BBBF sites developed parent education and support programs designed to meet the particular needs of the local residents, and none was strictly based on manualized, fixed number of session programs, such as the recently popular Incredible Years (Webster-Stratton, 1992) or Triple-P (Sanders, 1999) parent training programs. Rather, each site modified and adjusted programs in such a way as to allow them to offer such a broad array of child, parent/family, and community programs within their allocated budget from the government. Again, quoting from McCall and Green's (2004) *Social Policy Report*, "Experimenter-controlled uniform treatment administration insures that we know precisely the nature of the treatment documented to work by the evaluation, but it prohibits tailoring treatment to the individual needs of participants, which is a major 'best practice' of service delivery" (p. 1). Tailoring programs to individual needs of participants was a hallmark of the programs in the BBBF project.

This approach to program development and implementation clearly exchanged intensity, narrow focus, and strict adherence to prescribed program material and procedures for breadth, flexibility, and local involvement in program design. As mentioned above, a more focused and intense parent training program, such as that implemented by the Fast Track program (CPPRG, 1992) or the Montreal Prevention Experiment (MPE; Tremblay et al., 1992), may have been more effective in improving parenting skills, allowing them to deal more successfully with their children's emotional and behavior problems at home. However, there are trade-offs between the "bottom-up," broad ecological approach of BBBF and the "top-down," intense focus approach that characterizes the Fast Track, High/Scope Perry Preschool Project (PPP), Chicago Child–Parent Center (CPC), and MPE

127

programs. In particular, the top-down approach, using university-based professionals in project design and implementation, relies heavily on highly trained personnel. When a study is completed and the professional personnel leave, there is little chance that the program will continue. Also, an intervention focused on only one or two aspects of children's development overlooks the possible positive effects on parents or the local neighborhood. For example, in the PPP, although there was a heavy emphasis on teachers carrying out regular and frequent visits to the children's parents in their homes, no information was collected (or at least not reported) on any parent outcome measures. This was also the case for the MPE, where parent training was one of the two intervention strategies used (the other was social skills training for the boys), but no parent outcome measures were reported.

There are also important differences in program costs between BBBF and these other more intensive but narrowly focused programs, as discussed in chapter V. A large proportion of the program budget would have been required for each BBBF site to implement an intensive parent-training program such as that used in Fast Track. Consequently, there would have been few resources for the other parent-, child-, and community-focused programs that appear to have had important long-term impacts on all these groups.

Attribution of Program Effects

In chapter I it was emphasized that BBBF is not a series of particular programs or services. Given the variety of child-, parent/family-, and community-focused programs developed and implemented in each community, it is best viewed as an initiative or strategy for mobilizing disadvantaged neighborhoods around early child development and prevention. Therefore, it is impossible to attribute the observed outcomes to particular programs or activities but rather to the core elements of the strategy. These core elements of BBBF, described in detail in chapter I, were (a) ecological and holistic programs aimed at children, parents/families, and communities; (b) programs that are universally accessible to all children and families in the age range of 4–8 in the community; (c) a high level of resident participation; and (d) integration of services in prevention programming. What was evaluated in our research was the effectiveness of this strategy as implemented in three culturally different disadvantaged neighborhoods. It is for this reason that we emphasized in our analyses patterns of similar outcomes in all three BBBF communities more than differences among the three BBBF sites.

Comparison Site Limitations

There were important differences among the comparison groups used in the present study and those used in other studies of preschool programs that may have limited the ability of BBBF to demonstrate larger effects. As noted in chapter II, the purpose of establishing comparison sites for the BBBF communities was to provide protection against being misled by changes taking place provincially or regionally, which did not result from BBBF programs. Still, it was unavoidable that there would be a variety of other programs and initiatives to promote the development of young children and families in the comparison neighborhoods. In fact, most neighborhoods have a variety of such activities from time to time. For example, in Etobicoke, a community organization, the Braeburn Neighbourhood Place and Boys and Girls Club, has been in operation for 30 years and operates a number of programs for children of elementary school age. A community development worker works to involve residents in this organization and to make partnerships with other organizations like the Children's Aid Society and Metro Toronto Housing. At the school level, the Braeburn Junior School offers programs such as before- and after-school programs, child nutrition programs, homework programs, and sports activities. There are also youth programs for those over the age of 12 and a youth committee. There is an emergency food bank, a supplementary food program, and a community garden. There is also a summer camp program that focuses on reinforcing academic skills learned in school.

The Ottawa–Vanier comparison site also offers a number of programs for low-income families. For example, a prevention program called *Six Ans Gagnant* operates out of a community center. The program begins when mothers are pregnant and continues until children reach 6 years of age. The program focuses on single mothers who are on social assistance; mothers are offered classes on nutrition, children's physical and psychological development, and early literacy. For elementary school–aged children, there is 3-year literacy program in one of the schools in the community with a high level of illiteracy. At the community level, there is a Coalition of Community Health and Resource Centre of Ottawa, established in 1980. This coalition coordinates services for low-income families in the area and involves community members in social action.

Also, all children from the comparison sites and from the BBBF sites were enrolled in a high-quality, half-day, JK and Senior Kindergarten (SK) programs offered by the Ontario Ministry of Education to all 4- and 5-year-old children during the regular school year. These kindergarten programs are operated in primary schools with highly trained primary school teachers at a funding level of approximately US$4,320 per child annually. Parent reports indicated that nearly all, 97%–100%, of the children in the BBBF and comparison sites participated in both the JK and SK programs. The BBBF programs were offered in addition to these ongoing JK and SK programs and other existing services for young children and families offered in each community; any improved child outcomes for the BBBF sites were over and above those associated with these existing programs. That is, the present study evaluated the "value added" by BBBF programs to the effects of these other programs and services.

In other longitudinal studies of preschool programs, most notably CPC and PPP, the control/comparison group children were not enrolled in other high-quality programs, such as the JK/SK programs in the present study, when the major preschool programs were provided to the intervention group children. It is likely much easier to demonstrate positive effects for early childhood programs when the intervention group received up to 2 years of high-quality and expensive programs for the preschool children and their parents, whereas the control group received little if any support. Specifically, CPC children received either 1 or 2 years of half-day preschool at ages 3–4, along with extensive parent support; the comparison group did not receive any preschool at age 3 or 4 years and parents did not receive any program support. Reynolds (2000) and Reynolds et al. (2007) noted that all children in the CPC comparison group received full-day kindergarten, and 15–20% of children in this group were enrolled in Head Start (i.e., pre-school). Thus, the comparison group was described as having received "treatment as usual" (Reynolds, 2000, p. 55). It is clear, however, that "treatment as usual" only affected 20% of the CPC comparison group in contrast to the BBBF comparison group, where all the children attended 2 years of half-day kindergarten starting at age 4.

In the PPP, children were randomly assigned to high-quality preschool or no preschool. Children in the control group did not receive any pre-school and their parents did not receive home visits, thereby potentially increasing the size of effects from the intervention.

Interestingly, a later study involved a comparison of the High/Scope "open framework curriculum approach" used in the original Perry Preschool study with a traditional nursery program/"child-centered approach," using a different sample of children (Schweinhart, Weikart, & Larner, 1986). The longitudinal follow-up of the curriculum study showed that up to age 15 there were no significant differences between the High/Scope curriculum group and the traditional nursery curriculum group on any of the outcome domains measured. The outcomes included intellectual and scholastic performance over time and self-reports at age 15 of various aspects of social behavior and attitudes. A further follow-up at age 23 again revealed no significant differences between the High/Scope and traditional nursery curriculum groups (Schweinhart & Weikart, 1997). If the original PPP study had included a traditional nursery school curriculum group as a control, the magnitude of differences between the two groups may have been substantially different.

These findings emphasize the importance of examining the nature of the comparison conditions against which any intervention is evaluated.

As described previously, the present study evaluated the value added by BBBF programs to the effects of a variety of other programs and services, including the half-day JK and SK programs for children in both the BBBF and comparison sites.

Outcome Measures

In this monograph, results from 61 outcome measures have been reported. These measures have been chosen to reflect the overall goals of reducing emotional and behavioral problems and promoting the healthy development of young children and strengthening parents, families, and the neighborhood in responding to the needs of their children. The inclusion of so many outcome measures may raise methodological concerns for some readers. First, there may be concern about the quality and appropriateness of the measures. Second, testing so many outcomes inevitably raises the possibility of obtaining statistically significant outcomes that are really the product of random fluctuations. We will address each of these concerns in the following paragraphs.

Selection of Measures

The measures available to assess the outcomes of BBBF are likewise best understood historically. Before the programs were in place the RCU needed to gather baseline data, which had to cover the major domains BBBF hoped to influence: children, their families, and their communities. Within each of these domains, the RCU developed a list of the constructs, reviewed measures available that purported to assess those constructs, chose some of them, revised others, and created our own measures for a small number. The measures were incorporated in draft questionnaires which were circulated to the BBBF sites, to RCU members, and government staff for consultation. This consultative process resulted in measures being dropped and others added. Given the range of possibilities, it was perhaps inevitable that a great range of outcomes would be included in the measurement package.

The RCU is confident in the selection of its measures. As described in chapter II, the 29 scales used in this study all demonstrated strong psychometric properties. Also, approximately two thirds of the outcomes reported in this monograph were also used in the NLSCY. The NLSCY is a federally funded longitudinal survey of Canadians from birth to adulthood. This survey began in 1994 and involves more than 15,000 individuals who are interviewed every 2 years. Data from the NLSCY can be weighted to be representative of all Canadian children. Thus, by having common measures with the NLSCY, we can place the outcomes of the BBBF project in a national perspective (see BBBF: Project Sustainability Report, 2005, at http://bbbf. queensu.ca/pdfs/SUSTAINABILITY.PDF for an example of these analyses).

Type I Errors

The sheer number of outcomes analyzed may lead some readers to wonder if some of the significant findings reported are really the product of random fluctuations (Type I errors). While it is possible to use Bonferoni tests in order to reduce the probability of Type I errors, it greatly enhances the probability of Type II errors (for more explanation of this issue, see Rothman 1990 and Perneger 1998). Another strategy might be to only report those findings which are significant below a threshold p value below .01. In fact, because the test for cross-site and within-site patterning we have used in this monograph is based on a multinomial distribution, the actual p values we have been working with have been more conservative than the nominal values. Our nominal p value of .01 is actually .006, and our nominal p value of .05 is actually .038.

Also, our approach in this monograph has not been to focus on individual results at individual sites but rather to focus on patterns in the data: cross-site patterns, in which all three comparisons show results in the same direction, at least one of them significant at .05, or within-site patterns, in which results for several outcomes in the same domain favor or disfavor a BBBF site. Placing our focus on patterns has served the purpose of drawing attention away from what may well be single-site single-measure random fluctuations and thus help to solve the problem of Type I errors that may concern readers.

POLICY IMPLICATIONS

One of the most important implications of the results of the BBBF initiative is that local residents in disadvantaged communities, along with collaborating professionals, have the capacity to develop prevention programs that suit their needs, if adequate resources are provided and decision making is ceded to the community. In the case of the BBBF project, the three demonstration sites were selected through a competitive process, and it is likely that this resulted in three communities that had motivated local residents and professionals who were particularly interested in improving their community. We have presented information earlier in this chapter that the selected comparison sites also had independently developed several interesting and potentially valuable initiatives to promote the development of young children and families in their neighborhoods. Most neighborhoods have a variety of such activities from time to time.

One implication of the current study is that if other communities are interested in undertaking an initiative similar to the BBBF project, a certain amount of preparation, local planning, and community development will be required. This is, in fact, what the three BBBF communities engaged in for 2.5 years before they were able to have their programs fully operating. We are currently developing and field testing a manual and other training materials that specify the strategies, challenges, and lessons learned from our qualitative and quantitative research concerning the development and implementation of the BBBF initiative. These materials will be used as a tool for a pan-Canadian dissemination of the BBBF model and will also available to people in other countries who may be interested in learning about or adopting the BBBF model in their locales. In preparation for implementing the BBBF prevention model, a community will need to spend time and resources planning and organizing using the information in our training materials. This upfront preparation for mobilizing a local community prevention initiative is similar to the communities that care (CTC) prevention model (Hawkins & Catalano, 2002).

The CTC model consists of a strategy for mobilizing communities to implement evidence-based programs designed to reduce adolescent substance abuse, delinquency, violence, teen pregnancy, and school dropout and to foster positive development in adolescent youth. The CTC model is primarily focused on preparing communities to implement prevention interventions that address the specific concerns of local adolescent problem behaviors; less focus is on parent/family and community outcomes. Nonetheless, extensive time, effort, and local resources are directed toward building community decision-making capacity for developing, implementing, and evaluating preventive interventions for adolescent problem behaviors. The CTC model has been compared with a computer operating system, and this also serves as a good analogy for the BBBF prevention model.

There is a growing awareness regarding the importance of early childhood experiences for the health and well-being of our society (Keating & Hertzman, 1999; McCain & Mustard, 1999, 2002; Shonkoff & Phillips, 2000). Thus, providing adequate public financing for high-quality early childhood development programs would seem to be of primary importance. It has now been well documented (e.g., Dodge, 2004; Heckman, 2000, 2004, 2006) that investments in early childhood programs can have substantially greater long-term economic benefits than program investments for older children, adolescents, and adults, as Figure 4 illustrates (Heckman, 2006).

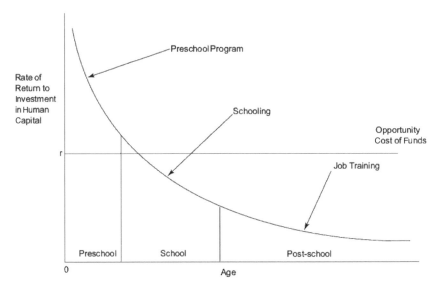

FIGURE 4.—Rates of return to human capital investment initially setting investment to be equal across all ages. *Source*: Heckman (2006).

In 1990, the BBBF longitudinal study was planned by the Ontario Government as a 25-year study, to follow program and comparison children through adolescence into early adulthood in order to allow for an analysis of these cost-saving outcomes (Government of Ontario, 1990). It was to be the first of its kind in Canada to determine whether the long-term monetary benefits or government savings for an early childhood prevention project would offset program costs. We now have evidence that investing in early childhood prevention programs in Canada can be a worthwhile endeavor.

Over the past 10 years, Canada has made progress on providing more funds for early child development projects (Government of Canada, 2000, 2003) to help provincial and territorial governments improve and expand early childhood development programs and services. Yet there is little indication that a comprehensive and coordinated system of high-quality early childhood development programs for all children from birth to school entry has been realized in any jurisdiction in Canada (Organization for Economic Co-operation and Development Directorate for Education, 2004). Similar observations have been made regarding early childhood services in the United States (Halfon, DuPlessis, & Inkelas, 2007) and the United Kingdom (Potter, 2007). Whether the current financial and political climate will allow the financing of such an ambitious yet highly desirable system is a major question. However, major proposals and initiatives in the United States, including the Obama–Biden "Comprehensive Zero to Five plan" (U.S.

Whitehouse, 2009) and funding by the Maternal and Child Health Bureau (2002) for the development of state early childhood comprehensive systems, as well as the proposal for an integrated children's system in the United Kingdom (U.K. Government, 2008), are encouraging.

We can only hope that research on early childhood programs, such as that reported here on the BBBF project, will provide the evidence and political support necessary for the development and financing of truly comprehensive systems for early childhood development.

CONCLUSIONS

The hallmark of the BBBF project is the three locally developed and operated organizations. Faced with an extremely broad and complex mandate, high expectations, and relatively little explicit direction, each of the communities developed an organization characterized by significant and meaningful local resident involvement in all decisions. This alone represents a tremendous accomplishment in neighborhoods in which, 20 years ago, many local residents viewed government programs and social services with skepticism, suspicion, or hostility. In developing their local organizations, BBBF projects have not only actively involved many local residents but have also played a major role in forming meaningful partnerships with other service organizations. They have developed a wide range of programs, many designed to respond to the locally identified needs of young children and their families and others to the needs of the neighborhood and broader community. As they strengthened and stabilized over the 7-year period from 1991 to 1998, each BBBF project increasingly gained the respect and support not only of local residents, service providers, and community leaders but also of the Ontario provincial government, which, in 1997, transferred all projects from demonstration to annualized funding, thus recognizing them as sustainable.

Based on data collected in the BBBF sites in 2003, Nelson, Pancer, Peters, et al. (2005) reported that all three projects were sustainable and were functioning effectively. They noted that this sustainability likely resulted to a great extent from the solid involvement of local neighborhood residents. Nelson, Pancer, Peters, et al. (2005) also report findings for data from a group of children born 5 years later than the longitudinal sample described in this monograph; results generally indicated more positive outcomes for children from schools in BBBF neighborhoods than for children from schools in the comparison communities. The size of these differences was generally greater than they had been 5 years earlier (Nelson, Pancer, Peters, et al., 2005). These findings support the view that the BBBF programs not only continued to

135

have positive impacts on children's social, emotional, behavioral, and academic functioning but that these impacts strengthened over this 5-year period. As of 2009, all three BBBF sites are continuing to function effectively.

The medium- and long-term findings reported in this monograph provide solid evidence that a universal, comprehensive, community-based prevention strategy, based on an ecological model of child development, can successfully promote the long-term development of young children and their families from disadvantaged neighborhoods, at a modest cost, and with the potential to begin to return the investment within a period as short as 7 years after program completion.

APPENDICES

TABLE OF PROGRAMS OFFERED AT THE THREE BETTER BEGINNINGS, BETTER FUTURES SITES AS OF 1998

Program Title	Participants	Service Provider/ Coordinator/Facilitator	Major Program Activities
Cornwall			
Child- and family-focused programs			
1. Playground (summer games)	Children ages 4–12	BBBF, L'Estrie Family Resource Center Coordinator, staff instructors, volunteers	8-week long summer program of athletic, recreational, and cultural activities, field trips, and puppet shows on conflict resolution, etc. A parent work group has input into activities implemented
2. Holiday activities	Kindergarten to Grade 2 children	BBBF, parent volunteers, L'Estrie Family Resource Center, school councils	Offers interesting day trips and educational activities for children on civic holidays and professional development days (trips to zoo, museums, outdoor games, crafts, films, etc.)
3. Community toy library	Community families	Toy librarian, community volunteers	For an annual fee of $20, families can borrow educational games, family resource films, books, etc. as often as they like. Volunteers do a lot of fundraising for the library
4. Theme boxes (now part of the toy library)	Community families and teachers	Project coordinator, teacher, parents	Many different theme boxes containing games and learning activities based on a theme (jobs, jungle animals, etc.). Can be borrowed by families or for use in classrooms

137

APPENDIX A (Contd.)

Program Title	Participants	Service Provider/ Coordinator/Facilitator	Major Program Activities
5. Family visits	Community families	Family workers	Family workers maintain regular contact with interested families to offer support, information about child development, community services and resources. Also runs seminars on various topics related to family development
6. Family activity center	Community families	BBBF staff, community volunteers	Objectives are to develop and improve parental competence and create good family relationships for optimal child development. Volunteers decide what activities they want and how to implement them (e.g., workshops, seminars, day trips)
7. Saturday playtime	Children ages 4–8	BBBF educator	Activities held every Saturday morning at community schools (arts, music, cooking, etc.)
8. Family vacation camp	Community families	BBBF staff, community volunteers	Sessions are offered to families in summer and March breaks. Volunteers are in charge of rules of conduct, raising funds to support activities, planning and implementing activities, etc.
School-based programs			
9. School activities center	Children in kindergarten to Grade 2	Educational assistants	Objective is promotion of the French language and the Francophone culture by supplying an educational assistant into the schools to help the teachers provide high quality activities for the children
10. Mini-breakfast	Children in kindergarten to Grade 2	BBBF staff	Children can have a healthy breakfast (muffins, fruits, juice, milk, cheese) when they arrive at school. Pamphlets and other information on healthy eating are distributed to families

APPENDIX A (Contd.)

Program Title	Participants	Service Provider/ Coordinator/Facilitator	Major Program Activities
11. Homework support	Community families	Educators, volunteers, coordinator	Parents and children meet together at the family activity center. They have a snack and then do homework together with the help of trained educators
Community-focused programs			
12. Community action group	Community members	BBBF, community volunteers	Organizes social activities, community gardens, environmental programs, supports different local programs like French week and fundraises, increases visibility and accessibility of BBBF, etc.
Highfield			
Child- and family-focused programs			
1. Family resource center drop-in	Families with children ages 0–4	1 family support coordinator, 1 parent volunteer, 1 nurse from Rexdale Health Center	4 mornings per week (2-hr sessions), families can participate in activities (crafts, etc.), special events, and summer outings. A nurse visits 2 × per month to talk about women's and children's health
2. Home visits	Families of children from kindergarten to Grade 2	4 EWs	Families visited before child entering junior kindergarten to provide information about area services, encouragement, referrals, and general support. Home Visitors spend. 5 days per week in kindergarten classroom. After the child is in kindergarten, home visits focus on school-related issues
3. Summer and March break program	Children from kindergarten to Grade 2	1 EW, 4 volunteers	Fun and educational activities provided for children to prepare them for school

139

APPENDIX A (Contd.)

Program Title	Participants	Service Provider/ Coordinator/Facilitator	Major Program Activities
4. Toy lending library	Families that use the drop-in	1 librarian, 3–4 parent volunteers	Library is open 4 days per week. Materials include over 500 toys, games, and puzzles. "Take a Book Program" has question sheets to get parents talking to kids about books. Also parenting resource books and activities to do with children
5. Play groups	Families with children in kindergarten	2 child and family EWs	Activities are unstructured, with an emphasis on providing nurturing and educational environment where families can learn and interact together
6. Preschool computer program	Children ages 2–4.5 years who attend drop-in	BBBF main service provider, 1 parent volunteer	Operates during drop-in hours on a first come first served basis. Children each have 5 min on the computer
7. Preschool literacy	Children ages 2–4.5 years who attend drop-in	In-school coordinator, family support coordinator, school librarian, 1 kindergarten teacher; BBBF funded	Intended to encourage preschoolers to read, support families, assist with transition to kindergarten by familiarizing family with school personnel
8. Before-and-after-school program	Children ages 4–8 and 9–12	Community development coordinator, recreation staff	Age-appropriate recreational activities and nutritional snacks provided for children at the primary school level
School-based programs 9. Health and nutrition program	All children at Highfield Junior School get snacks 3 × per week	1 nutrition coordinator, 3 paid parents, 10 parent volunteers, funding from BBBF, the school, parent donations, and other sources	Hold nutrition assemblies, fairs, and other activities. Workshops for parents, Hot Lunch Program ($.50 per lunch), providing sandwiches for kids without lunches, fitness activities, play days, etc.

APPENDIX A (Contd.)

Program Title	Participants	Service Provider/ Coordinator/Facilitator	Major Program Activities
10. Educational assistants, parent volunteers, and academic/language development	Children from kindergarten to Grade 2	4 EWs, 1 certified teacher, 2 assistants for kindergarten classes, 6–10 volunteers	4 EWs spend time in kindergarten classes to increase children's exposure to English and adult support, summer enrichment programs, After-school enrichment reading programs, family literacy nights, made dual language tapes to be used by families
11. Classroom social skills, intervention, storytelling and drama	School classes	In-school coordinator, university students, funded by BBBF, Highfield Junior School, Lion's Club	Including a curriculum-based social/citizenship skills intervention. Also, Grade 3 students visit a seniors' lodge $1 \times$ per week and spend time with seniors. EW and Parent Volunteers help children to develop better social skills. 2 drama trips per year for kindergarten classes
12. Home-school connection and parental involvement	Parents of children in project school	BBBF project manager, in-school coordinator and other coordinators and staff, parent volunteers	Parents participate in in-school and nutrition committees, School Council, Inner City Committee, School Design Committee, Snack Program, and some have been hired as EW and Research Assistants
13. Community and ethnocultural relations	School and Community members	In-school coordinator, EWs, BBBF, Highfield Junior School	Special events held at school to increase the exposure and participation of various cultures in the community, e.g., annual multicultural caravan
Parent-focused programs			
14. Parent relief	Community residents (space for 5–10 children at a time)	BBBF main service provider, 2 paid parents	Child care is offered 2 days per week (09:00 a.m.–11:30 a.m.) for parents needing a break. Parents must book ahead because space is usually filled to capacity
15. Parents' group	Parents who participate in drop-in or who have children at Highfield	Family support coordinator, CAS family support team, nurse & nutritionist from Rexdale Health Center	Parents meet weekly to socialize, organize special events, do crafts, or have workshops (e.g., women's issues, childhood illnesses, discipline, nutrition)

APPENDIX A (Contd.)

Program Title	Participants	Service Provider/ Coordinator/Facilitator	Major Program Activities
Community-focused programs			
16. Resident participation and leadership	Community parents	Community development coordinator and staff; community development committee	Parents are informally encouraged to join project committees, to get involved in planning community events, to advocate for the community (e.g., lighting, bus shelters, etc.). Parents are given skill development and leadership building workshops
17. Welcome baskets	Community families	BBBF	Baskets contain info about BBBF, other community services, and goodies. Given to new families through the schools in BBBF area to welcome them and encourage involvement in the project and the community
18. Language and prevocational skills	Community residents	BBBF refers students to the English as Second Language (ESL) program run by the school board	ESL Program has been running for several years. A Hindi class also ran for 1 year
19. Neighborhood safety	Community residents	Community development coordinator and staff, parents	Several community safety forums held. Have implemented security guards, improved lighting, removal of derelict cars, crossing guard, etc.
20. Social and recreational programs	Community residents	BBBF staff	Before-and-after school programs, March Break programs, fun activities and ballet lessons for kids, aerobics and bus trips for parents
21. Ethnocultural programs and activities	Community residents	Community development coordinator and staff	Several different cultural events (e.g., Diwali, Holi, Black History Month). Also staff are hired that have cultural backgrounds similar to residents

APPENDIX A (Contd.)

Program Title	Participants	Service Provider/ Coordinator/Facilitator	Major Program Activities
Sudbury			
Child- and family-focused programs			
1. After school/holiday programs	Children ages 4–8	9 part-time child care Workers, College Boreal Placement Students, 3 cooks, 2–4 volunteers, City Parks, and Recreation	Daily program provides a safe place for 100 children to play after school and on school holidays. Snacks and special activities are offered. Children are encouraged to solve problems and conflicts fairly
2. Summer programs	Programs are offered at 3 sites in the community	9 part-time child care workers	Offered 8 per week 09:00 a.m.–03:00 p.m., kids participate in activities similar to the After School programs, but with more emphasis on outdoor activities
3. BBBF membership and volunteer	Open invitation to all community residents to become a member of BBBF	Membership coordinator	The coordinator visits the community residents to explain BBBF and receive feedback from them on the program. Responsible for running 3 membership meetings a year
4. L'Arc-en-ciel du Moulin a Fleur	Families with children ages 0–5	1 Francophone community worker, 1 child care worker. Parents who bring their children monitor their children	Mom and tots drop-in program with participant-driven activities. Organized workshops and presentations are very successful
5. Family visiting program	Community members	2 S-BBBF staff (1 Anglophone, 1 Francophone)	Advocates and supports families' needs, provides support to child care teams, do presentations for other agencies, schools
6. Travelling road show	Open to all community residents	2 BBBF staff, 3–5 parent volunteers	Staff visit 3 different sites 1 per week to play with children while parents discuss parenting problems and solutions, and organize events
7. Halloween haunted house	Whole community	3 part-time child care staff, community workers	Extend after-school program at Halloween to open Haunted House constructed by staff

143

APPENDIX A (Contd.)

Program Title	Participants	Service Provider/Coordinator/Facilitator	Major Program Activities
School-based programs			
8. Peaceful playgrounds program	Children in kindergarten to Grade 6 in 3 local schools	2 BBBF staff, 1 placement student	Teach cooperative games, teach kids how to listen to each other, how to vote democratically, etc. A week is allotted to an anger management course, as well as peer mediation skills for teachers and children
9. Native cultural program	Children in Grades 1–3 at 2 schools	2 BBBF staff, 4 placement students	Through traditional methods kids are taught about equality of all cultures, and to respect each other, self, and mother Earth
10. Early bird breakfast and play program	Focus is on children ages 4–8, but no one is turned away. Approximately 250 children participate daily.	3 BBBF staff, child care workers, volunteers	Nutritious food is served and children participate in crafts and physical activities
11. Multicultural support program	2 Francophone schools, 3 different classes	1 BBBF part-time staff from Rwanda working as a teacher's aide	Children are exposed to different cultures in an informal way. Teacher's aide is currently translating a Rwandan children's book which will be used in the classes
Parent-focused programs			
12. Christmas baskets	Whole Donovan/Flour Mill community	Community workers, family support workers	Assistance in the way of gifts and food at Christmas
13. Babysitting and transportation	Community members	Family support worker	Provide child care and transportation to permit parents to participate in programs, committees
14. Can skate	Community members		Free skating every winter in partnership with the City. Skates provided
Community-focused programs			
15. Community kitchen program	Community residents	1 BBBF staff, parent volunteers, funding from Steel Workers Humanities Fund	Participants plan menu, then cook and clean while staff watch children. Staff shop for groceries and supplies. Each participant takes food home

APPENDIX A (Contd.)

Program Title	Participants	Service Provider/ Coordinator/Facilitator	Major Program Activities
16. The environmental program	Parents and children	1 BBBF staff, EJLB Grant, placement students, summer students	Offers information about caring for the environment. Annual development of community gardens, which involves participation of children, school yard naturalization, park and stream rehabilitation, recycling, local walks to recognize indigenous plants, animals
17. Research program	Community members	2 BBBF staff, 1–2 volunteers	Offers the community the possibility to develop local research projects and use the data from the activities to initiate other programs
18. Mediation group	Parents in the community	Community workers	Encourages dialogue among community workers and parents in order to deal with disagreements through effective conflict resolution techniques
19. Myths and mirrors community arts program	Community; all ages	1 Community development worker, 20 volunteers, placement students	Community Arts programs featuring giant puppets, mask making, large-scale community art projects and celebrations, theatre, festivals, costumes, parades. Now an independently incorporated organization
20. Community development	Native community Francophone community	1 Native Community Worker 1 Francophone Community Worker	To organize respective communities, help identify community needs, liaise with respective caucuses, implement programs and initiatives in community, advocate, provide support to child care workers
21. Preteen program	Pre-teens in the community	Adults and teens from community	2 Programs (English and French) offer activities appropriate for pre-teen age group
22. GEODE (Grassroots Economic Opportunities Development and Evaluation)	Whole community	1 part-time community organizer; volunteers: Bronfman funding	To provide community economic development opportunities to low income people including a "Good Food Box," community shared agriculture, a green dollar bartering system for individuals and non-profit organizations. Now an independently incorporated organization

145

APPENDIX A (Contd.)

Program Title	Participants	Service Provider/ Coordinator/Facilitator	Major Program Activities
23. Fundraising	Community members	Project coordinator	Raise funds for programs via small bake sales to large mail campaigns
24. Committee training	Community members	Project coordinator	To provide training and expertise and ensure community ownership by having all Council Committees run by Council and Community Members, i.e., Finance Committee, Personnel Committee, Program Committee, Membership Committee, Ad Hoc Committees, Newsletter Committee
25. General training	BBBF council members, staff, community members	Project coordinator, community workers, Membership coordinator	Provide training on Community Development, First Aid, CPR, Communication, Racism, Child Care Techniques, Chairing and Facilitating Meetings, Consensus Process, How to be a Council Member, Healthy Eating, Environment, Advocacy, Legal Issues, Welfare
26. Volunteer recognition	Volunteers	1 volunteer coordinator	Annual celebration to recognize efforts of volunteers
27. Community advisory committee	Friends of Better Beginnings, Better Futures (including many service providers)	Project coordinator	A group of over 50 community leaders to provide advice and support on an on-going basis

EW, enrichment worker.

APPENDIX B

EXAMINATION OF ATTRITION BIAS FROM GRADE 6 TO GRADE 9: DIFFERENCES IN SOCIO-DEMOGRAPHIC VARIABLES BETWEEN CASES RETAINED AND CASES LOST

Variables	Full Sample	Sample (Retained)	Retained (Mean)	Lost (Mean)	Mean Difference	Effect Size	p
Gender of respondent	730	626	0.93	0.88	0.04	.17	ns
Respondent's year of birth	726	623	1,962.1	1,962.8	−0.70	−.14	ns
Gender of child	730	626	0.47	0.42	0.05	.10	ns
Single parent throughout	730	626	0.20	0.27	−0.07	−.17	ns
Two parents throughout	730	626	0.65	0.73	−0.08	−.16	ns
Number of years in neighborhood	730	626	5.48	4.78	0.70	.19	ns
Respondent's education	725	623	13.93	14.07	−0.14	−.07	ns
Monthly income ($)	726	625	3,569	3,614	−45.00	−.02	ns
Monthly food costs ($)	704	616	544	525	19.00	.09	ns
Monthly housing costs ($)	682	601	1,052	1,001	51.00	.11	ns
In-public housing	728	625	0.16	0.17	−0.02	−.05	ns
Respondent working full-time	728	625	0.60	0.63	−0.03	−.08	ns
Partner working full-time	575	500	0.83	0.87	−0.04	−.11	ns
Respondent seeking work	243	219	0.32	0.29	0.03	.07	ns
Partner seeking work	97	89	0.30	0.13	0.18	.40	ns
Cultural group							
Anglophone	730	626	0.34	0.26	0.08	.17	ns
Francophone	730	626	0.36	0.35	0.01	.03	ns
Native	730	626	0.04	0.01	0.03	.17	ns
Other ethnicity	730	626	0.38	0.38	0.01	.01	ns
Immigrant	730	626	0.40	0.42	−0.02	−.04	ns

Note.—*ns* = not significant.

APPENDIX C
RELIABILITIES OF SCALES USED IN DATA COLLECTION WITH GRADES 3, 6, AND 9 CHILDREN, THEIR PARENTS, AND TEACHERS

Scale	Source	Number of Items (Range of Scores)	Reliability Coefficient (Cronbach's α)		
			Grade 3	Grade 6	Grade 9
Prosocial Scale (Parent Ratings of Youth)	NLSCY	10 items (0–20) Higher score indicates more prosocial behavior	NA	.86	.88
Conflict Resolution Scale (Parent Ratings of Youth)	NLSCY	8 items (8–32) Higher score indicates less conflict resolution	NA	NA	.78
Self Esteem Scale (Youth Self-Report)	NLSCY	4 items (4–20) Higher score indicates higher self-esteem	NA	.75	.85
Conflict Management Subscale (Teacher Ratings of Youth)	Subscale from Social Skills Rating Scale (Gresham & Elliott, 1990)	6 items (0–12) Higher score indicates more conflict management	.82	.89	.89
Emotional-Anxiety Disorder Scale (Parent Ratings of Youth)	NLSCY	8 items (0–16) Higher score indicates more emotional-anxiety behavior	.81	.85	.86
Physical Aggression Scale (Parent Ratings of Youth)	NLSCY	6 items (0–12) Higher score indicates more physical aggression behavior	.85	.85	.85
Indirect Aggression Scale (Parent Ratings of Youth)	NLSCY	5 items (0–10) Higher score indicates more indirect aggression behavior	.84	.83	.87

APPENDIX C (Contd.)

Scale	Source	Number of Items (Range of Scores)	Reliability Coefficient (Cronbach's α)		
			Grade 3	Grade 6	Grade 9
Hyperactivity/Inattention Scale (Parent Ratings of Youth)	NLSCY	8 items (0–16) Higher score indicates more hyperactivity-inattention behavior	.89	.89	.90
Delinquency Scale (Parent Ratings of Youth)	NLSCY (NLSCY labeled this scale "Property Offence")	6 items (0–12) Higher score indicates more delinquency behavior	NA	.73	.75
Oppositional-Defiant Scale (Parent Ratings of Youth)	From Child Behaviour Problems Subscales of Revised Ontario Child Health Study (Boyle et al., 1993)	8 items (0–16) Higher score indicates more oppositional-defiant behavior	.85	.89	.89
Depression (Parent Ratings of Youth)	Scale is part of the Child Behaviour Problems Subscales of the Revised Ontario Child Health Study (Boyle et al., 1993)	3 items (0–6) Higher score indicates more depression behavior	.60	.65	.69
Emotional–Anxiety Disorder Scale (Teacher Ratings of Youth)	NLSCY	5 items (0–10) Higher score indicates more emotional-anxiety behavior	.89	.89	.84
Hyperactivity/Inattention Scale (Teacher Ratings of Youth)	NLSCY	7 items (0–14) Higher score indicates more hyperactivity-inattention behavior	.92	.92	.92
Emotional–Anxiety Disorder Scale (Youth Self-Report)	NLSCY	7 items (0–14) Higher score indicates more emotional-anxiety behavior	NA	.75	.80

149

APPENDIX C (Contd.)

Scale	Source	Number of Items (Range of Scores)	Reliability Coefficient (Cronbach's α)		
			Grade 3	Grade 6	Grade 9
Physical Aggression Scale (Youth Self-Report)	NLSCY	6 items (0–12) Higher score indicates more physical aggression behavior	NA	.79	.76
Indirect Aggression Scale (Youth Self-Report)	NLSCY	5 items (0–10) Higher score indicates more indirect aggression behavior	NA	.75	.64
Hyperactivity/Inattention Scale (Youth Self-Report)	NLSCY	6 items (0–12) Higher score indicates more hyperactivity-inattention behavior	NA	.73	.73
Delinquency Scale (Youth Self-Report)	RCU, based on items from NLSCY	10 items (0–28) Higher score indicates more delinquency behavior	NA	.72	.84
Delinquent Friends Scale (Youth Self-Report)	RCU, based on items from NLSCY	9 items (0–27) Higher score indicates more delinquency by friends	NA	NA	.88
Student Preparedness Scale (Teacher Ratings of Youth)	NLSCY	4 items (4–20) Higher score indicates less preparedness for learning at school	NA	.85	.88
Adaptive Functioning Scale (Teacher Ratings of Youth)	RCU created scale by combining items from Achenbach et al., 1987	4 items (4–28) Higher score indicates more adaptive functioning	.86	.87	.91
Social Support Scale (Parent Self-Report)	From the 24-item Social Provisions Scale	6 items (6–24) Higher score indicates more social support	.80	.83	.85

150

APPENDIX C (Contd.)

Scale	Source	Number of Items (Range of Scores)	Reliability Coefficient (Cronbach's α)		
			Grade 3	Grade 6	Grade 9
Depression Scale (Parent Self-Report)	Derived from the 20-item CES-D Scale Radloff, 1977 (Cutrona & Russell, 1987)	12 items (12–48) Higher score indicates more depression	.84	.87	.90
Family Functioning Scale (Parent Self-Report)	Derived from 12-item Family Functioning Scale (Epstein, Baldwin, & Bishop, 1983)	7 items (7–28) Higher score indicates higher family functioning	.88	.82	.78
Hostile-Ineffective Parenting Scale (Parent Self-Report)	NLSCY	7 items (0–28) Higher score indicates more hostile-ineffective parenting	.74	.78	.80
Parent Monitoring Scale (Youth Self-Report)	RCU, based on items from NLSCY	3 items (0–12) Higher score indicates higher parent monitoring	NA	NA	.79
Neighborhood Activities Scale (Parent Self-Report)	RCU	6 items (0–12) Higher score indicates more neighborhood activities	.78	.80	.85
Sense of Community Involvement Scale (Parent Self-Report)	From the 9-item scale Sense of Community Involvement Scale (Buckner, 1988)	5 items (5–20) Higher score indicates less community involvement.	.79	.78	.81
Neighborhood Satisfaction Scale (Parent Self-Report)	Items in Quality of Life Surveys (Institute for Social Research, 1981)	5 items (4–30) Higher score indicates greater neighborhood satisfaction	.74	.88	.81

Note.—NLSCY = Canadian National Longitudinal Survey of Children and Youth; RCU = BBBF Research Coordination Unit.

APPENDIX D

Adjusted Means (Standard Deviations) for All Outcome Measures at Grades 3, 6, and 9, by Cohort

Measure	BBBF Cohort Combined Mean (SD)			Comparison Cohort Combined Mean (SD)		
	Grade 3	Grade 6	Grade 9	Grade 3	Grade 6	Grade 9
Child social functioning						
Parent-rated						
Prosocial Behavior Scale	6.7 (6.5)	13.0 (3.9)**	12.2 (4.3)	6.5 (5.5)	11.6 (4.3)	12.2 (4.2)
Number of people important to child		6.7 (5.9)**	6.8 (6.1)**		4.9 (3.7)	5.2 (3.9)
Conflict Resolution Scale			14.7 (4.4)*			15.6 (4.5)
Child-rated						
Self-Esteem Scale		16.9 (2.6)	15.9 (3.1)**		17.0 (2.5)	16.8 (2.5)
Extracurricular activities		7.4 (3.5)	7.7 (4.1)		7.2 (3.2)	8.1 (4.2)
Teacher-rated						
Self-Control/Conflict Management Scale	4.0 (2.0)	9.4 (2.7)**	9.4 (2.8)	3.9 (2.0)	8.4 (2.5)	8.8 (2.9)
Child emotional and behavioral problems						
Parent-rated						
Emotional–Anxiety Disorder Scale	2.9 (2.8)	3.3 (2.9)	2.8 (2.8)	2.7 (2.4)	2.8 (2.8)	2.7 (2.6)
Physical Aggression Scale	1.4 (2.0)	1.6 (2.1)**	1.2 (1.8)	1.4 (1.9)	1.1 (1.6)	1.0 (1.6)
Indirect Aggression Scale	1.5 (1.8)	1.5 (1.8)**	1.1 (1.7)	1.5 (1.8)	1.1 (1.3)	1.0 (1.3)
Hyperactivity–Inattention Scale	4.0 (3.4)	3.8 (3.4)	3.1 (3.2)	3.9 (3.2)	3.6 (3.1)	3.0 (3.1)
Delinquency Scale		0.9 (1.4)	1.0 (1.6)		1.0 (1.5)	1.0 (1.3)
Oppositional Defiant Scale	4.9 (3.0)	5.2 (3.5)	5.0 (3.4)	5.1 (3.3)	5.0 (3.4)	4.9 (3.3)
Depression Scale	0.9 (1.1)	1.3 (1.2)**	1.1 (1.1)	0.9 (1.0)	1.1 (1.2)	1.0 (1.0)
Teacher-rated						
Emotional–Anxiety Disorder Scale	2.4 (3.1)**	3.6 (3.5)	2.0 (2.5)*	3.3 (3.6)	3.4 (3.2)	2.6 (2.3)
Hyperactivity–Inattention Scale	3.3 (3.5)**	4.2 (3.5)**	4.3 (3.9)**	4.2 (3.7)	5.3 (3.9)	5.7 (3.8)

APPENDIX D (Contd.)

Measure	BBBF Cohort Combined Mean (SD)			Comparison Cohort Combined Mean (SD)		
	Grade 3	Grade 6	Grade 9	Grade 3	Grade 6	Grade 9
Child-rated						
Emotional–Anxiety Disorder Scale		3.8 (2.8)	4.0 (2.8)**		3.8 (2.6)	3.2 (2.7)
Physical Aggression Scale		2.0 (2.2)*	2.0 (2.1)		1.6 (2.1)	1.7 (1.7)
Indirect Aggression Scale		1.5 (1.8)	1.7 (1.7)		1.1 (1.3)	1.8 (1.8)
Hyperactivity—Inattention Scale		4.0 (2.4)	4.2 (2.5)		4.1 (2.7)	4.0 (2.6)
Delinquency Scale		1.4 (1.7)	2.5 (3.6)		1.2 (1.6)	2.0 (2.4)
Ever arrested/taken to police station			0.1 (0.3)			0.1 (0.3)
Delinquent Friends Scale			5.4 (4.7)			4.7 (3.8)
School functioning						
Parent-rated						
Child repeated a grade		0.1 (0.3)	0.1 (0.3)**		0.1 (0.3)	0.2 (0.3)
Teacher-administered						
Student Preparedness Scale	12.0 (2.9)	10.0 (3.8)	9.1 (3.8)*	12.0 (3.3)	10.7 (4.0)	10.1 (3.6)
Adaptive Functioning Scale		16.3 (4.6)	17.4 (6.1)*		15.8 (4.7)	16.0 (6.1)
Child suspended since last fall		0.1 (0.3)*	0.2 (0.4)		0.1 (0.3)	0.2 (0.3)
How far hope child will go in school		4.0 (1.2)	4.0 (1.2)**		3.9 (1.2)	3.6 (1.3)
Child's current academic achievement			3.0 (1.3)			3.2 (1.3)
Standardized mathematics test	2.2 (0.7)	2.6 (0.8)*	2.5 (0.8)	2.1 (0.7)	2.4 (0.7)	2.4 (0.7)
Child received special education/services	0.3 (0.4)	0.2 (0.4)*	0.2 (0.4)*	0.3 (0.4)	0.3 (0.4)	0.3 (0.4)
Child limitations due to learning disability		0.1 (0.3)	0.1 (0.3)		0.1 (0.4)	0.1 (0.3)
Child health and health risk behaviors						
Parent-rated						
General health rating	1.6 (0.7)	1.7 (0.7)*	1.7 (0.8)	1.5 (0.7)	1.6 (0.7)	1.8 (0.7)
Number of chronic conditions	0.8 (1.1)**	1.0 (1.2)**	0.9 (1.2)*	0.6 (0.9)	0.7 (1.0)	0.7 (0.9)

APPENDIX D (Contd.)

Measure	BBBF Cohort Combined Mean (SD)			Comparison Cohort Combined Mean (SD)		
	Grade 3	Grade 6	Grade 9	Grade 3	Grade 6	Grade 9
Child limited by health problems	0.1 (0.3)	0.1 (0.3)	0.1 (0.3)	0.1 (0.2)	0.1 (0.3)	0.1 (0.3)
Child's exposure to second-hand smoke		6.5 (11.4)	6.7 (15.0)		8.1 (12.1)	7.2 (14.5)
Child-rated						
Body mass index	18.1 (3.4)**	20.4 (4.5)	22.7 (4.8)	17.4 (2.9)	20.7 (4.4)	22.5 (4.6)
Breakfast consumption		0.7 (0.5)	0.4 (0.5)		0.7 (0.5)	0.5 (0.5)
Meets all four food groups recommendations		0.1 (0.3)	0.0 (0.1)		0.1 (0.2)	0.0 (0.1)
Alcohol consumption		0.1 (0.3)	2.9 (1.9)		0.1 (0.3)	2.8 (1.6)
Smoking experience		1.2 (0.5)	1.6 (0.8)		1.2 (0.4)	1.5 (0.6)
Number of times injured in past 12 months		0.9 (1.2)	0.8 (1.1)		1.0 (1.3)	0.5 (0.9)
Experience with marijuana			0.6 (1.4)			0.6 (1.1)
Stress index			1.9 (1.3)			1.8 (1.2)
Ever had consensual sex			0.2 (0.4)			0.2 (0.3)
Parent health and health risk behaviors						
Parent-rated						
Self-rated health	2.2 (1.0)	2.3 (0.9)**	2.5 (0.9)	2.0 (0.9)	2.1 (0.9)	2.5 (0.9)
Body mass index	26.2 (5.1)	25.9 (5.3)	25.9 (4.9)	26.0 (5.3)	25.7 (4.6)	25.9 (5.0)
Smoking	0.6 (0.7)	0.5 (0.7)	0.4 (0.6)	0.6 (0.7)	0.5 (0.6)	0.4 (0.6)
Problems with Professional Service Index	0.1 (0.4)	0.2 (0.4)	0.2 (0.4)	0.1 (0.3)	0.2 (0.4)	0.2 (0.4)
Parent/family functioning						
Parent-rated						
Social Support Scale	20.8 (2.5)	21.2 (2.4)**	21.2 (2.5)**	21.0 (2.3)	20.1 (2.8)	20.1 (2.6)
Depression Scale	19.6 (6.0)	18.4 (6.2)	18.6 (6.2)	18.8 (5.5)	19.0 (6.7)	19.0 (6.7)
Marital satisfaction	8.7 (1.5)	8.3 (1.7)	8.5 (1.4)*	8.6 (1.5)	8.4 (1.4)	8.1 (1.5)
Family Functioning Scale	23.1 (3.5)**	23.6 (2.9)**	23.7 (2.9)**	23.9 (3.1)	22.6 (2.9)	22.9 (2.7)

APPENDIX D (Contd.)

Measure	BBBF Cohort Combined Mean (SD)			Comparison Cohort Combined Mean (SD)		
	Grade 3	Grade 6	Grade 9	Grade 3	Grade 6	Grade 9
Stressful life events	1.6 (1.6)	1.5 (1.5)**	1.6 (1.5)	1.6 (1.4)	2.0 (1.6)	1.6 (1.4)
Financial stress	0.5 (0.8)	0.5 (0.8)	0.8 (0.8)	0.5 (0.7)	0.5 (0.7)	0.9 (1.0)
Hostile-Ineffective Parenting Scale	7.9 (3.7)	8.2 (3.9)**	13.0 (3.8)	7.9 (4.4)	7.1 (3.9)	13.1 (4.3)
Child-rated						
Parent Monitoring Scale			9.1 (2.8)**			10.0 (2.3)
Community involvement and neighborhood quality						
Parent-rated						
Neighborhood Activities Scale	2.6 (2.1)	3.3 (2.7)*	3.4 (2.7)	2.5 (2.1)	2.8 (2.5)	3.0 (2.3)
Parent's Social Activities Index	10.1 (10.7)*	7.8 (7.1)	7.3 (7.7)	8.6 (7.6)	8.2 (11.0)	6.3 (8.1)
Sense of Community Involvement Scale	10.2 (2.1)	9.8 (2.2)**	9.5 (2.5)	10.3 (2.2)	10.5 (1.8)	10.2 (1.9)
Neighborhood Satisfaction Scale	19.5 (4.8)	21.1 (4.5)**	21.7 (4.6)**	20.2 (4.7)	19.4 (4.5)	19.6 (4.0)
Health Care and Social Services Utilization Index	1.0 (1.0)**	1.6 (1.1)**	1.6 (1.2)	0.8 (0.7)	1.3 (1.0)	1.7 (1.3)

Note.—All means were adjusted for gender and birth year of respondent (typically the mother), gender of child, number of siblings, number of parents in the home, respondents' education, family income, cultural category (Anglophone, Francophone, Native, and other), and immigrant status. All values rounded up to the nearest tenth. A blank space indicates that data for that measure were not collected at that time point. The range of sample sizes for the BBBF and Comparison cohorts, respectively, was as follows:

Grade 3: Parent ratings (BBBF n = 322–480 and Com. n = 179–290); teacher ratings (BBBF n = 259–408 and Com. n = 149–255).

Grade 6: Parent ratings (BBBF n = 276–459 and Com. n = 114–254); teacher ratings (BBBF n = 347–459 and Com. n = 137–165); child ratings (BBBF n = 296–433 and Com. n = 159–238).

Grade 9: Parent ratings (BBBF n = 193–431 and Com. n = 53–218); teacher ratings (BBBF n = 131–305 and Com. n = 71–127); child ratings (BBBF n = 250–339 and Com. n = 122–167).

*Significant cross-site pattern between BBBF and Comparison cohorts at $p < .05$ level.

**Significant cross-site pattern between BBBF and Comparison cohorts at $p < .01$ level.

APPENDIX E

YEARLY COST CALCULATIONS FOR 12 MONETIZABLE MEASURES IN $CDN FROM JUNIOR KINDERGARTEN TO GRADE 9

Year:	1993	1994	1995	1996	1997	1998	1999	2000	2001	2002	2003	Total
Grade:	JK	SK	G 1	G 2	G 3	G 4[a]	G 5[a]	G6	G 7[a]	G 8[a]	G 9	(JK–G9)
Visits to a family physician												
BB												
Mean ($)	25[a]	27	26	21	15	18	19	20	19	15	14	219
95% CI		(24, 29)	(24, 28)	(19, 23)	(14, 16)			(18, 21)			(13, 15)	—
n	238	160	189	212	373	386	386	366	386	386	386	
Com.[b]												
Mean ($)	22[a]	21	26	23	18	19	19	18	18	17	16	217
95% CI		(19, 24)	(23, 28)	(20, 25)	(16, 20)			(16, 20)			(14, 18)	—
n	223	189	201	208	215	223	223	211	223	223	223	
Hospital emergency room use												
BB												
Mean ($)	112	73	47	42	31	38	41	41	39	30	25	519
95% CI	(92, 132)	(56, 89)	(34, 61)	(30, 54)	(23, 39)			(33, 50)			(18, 31)	—
n	130	159	185	200	356	367	367	346	367	367	367	
Com.												
Mean ($)	65	58	24	31	22	26	27	26	27	28	28	362
95% CI	(46, 84)	(44, 71)	(14, 33)	(21, 40)	(14, 30)			(18, 35)			(19, 37)	—
n	118	186	200	204	213	219	219	207	219	219	219	
Number of serious injuries												
BB												
Mean ($)	302	329	385[a]	390	364	507	695	579	1,324	3,731	4,842	13,448
95% CI	(60, 543)	(127, 531)		(190, 591)	(171, 557)			(373, 785)			(4,416, 5,267)	—
n	106	128	152	148	203	208	208	200	208	208	208	
Com.												
Mean ($)	487	470	492[a]	482	393	513	580	397	1,145	3,470	4,529	12,958
95% CI	(116, 858)	(243, 696)		(252, 711)	(200, 586)			(222, 572)			(4,145, 4,913)	—
n	81	131	146	143	143	146	146	140	146	146	146	
Number of overnight stays in hospital												
BB												
Mean ($)	157	77	106[a]	126	109	96	46	16	32	48	50	863

APPENDIX E (Contd.)

Year:	1993	1994	1995	1996	1997	1998	1999	2000	2001	2002	2003	Total (JK–G9)
Grade:	JK	SK	G 1	G 2	G 3	G 4[a]	G 5[a]	G6	G 7[a]	G 8[a]	G 9	
95% CI	(28, 287)	(4, 150)		(12, 240)	(−19, 237)			(3, 30)			(14, 86)	—
n	113	135	196	170	275	288	288	269	288	288	288	—
Com. Mean ($)	97	0	56[a]	92	106	84	39	18	24	20	15	551
95% CI	(−44, 239)	(0, 0)		(22, 161)	(19, 193)			(−1, 36)			(−16, 45)	—
n	82	133	161	153	157	161	161	152	161	161	161	—
Visits with a nurse practitioner												
BB Mean ($)	3[a]	4[a]	5	2	1	1	2	2	2	2	1	25
95% CI			(3, 6)	(1, 3)	(.3, 1)			(1, 2)			(1, 2)	—
n	237	237	187	203	353	384	384	364	384	384	384	—
Com. Mean ($)	1[a]	1[a]	1	2	1	1	1	1	1	1	1	12
95% CI			(−.2, 2)	(1, 3)	(0, 1)			(.6, 2)			(.7, 2)	—
n	221	221	199	205	203	221	221	209	221	221	221	—
Family involvement with Children's Aid Society												
BB Mean ($)	10[a]	11[a]	12	7	8[a]	8	7	6	6	6	6	87
95% CI			(10, 14)	(5, 9)				(4, 9)			(3, 8)	—
n	216	216	177	200	216	216	216	202	216	216	216	—
Com. Mean ($)	10[a]	10[a]	11	8	8[a]	7	5	5	5	5	5	79
95% CI			(9, 13)	(6, 10)				(3, 6)			(3, 7)	—
n	215	215	189	202	215	215	215	207	215	215	215	—
Use of special education services												
BB Mean ($)	NA	NA	1,765	2,657	1,880	1,906	1,607	1,438	1,456	1,303	1,199	15,211
95% CI			(1,214, 2,316)	(2,084, 3,231)	(1,419, 2,341)			(1,057, 1,817)			(911, 1,486)	—
n			132	137	200	273	273	233	273	273	273	—

APPENDIX E (Contd.)

Year:	1993	1994	1995	1996	1997	1998	1999	2000	2001	2002	2003	Total
Grade:	JK	SK	G 1	G2	G3	G 4[a]	G 5[a]	G6	G 7[a]	G 8[a]	G 9	(JK–G9)
Com.												
Mean ($)	NA	NA	2,673	2,988	1,869	2,104	2,044	1,961	1,968	1,857	1,782	19,246
95% CI			(1,961, 3,386)	(2,303, 3,673)	(1,319, 2,418)			(1,365, 2,556)			(1,331, 2,234)	—
n			104	101	112	119	119	82	119	119	119	—
Grade repetition (cumulative cost only, from JK to G9)												
BB												
Mean ($)												921
95% CI												712, 1,131
n												431
Com.												
Mean ($)												1,264
95% CI												943, 1,585
n												223
Cost of being arrested (Grade 9 only)												
BB												
Mean ($)												113	113
95% CI												74, 151	—
n												329	—
Com.												
Mean ($)												136	136
95% CI												81, 191	—
n												149	—
Cost of court appearance (Grade 9 only)												
BB												
Mean ($)												61	61
95% CI												34, 87	—
n												318	—

APPENDIX E (Contd.)

Year:	1993	1994	1995	1996	1997	1998	1999	2000	2001	2002	2003	Total
Grade:	JK	SK	G 1	G2	G3	G 4[a]	G 5[a]	G6	G 7[a]	G 8[a]	G 9	(JK–G9)
Com.												
Mean ($)											35	35
95% CI											15, 54	—
n											147	—
Amount of annual social assistance received by parents (when children in Grade 9)												
BB												
Mean ($)											1,370	1,370
95% CI											(987, 1,753)	—
n											431	
Com.												
Mean ($)											1,646	1,646
95% CI											(1,160, 2,132)	—
n											219	
Amount of annual Ontario disability payments received by parents (when children in Grade 9)												
BB												
Mean ($)											725	725
95% CI											(412, 1,038)	—
n											417	
Com.												
Mean ($)											932	932
95% CI											(511, 1,353)	—
n											212	

Note.— BB = Three BBBF Project Sites; CI = confidence interval; Com. = 2 comparison sites; NA = not applicable.

[a]Values were interpolated as no data collection occurred that year; it is not possible to calculate confidence intervals for interpolated costs.

[b]All values were adjusted for birth year and gender of the interview respondent, gender of child, number of siblings, marital status, single parent status, respondents' education, employment status, family income, cultural category (Anglophone or Francophone), and immigrant status. The cost values are based on the value of each outcome as outlined in Chapter V (e.g., $29.44 for a visit to a family physician), multiplied by frequency of occurrence of that outcome for each child in our longitudinal sample for that year (e.g., 0 = no family physician visit or 1 = yes, visited family physician). All dollars are present value in 2003 Canadian dollars discounted at 3%.

REFERENCES

Achenbach, T. M., McConaughy, S. H., & Howell, C. T. (1987). Child/adolescent behavioral and emotional problems: Implications of cross–informant correlations for situational specificity. *Psychological Bulletin*, **101**(2), 213–232.

Albano, A., Chorpita, B., & Barlow, D. (1996). Childhood anxiety disorders. In E. J. Mash & R. A. Barkley (Eds.), *Child psychopathology* (1st ed., pp. 196–241). London, U.K.: Guildford Press.

Anderson, L. M., Shinn, C., Fullilove, M. T., Scrimshaw, S. C., Fielding, J. E., Normand, J., et al. (2003). The effectiveness of early childhood development programs. A systematic review. *American Journal of Preventive Medicine*, **24**(3, Suppl.), 32–46.

Aneshensel, C. S., & Sucoff, C. A. (1996). The neighborhood context of adolescent mental health. *Journal of Health and Social Behavior*, **37**, 293–310.

Angus, D. E., Cloutier, J. E., Albert, T., Chenard, D., Shariatmadar, A., Pickett, W., et al. (1998). *The economic burden of unintentional injury in Canada*. Toronto, Canada: SmartRisk Foundation.

Aos, S., Lieb, R., Mayfield, J., Miller, M., & Pennucci, A. (2004). *Benefits and costs of prevention and early intervention programs for youth*. Olympia, WA: Washington State Institute for Public Policy.

Barnes, J. (2007). How Sure Start Local Programme areas changed. In J. Belsky, J. Barnes & E. Melhuish (Eds.), *The national evaluation of Sure Start: Does area-based early intervention work?* (pp. 173–194). Bristol, U.K.: Policy Press/University of Bristol.

Barnes, J., Katz, I., Korbin, J. E., & O'Brien, M. (2006). *Children and families in communities: Theory, research, policy and practice*. Chichester, U.K.: John Wiley.

Barnett, W. S. (1996). *Lives in the balance: Age-27 benefit-cost analysis of the High/Scope Perry Preschool Program* [Monographs of the High/Scope Educational Research Foundation, 11]. Ypsilanti, MI: High/Scope Press.

Barnett, W. S., & Masse, L. N. (2007). Comparative benefit-cost analysis of the Abecedarian program and its policy implications. *Economics of Education Review*, **26**, 113–125.

Beauvais, C., & Jenson, J. (2003). *The well-being of children: Are there "neighborhood effects"?* (Discussion paper F/31). Ottawa, Canada: Canadian Policy Research Networks. Retrieved from http://www.cprn.org/doc.cfm?doc=156&l=en

Bell, L. G., & Bell, D. C. (2005). Family dynamics in adolescence affect midlife well-being. *Journal of Family Psychology*, **19**, 198–207.

Belsky, J., Melhuish, E., Barnes, J., Leyland, A. H., Romaniuk, H., & the National Evaluation of Sure Start Research Team. (2006). Effects of Sure Start Local Programmes on children and families: Early findings from a quasi-experimental, cross sectional study. *British Medical Journal*, doi:10.1136/bmj.38853.451748

Benson, P. L., Leffert, N., Scales, P. C., & Blyth, D. A. (1998). Beyond the village rhetoric: Creating healthy communities for children and adolescents. *Applied Development Science*, **2**(3), 138–159.

Bentler, P. M. (1990). Comparative fit indexes in structural models. *Psychological Bulletin*, **107**(2), 238–246.

Beswick, J. F., & Willms, J. D. (2008). *The critical transition from "learning-to-read" to "reading-to-learn."* Manuscript submitted for publication.

Birmaher, B., Ryan, N. D., Williamson, D. E., Brent, D. A., Kaufman, J., Dahl, R., et al. (1996). Childhood and adolescent depression: A review of the past 10 years. Part I. *Journal of the American Academy of Child and Adolescent Psychiatry*, **35**, 1427–1439.

Black, M. M., & Krishnakumar, A. (1998). Children in low-income, urban settings. Interventions to promote mental health and well-being. *American Psychologist*, **53**, 635–646.

Blyth, D. A., & Leffert, N. (1995). Communities as contexts for adolescent development: An empirical analysis. *Journal of Adolescent Research*, **10**, 64–87.

Blyth, D. A., & Roehlkepartain, E. C. (1993). *Healthy communities; healthy youth: How communities contribute to positive youth development*. Minneapolis, MN: Search Institute.

Boisjoli, R., Vitaro, F., Lacourse, E., Barker, E. D., & Tremblay, R. E. (2007). Impact and clinical significance of a preventive intervention for disruptive boys: 15-year follow-up. *British Journal of Psychiatry*, **191**, 415–419.

Bouchard, C. (2005). Searching for impacts of a community-based initiative: The evaluation of "1, 2, 3 GO!." In J. Scott & H. Ward (Eds.), *Safeguarding and promoting the well-being of children, families, and their communities* (pp. 228–241). London, U.K.: Jessica Kingsley Publications.

Boyle, M. H., Offord, D. R., Racine, Y. A., Fleming, J. E., Szatmari, P., & Sanford, M. (1993). Evaluation of the revised Ontario Child Health Study scales. *Journal of Child Psychology and Psychiatry*, **34**(2), 189–213.

Bramlett, R. K., Scott, P., & Rowell, R. K. (2000). A comparison of temperament and social skills in predicting academic performance in first graders. *Special Services in the Schools*, **16**(1–2), 147–158.

Bronfenbrenner, U. (1977). Toward an experimental ecology of human development. *American Psychologist*, **32**(7), 513–531.

Bronfenbrenner, U. (1979). *The ecology of human development*. Cambridge, MA: Harvard University Press.

Bronfenbrenner, U. (1986a). Recent advances in research on the ecology of human development. In R. K. Silbereisen, K. Eyferth, & G. Rudinger (Eds.), *Development as action in context: Problem behavior and normal youth development* (pp. 287–309). Heidelberg, Germany: Springer-Verlag.

Bronfenbrenner, U. (1986b). Ecology of the family as a context for human development: Research perspectives. *Developmental Psychology*, **22**(6), 723–742.

Bronfenbrenner, U., & Morris, P. A. (2006). The bioecological model of human development. In W. Damon & R. M. Lerner (Eds.), *Theoretical models of human development. Handbook of child psychology* (Vol. 1, 6th ed., pp. 793–828). Hoboken, NJ: John Wiley.

Brooks-Gunn, J. (2003). Do you believe in magic? What we can expect from early childhood intervention programs. *Social Policy Report*, **17**, 3–14.

Browne, G., Gafni, A., & Roberts, J. (2002). *Approach to the measurement of costs (expenditures) when evaluating health and social programs* (Working Paper Series 01-03). Hamilton, Canada: McMaster University, System-Linked Research Unit on Health and Social Service Utilization.

Bruner, C. (2004). *Many happy returns: Three economic models that make the case for school readiness*. Des Moines, IA: State Early Childhood Policy Technical Assistance Network.

Buckner, J. C. (1988). The development of an instrument to measure neighborhood cohesion. *American Journal of Community Psychology*, **16**, 771–791.

Buehler, C. (2006). Parents and peers in relation to early adolescent problem behavior. *Journal of Marriage and the Family*, **68**, 109–124.

Bursuck, W. D., & Asher, S. R. (1986). The relationship between social competence and achievement in elementary school children. *Journal of Clinical Child Psychology*, **15**(1), 41–49.

Bushnik, T., Barr-Telford, L., & Bussiere, P. (2004). *In and out of high school: First results from the second cycle of the Youth in Transition Survey, 2002*. Statistics Canada catalogue no. 81-595-MIE—No. 014. Ottawa, Canada: Statistics Canada. Retrieved from http://dsp-psd.tpsgc.gc.ca/Collection/Statcan/81-595-MIE/81-595-MIE2004014.pdf

Cameron, G., Pancer, M., McKenzie-Mohr, S., & Cooper, D. (1993). *Communities coming together: Proposal development in the Better Beginnings, Better Futures Project*. Kingston, ON: Better Beginnings, Better Futures Research Coordination Unit.

Camilli, G., Vargas, S., Ryan, S., & Barnett, W. S. (2010). *Meta-analysis of the effects of early education interventions on cognitive and social development*. Teachers College Record, 112. Retrieved from http://www.tcrecord.org ID Number: 15440

Capaldi, D., & Patterson, G. R. (1987). An approach to the problem of recruitment and retention rates for longitudinal research. *Behavioral Assessment*, **9**(2), 169–177.

Carnegie Task Force on Meeting the Needs of Young Children. (1994). *Starting points. Meeting the needs of our youngest children*. New York, NY: Carnegie Corporation of New York.

Catalano, R. F., Berglund, M. L., Ryan, J. A., Lonczak, H. S., & Hawkins, D. (2002). Positive youth development in the United States: Research findings on evaluations of positive youth development programs. Retrieved from http://www.journals.apa.org/prevention/volume5/pre0050015a.html

Christakis, N. A., & Fowler, J. H. (2007). The spread of obesity in a large social network over 32 years. *The New England Journal of Medicine*, **357**(4), 370–379.

Coffey, C. (2003). *The business case for early childhood education and care: Building a bridge to economic prosperity*. Retrieved from http://www.rbc.com/newsroom/20031104coffey.html

Cohen, J. (1977). *Statistical power analysis for the behavioral sciences* (Rev. ed.). New York: Academic Press.

Coie, J. D., & Jacobs, M. R. (1993). The role of social context in the prevention of conduct disorder. *Development and Psychopathology*, **5**(1–2), 263–275.

Conduct Problems Prevention Research Group. (1992). A developmental and clinical model for the prevention of conduct disorder: The Fast Track Program. *Development and Psychopathology*, **4**(4), 509–527.

Conduct Problems Prevention Research Group. (1999). Initial impact of the Fast Track prevention trial for conduct problems: I. The high-risk sample. *Journal of Consulting and Clinical Psychology*, **67**(5), 631–647.

Conduct Problems Prevention Research Group. (2002a). The implementation of the Fast Track Program: An example of a large-scale prevention science efficacy trial. *Journal of Abnormal Child Psychology*, **30**(1), 1–17.

Conduct Problems Prevention Research Group. (2002b). Evaluation of the first 3 years of the Fast Track prevention trial with children at high risk for adolescent conduct problems. *Journal of Abnormal Child Psychology*, **30**(1), 19–35.

Conduct Problems Prevention Research Group. (2007). Fast Track randomized controlled trial to prevent externalizing psychiatric disorders: Findings from grades 3 to 9. *Journal of the American Academy of Child and Adolescent Psychiatry*, **46**(10), 1250–1262.

Connor, S., & Brink, S. (1999). *Understanding the early years: Community impacts on child development*. Ottawa, ON: Applied Research Branch, Strategic Policy, Human Resources Development Canada (W-99-6E).

Cook, T. D., & Campbell, D. T. (1977). *Quasi-experimental design and analysis issues for field settings*. Boston: Houghton Mifflin.

Cormier, N. (2005). *L'initiative communautaire 1, 2, 3 GO! pour tout-petits: Analyse d'impacts sure le partenariat perçu et activé par les intervenants* (Unpublished doctoral dissertation). Département de psychologie, Université du Québec à Montréal, Montréal, Canada.

Crooks, C., & Peters, R. DeV (2002). Summary of several methods of summarizing outcome findings from Mrazek & Brown's evidence-based literature review of psychosocial prevention and early intervention programs for young children. In C. C. Russell (Ed.), *The state of knowledge about prevention/early intervention*. Toronto, Canada: Invest in Kids Foundation (pp. 305–382). Retrieved from http://www.investinkids.ca/parents/about-us/our-research/article type/articleview/articleid/1230/review-of-preventionearly-intervention-research.aspx

Cutrona, C. E., & Russell, D. W. (1987). The provisions of social relationships and adaptation to stress. In W. H. Jones & D. Perlman (Eds.), *Advances in personal relationships* (Vol. I, pp. 37–67). New York: JAI Press.

Dodge, D. (2004). Human capital, early childhood development and economic growth. In R. E. Tremblay, R. G. Barr & R. DeV. Peters (Eds.), *Encyclopedia on early childhood development* [online]. Montreal, Canada: Centre of Excellence for Early Childhood Development. Retrieved from http://www.child-encyclopedia.com/documents/DodgeANG.pdf

Dupere, V., Lacourse, E., Willms, J. D., Leventhal, T., & Tremblay, R. E. (2008). Neighborhood poverty and early transition to sexual activity in young adolescents: A developmental ecological approach. *Child Development*, **79**(5), 1463–1476.

Durlak, J. A., Taylor, R. D., Kawashima, K., Pachan, M. K., DuPre, E. P., Celio, et al. (2007). Effects of positive youth development programs on school, family, and community systems. *American Journal of Community Psychology*, **39**(3–4), 269–286.

Eisenberg, N., & Fabes, R. A. (1998). Prosocial development. In D. Eisenberg (Ed.), *Social, emotional, and personality development. Volume 3: Handbook of child psychology* (5th ed., pp. 701–778). New York: Wiley.

Epstein, N. B., Baldwin, L. M., & Bishop, D. S. (1983). The McMaster Family Assessment Device. *Journal of Marital and Family Therapy*, **9**, 171–180.

Evers, S., Taylor, J., Manske, S., & Midgett, C. (2001). Eating and smoking behaviors of school children in southwestern Ontario and Charlottetown, PEI. *Canadian Journal of Public Health*, **92**, 433–436.

Eyberg, S. M., Nelson, M. M., & Boggs, S. R. (2008). Evidenced-based psychosocial treatment for children and adolescents with disruptive behavior. *Journal of Clinical Child and Adolescent Psychology*, **37**(1), 215–237.

Fad, K. S., & Ryser, G. R. (1993). Social/behavioral variables related to success in general education. *Remedial and Special Education*, **14**(1), 25–35.

Fauber, R., Forehand, R., Thomas, A. M., & Wierson, M. (1990). A mediational model of the impact of marital conflict on adolescent adjustment in intact and divorced families: The role of disrupted parenting. *Child Development*, **61**, 1112–1123.

Foster, E. M., & Jones, D. E. (2005). *The economic analysis of prevention: An illustration involving the Fast Track Project*. Unpublished manuscript. Retrieved from http://www.unc.edu/~emfoster/papers/FT_ceac.pdf

Fowler, J. H., & Christakis, N. A. (2008). Dynamic spread of happiness in a large social network: Longitudinal analysis of the Framingham Heart Study social network. *British Medical Journal*, doi:10.1136/bmj.a2338

Frazier, P. A., Tix, A. P., & Barron, K. E. (2004). Testing moderator and mediator in counselling psychology. *Journal of Counselling Psychology*, **51**(1), 115–134.

Friedman, J. H. (2001). Greedy function approximation: A gradient boosting machine. *Annals of Statistics*, **29**, 1189–1232.

Galambos, N. L., Barker, E. T., & Almeida, D. M. (2003). Parents *do* matter: Trajectories of change in externalizing and internalizing problems in early adolescence. *Child Development*, **74**, 578–594.

Garber, J., Robinson, N. S., & Valentiner, D. (1997). The relation between parenting and adolescent depression: Self-worth as a mediator. *Journal of Adolescent Research*, **12**, 12–33.

Geeraert, L., Van den Noortgate, W., Grietans, H., & Onghena, P. (2004). The effects of early prevention programs for families with young children at risk for physical child abuse and neglect: A meta-analysis. *Child Maltreatment*, **9**, 277–291.

Gorman-Smith, D., Tolan, P. H., Loeber, R., & Henry, D. B. (1998). Relation of family problems to patterns of delinquent involvement among urban youth. *Journal of Abnormal Child Psychology*, **26**, 319–333.

Government of Canada. (2000). *First Ministers' meeting communiqué on early childhood development*. Retrieved from http://www.scics.gc.ca/cinfo00/800038004_e.html

Government of Canada. (2003). *Multilateral framework on early learning and child care*. Retrieved from http://www.ecd-elcc.ca/en/elcc/elcc_multiframe.shtml

Government of Ontario. (1990). *"Better Beginnings, Better Futures" Project: Policy research demonstration project: Primary prevention. Request for proposals: Research sites*. Toronto, Canada: Queen's Printer for Ontario.

Gray, M. R., & Steinberg, L. (1999). Unpacking authoritative parenting: Reassessing a multidimensional construct. *Journal of Marriage and the Family*, **61**, 574–587.

Greenwald, R. L., Bank, L., Reid, J. B., & Knutson, J. F. (1998). A discipline-mediated model of excessively punitive parenting. *Aggressive Behavior*, **23**, 259–280.

Gresham, F. M. (1992). Social skills and learning disabilities: Causal, concomitant, or correlational? *School Psychology Review*, **21**, 348–360.

Gresham, F. M., & Elliott, S. N. (1990). *Social skills rating system manual*. Circle Pines, MN: American Guidance Services.

Grotevant, H. D., & Cooper, C. R. (1986). Individuation in family relationships. *Human Development*, **29**, 82–100.

Halfon, N., DuPlessis, H., & Inkelas, M. (2007). Transforming the U.S. child health system. *Health Affairs*, **26**, 315–330.

Harris, J. R. (1998). *The nurture assumption: Why children turn out the way they do*. New York: Free Press.

Hawe, P., Shiell, A., & Riley, T. (2004). Complex interventions: How "out of control" can a randomised controlled trial be? *British Medical Journal*, **328**, 1561–1563.

Hawkins, J. D., & Catalano, R. F. (2002). *Investing in your community's youth: An introduction to the Communities That Care system*. South Deerfield, MA: Channing Bete Company.

Health Canada. (2007). *Eating well with Canada's food guide*. Ottawa, Canada: Minister of Supply and Services Canada.

Heckman, J. J. (2000). Policies to foster human capital. *Research in Economics*, **54**, 3–56.

Heckman, J. J. (2004). Invest in the very young. In R. E. Tremblay, R. G. Barr & R. DeV. Peters (Eds.), *Encyclopedia on early childhood development* [online]. Montreal, Canada: Centre of Excellence for Early Childhood Development. Retrieved from http://www.child-encyclopedia.com/pages/PDF/HeckmanANGxp.pdf

Heckman, J. J. (2006). Skill formation and the economics of investing in disadvantaged children. *Science*, **312**, 1900–1902.

Hepworth, P. (2000). Jack's troubled career: The costs to society of a young person in trouble. *Prevention Newsletter*, *2*, 10–11. Ottawa: Government of Canada, National Crime Prevention Centre.

Herman, M. R., Dornbusch, S. M., Herron, M. C., & Herting, J. R. (1997). The influence of family regulation, connection, and psychological autonomy on six measures of adolescent functioning. *Journal of Adolescent Research*, **12**, 34–67.

Hinshaw, S. P. (2002). Commentary: Prevention/intervention trials and developmental theory: Commentary on the Fast Track section. *Journal of Abnormal Child Psychology*, **30**(1), 53–59.

Hinshaw, S. P., & Lee, S. S. (2003). Conduct and oppositional defiant disorders. In E. J. Mash & R. A. Barkley (Eds.), *Child psychopathology* (2nd ed., pp. 144–198). New York: Guilford Press.

Hu, L., & Bentler, P. M. (1999). Cutoff criteria for fit indexes in covariance structure analysis: Conventional criteria versus new alternatives. *Structural Equation Modeling*, **6**, 1–55.

Hundert, J., Boyle, M. H., Cunningham, C. E., Duku, E., Heale, J., McDonald, J., et al. (1999). Helping children adjust—A Tri-Ministry Study: II. Program effects. *Journal of Child Psychology and Psychiatry*, **40**, 1061–1073.

Institute for Social Research. (1981). *Social change in Canada series*. Toronto, Canada: York University Press.

Institute of Medicine. (1994). *Reducing risks for mental disorders: Frontiers for preventive intervention research*. Washington, DC: National Academy Press.

Institute of Medicine. (2000). *From neurons to neighborhoods: The science of early childhood development*. Washington, DC: National Academy Press.

Karoly, L., Greenwood, P., Everingham, S., Houbé, J., Kilburn, M., Rydell, C., et al. (1998). *Investing in our children: What we know and don't know about the costs and benefits of early childhood interventions*. Santa Monica, CA: RAND Corporation.

Karoly, L. A., Kilburn, M. R., & Cannon, J. S. (2005). *Early childhood interventions: Proven results, future promises*. Santa Monica, CA: RAND Corporation.

Keating, D. P., & Hertzman, C. (Eds.). (1999). *Developmental health and the wealth of nations*. New York: Guildford Press.

Kendall, P. C., Chansky, T. E., Kane, M. T., Kim, R., Kortlander, E., Ronan, K., et al. (1992). *Anxiety disorders in youth: Cognitive-behavioral interventions*. New York: Macmillan.

Kohen, D. E., Hertzman, C., & Brooks-Gunn, J. (1998). *Affluent neighborhoods and school readiness*. Paper presented at investing in children: A research conference at the Applied Research Branch, Human Resources Development Canada (W-98-15Es). Ottawa, Canada.

Kumpfer, K. L., & Alvarado, R. (2003). Family-strengthening approaches for the prevention of youth problem behaviors. *American Psychologist*, **58**, 457–465.

Lacourse, E., Côté, S., Nagin, D. S., Vitaro, F., Brendgen, M., & Tremblay, R. E. (2002). A longitudinal-experimental approach to testing theories of antisocial behavior development. *Development and Psychopathology*, **14**, 909–924.

Leventhal, T., & Brooks-Gunn, J. (2000). The neighborhoods they live in: The effects of neighborhood residence on child and adolescent outcomes. *Psychological Bulletin*, **126**, 309–337.

Lister-Sharp, D., Chapman, S., Stewart-Brown, S., & Sowden, A. (1999). Health promoting schools and health promotion in schools: Two systematic reviews. *Health Technology Assessment*, **3**(22), 1–207.

Lochman, J. E. (2004). Contextual factors in risk and prevention research. *Merrill-Palmer Quarterly*, **50**(3), 311–325.

Lohman, T., Roche, A., & Martorell, R. (1988). *Anthropometric standardization reference manual*. Champaign, IL: Human Kinetics Books.

Lundahl, B. W., Nimer, J., & Parsons, B. (2006). Preventing child abuse: A meta-analysis of parent training programs. *Research in Social Work Practice*, **16**, 251–262.

Luthar, S. S., Sawyer, J. A., & Brown, P. J. (2006). Conceptual issues in studies of resilience: Past, present, and future research. *Annals New York Academy of Sciences*, **1094**, 105–115.

Lynch, R. G. (2005). Preschool pays: High-quality early education would save billions. *American Educator, Winter 2004/2005*. Retrieved from http://www.aft.org/pubs-reports/american_educator/issues/winter04-05/preschoolpays.htm

MacLeod, J., & Nelson, G. (2000). Programs for the promotion of family wellness and the prevention of child maltreatment: A meta-analytic review. *Child Abuse and Neglect*, **24**, 1127–1149.

Masse, L. N., & Barnett, W. S. (2002). *A benefit cost analysis of the Abecedarian Early Childhood Intervention*. New Brunswick, NJ: National Institute for Early Education Research.

Maternal & Child Health Bureau. (2002). *The early childhood comprehensive systems initiative.* Retrieved from http://www.state-eccs.org/

McCain, M. N., & Mustard, J. F. (1999). *Early Years Study: Reversing the real brain drain.* Toronto: Ontario Children's Secretariat. Retrieved from http://www.founders.net

McCain, M. N., & Mustard, J. F. (2002). *The Early Years Study three years later. From early development to human development: Enabling communities.* Toronto, Canada: Ontario Children's Secretariat. Retrieved from http://www.founders.net

McCain, M. N., Mustard, J. F., & Shanker, S. (2007). *Early Years Study 2: Putting science into action.* Toronto, Canada: Council for Early Child Development. Retrieved from http://www.founders.net

McCall, R. B., & Green, B. L. (2004). Beyond the methodological gold standards of behavioral research: Considerations for practice and policy. *Social Policy Report,* **18**(2), 3–12.

McCartney, K., & Rosenthal, R. (2000). Effect size, practical importance, and social policy for children. *Child Development,* **71**(1), 173–180.

McMahon, R. J., & the Conduct Problems Prevention Research Group. (2004). *Preventing severe conduct problems in school-aged youth: Elementary school outcomes, mediation, and moderation in the FAST TRACK Project.* Presented at the Society for Prevention Research Meeting, Quebec City, Canada.

Melhuish, E., Belsky, J., Leyland, A. H., Barnes, J., & the National Evaluation of Sure Start Research Team. (2008). Effects of fully-established Sure Start Local Programmes on 3-year old children and their families in England: A quasi-experimental observational cross sectional study. *Lancet,* **372**, 1641–1647.

Meredith, W. (1993). Measurement invariance, factor analysis and factorial invariance. *Psychometrika,* **58**, 525–543.

Moore, M. A., Boardman, A. E., Vining, A. R., Weimer, D. L., & Greenberg, D. H. (2004). Just give me a number! Practical values for the social discount rate. *Journal of Policy Analysis and Management,* **23**, 789–812.

Mrazek, P. J., & Brown, C. H. (2002). An evidenced-based literature review regarding outcomes in psychosocial prevention and early prevention in young children. In C. C. Russell (Ed.), *The state of knowledge about prevention/early intervention* (pp. 42–144). Toronto, Canada: Invest in Kids Foundation. Retrieved from http://www.investinkids.ca/ parents/about-us/our-research/articletype/articleview/articleid/1230/review-of-prevention early-intervention-research.aspx

Muthén, L. K., & Muthén, B. O. (1998). *Mplus user's guide.* Los Angeles, CA: Author.

Nastasi, B. K., & Hitchcock, J. (2009). Challenges of evaluating multilevel interventions. *American Journal of Community Psychology,* **43**, 360–376.

National Council on Welfare. (2004). *Welfare incomes 2003.* Retrieved from http://www. ncwcnbes.net/documents/researchpublications/ResearchProjects/WelfareIncomes/2003 Report_Spring2004/ReportENG.pdf

National Research Council Panel on Research on Child Abuse and Neglect. (1993). *Understanding child abuse and neglect.* Washington, DC: National Academy Press.

Nelson, G., Laurendeau, M. C., Chamberland, C., & Peirson, L. (2001). A review and analysis of programs to promote family wellness and prevent the maltreatment of pre-school and elementary school-aged children. In I. Prilleltensky, G. Nelson & L. Peirson (Eds.), *Promoting family wellness and preventing child maltreatment: Fundamentals for thinking and action* (pp. 220–272). Toronto, Canada: University of Toronto Press.

Nelson, G., Pancer, S. M., Hayward, K., & Kelly, R. (2004). Partnerships and participation of community residents in health promotion and prevention: Experiences of the Highfield Community Enrichment Project (Better Beginnings, Better Futures). *Journal of Health Psychology,* **9**, 213–227.

Nelson, G., Pancer, S. M., Hayward, K., & Peters, R. DeV. (2005). *Partnerships for prevention: The story of the Highfield Community Enrichment Project.* Toronto, Canada: University of Toronto Press.

Nelson, G., Pancer, S. M., Peters, R. DeV., Hayward, K., Petrunka, K., & Bernier, J. R. (2005). *Better Beginnings, Better Futures: Project sustainability.* Kingston, Canada: Better Beginnings, Better Futures Research Coordination Unit Technical Report.

Nelson, G., Westhues, A., & MacLeod, J. (2003). A meta-analysis of longitudinal research on preschool prevention programs for children. *Prevention and Treatment, 6.* Retrieved from http://journals.apa.org/prevention/volume6/toc-dec18-03.html

Nores, M., Belfield, C. R., Barnett, W. S., & Schweinhart, L. (2005). Updating the economic impacts of the High/Scope Perry Preschool Program. *Educational Evaluation and Policy Analysis, 27*(3), 245–261.

Offord, D. R. (1996). The state of prevention and early intervention. In R. DeV. Peters & R. J. McMahon (Eds.), *Preventing childhood disorders, substance abuse and delinquency* (pp. 329–344). Thousand Oaks, CA: Sage.

Offord, D. R., Kraemer, H. C., Kazdin, A. E., Jensen, P. S., & Harrington, R. (1998). Lowering the burden of suffering from child psychiatric disorder: Trade-offs among clinical, targeted and universal interventions. *Journal of the American Academy of Child and Adolescent Psychiatry, 37,* 686–694.

Olds, D. L. (1997). The Prenatal Early Infancy Project: Preventing child abuse in the context of promoting maternal and child health. In D. A. Wolfe, R. J. McMahon & R. DeV. Peters (Eds.), *Child abuse: New directions in prevention and treatment across the lifespan* (pp. 130–156). Thousand Oaks, CA: Sage.

Olds, D. L., Eckenrode, J., Henderson, C. R., Kitzman, H., Powers, J., Cole, R., et al. (1997). Long-term effects of home visitation on maternal life course, child abuse and neglect, and children's arrests: Fifteen year follow-up of a randomized trial. *Journal of the American Medical Association, 278,* 637–643.

Olds, D. L., Henderson, C. R., Cole, R., Eckenrode, J., Kitzman, H., Luckey, D., et al. (1998). Long-term effects of nurse home visitation on children's criminal and antisocial behavior. *Journal of the American Medical Association, 280*(14), 1238–1244.

O'Neil, R., Welsh, M., Parke, R. D., Wang, S., & Strand, C. (1997). A longitudinal assessment of the academic correlates of early peer acceptance and rejection. *Journal of Clinical Child Psychology, 26,* 290–303.

Ontario Ministry of Community and Social Services. (2007). *Ontario Disability Support Program.* Retrieved from http://www.mcss.gov.on.ca/mcss/english/pillars/social/odsp-isdirectives/ODSP_incomesupport.htm

Organization for Economic Cooperation and Development (OECD) Directorate for Education. (2004). *Early childhood education and care policy: Canada country note.* Retrieved from http://www.oecd.org/dataoecd/42/34/33850725.pdf

Pancer, S. M., & Cameron, G. (1994). Resident participation in the Better Beginnings, Better Futures Prevention Project: I. The impact of involvement. *Canadian Journal of Community Mental Health, 13*(2), 197–211.

Pancer, S. M., Cornfield, D., & Amio, J. (1999). *Programs for better beginnings* (Technical report). Kingston, Canada: Better Beginnings, Better Futures Research Coordination Unit. Retrieved from http://bbbf.queensu.ca/pdfs/es_pgm.pdf

Perneger, T. V. (1998). What's wrong with Bonferroni adjustments. *British Medical Journal, 316,* 1236–1238.

Peters, R. DeV., Arnold, R., Petrunka, K., Angus, D., Brophy, K., Burke, S., et al. (2000). *Developing capacity and competence in the Better Beginnings, Better Futures communities: Short-*

term findings report. Kingston, Canada: Better Beginnings, Better Futures Research Coordination Unit. Retrieved from http://bbbf.queensu.ca/pub.html#sterm

Peters, R. DeV., Petrunka, K., & Arnold, R. (2003). The Better Beginnings, Better Futures Project: A universal, comprehensive, community-based prevention approach for primary school children and their families. *Journal of Clinical Child and Adolescent Psychology, 32,* 215–227.

Pettit, G. S., Laird, R. D., Dodge, K. A., Bates, J. E., & Criss, M. M. (2001). Antecedents and behavior-problem outcomes of parental monitoring and psychological control in early adolescence. *Child Development, 72,* 583–598.

Piquero, A., Farrington, D. P., Welsh, B., Tremblay, R., & Jennings, W. (2008). *Effects of early family/parent training programs on antisocial behavior and delinquency: A systematic review.* Stockholm, Sweden: Swedish National Council for Crime Prevention.

Potter, C. A. (2007). Developments in UK early years policy and practice: Can they improve outcomes for disadvantaged children? *International Journal of Early Years Education, 15,* 171–180.

Quest International. (1990). *Lions-Quest Skills for Growing.* Granville, OH: Quest International.

Radloff, L. S. (1977). The CES-D scale: A self-report depression scale for research in the general population. *Applied Psychological Measurement, 1,* 385–401.

Ramey, C. T., & Campbell, F. A. (1984). Preventive education for high-risk children: Cognitive consequences of the Carolina Abecedarian Project. *American Journal on Mental Deficiency, 88,* 515–523.

Reynolds, A. J. (1992). Mediated effects of preschool intervention. *Early Education and Development, 3,* 139–164.

Reynolds, A. J. (1995). One year of preschool intervention or two: Does it matter? *Early Childhood Research Quarterly, 10,* 1–31.

Reynolds, A. J. (1997). *The Chicago Child–Parent Centers: A longitudinal study of extended early childhood intervention.* Madison: University of Wisconsin-Madison.

Reynolds, A. J. (2000). *Success in early intervention: The Chicago Child–Parent Centers program and youth through age 15.* Lincoln: University of Nebraska Press.

Reynolds, A. J. (2004). Research on early childhood interventions in the confirmatory mode. *Children and Youth Services Review, 26,* 15–38.

Reynolds, A. J., Ou, S., & Topitzes, J. W. (2004). Paths of effects of early childhood intervention on educational attainment and delinquency: A confirmatory analysis of the Chicago Child–Parent Centers. *Child Development, 75,* 1299–1328.

Reynolds, A. J., & Temple, J. A. (1995). Quasi-experimental estimates of the effects of a preschool intervention: Psychometric and econometric comparisons. *Evaluation Review, 19,* 347–373.

Reynolds, A. J., & Temple, J. A. (2008). Cost-effective early childhood development programs from preschool to third grade. *Annual Review of Clinical Psychology, 4,* 109–139.

Reynolds, A. J., Temple, J. A., Ou, S. R., Robertson, D. L., Mersky, J. P., Topitzes, J. W., et al. (2007). Effects of a school-based, early childhood intervention on adult health and well-being: A 19-year follow-up of low-income families. *Archives of Pediatric and Adolescent Medicine, 161,* 730–739.

Reynolds, A. J., Temple, J. A., Robertson, D. L., & Mann, E. A. (2002). Age 21 cost-benefit analysis of the Title I. Chicago Child–Parent Centers. *Educational Evaluation and Policy Analysis, 24*(4), 267–303.

Ridgeway, G., McCaffrey, D., & Morral, A. (2006). *Toolkit for weighting and analysis of nonequivalent groups: A tutorial for the twang package.* Retrieved from http://finzi.psych.upenn.edu/R/library/twang/doc/twang.pdf

Rogers, W. M., Schmitt, N., & Mullins, M. E. (2002). Correction for unreliability of multifactor measures: Comparison of alpha and parallel forms approaches. *Organizational Research Methods, 5,* 184–199.

Rothman, K. J. (1990). No adjustments are needed for multiple comparisons. *Epidemiology*, **1**, 15–21.

Russell, C. C. (Ed.). (2002). *The state of knowledge about prevention/early intervention*. Toronto, Canada: Invest in Kids Foundation. Retrieved from http://www.investinkids.ca

Rutter, M. (2006). Is Sure Start an effective preventive intervention? *Child and Adolescent Mental Health*, **11**(3), 135–141.

Sanders, M. R. (1999). Triple P—Positive Parenting Program: Towards an empirically validated multilevel parenting and family support strategy for the prevention of behavior and emotional problems in children. *Clinical Child and Family Psychology Review*, **2**, 71–90.

Sanders, M. R., Markie-Dodds, C., Turner, K. M. T., & Ralph, A. (2004). Using the Triple P system of intervention to prevent behavioural problems in children and adolescents. In P. Barnett & T. H. Ollendick (Eds.), *Handbook of interventions that work with children and adolescents: Prevention and treatment* (pp. 489–516). Chichester, U.K.: Wiley.

Sandler, I. (2001). Quality and ecology of adversity as common mechanisms of risk and resilience. *American Journal of Community Psychology*, **29**, 19–55.

Schneiders, J., Drukker, M., van der Ende, J., Verhulst, F. C., van Os, J., & Nicolson, N. A. (2003). Neighborhood socioeconomic disadvantage and behavioral problems from late childhood into early adolescence. *Journal of Epidemiology and Community Health*, **57**, 699–703.

Schorr, L. (1997). *Common purpose: Strengthening families and neighborhoods to rebuild America*. New York: Doubleday/Anchor Books.

Schweinhart, L. J., Barnes, H. V., & Weikart, D. P. (1993). *Significant benefits: The High/Scope Perry Preschool study through age 27* [Monographs of the High/Scope Educational Research Foundation, 10]. Ypsilanti, MI: High/Scope Press.

Schweinhart, L. J., Montie, J., Xiang, Z., Barnett, W. S., Belfield, C. R., & Nores, M. (2005). *Lifetime effects: The High/Scope Perry Preschool study through age 40* [Monographs of the High/Scope Educational Research Foundation, 14]. Ypsilanti, MI: High/Scope Press.

Schweinhart, L. J., & Weikart, D. P. (1997). The High/Scope preschool curriculum comparison study through age 23. *Early Childhood Research Quarterly*, **12**, 117–143.

Schweinhart, L. J., Weikart, D. P., & Larner, M. B. (1986). Consequences of three preschool curriculum models through age 15. *Early Childhood Research Quarterly*, **1**, 15–45.

Shepard, D. (1968). A two-dimensional interpolation function for irregularly-spaced data. *Proceedings of the 1968 Association for Computing Machinery National Conference*. Retrieved from http://portal.acm.org/citation.cfm?id=810616

Shonkoff, J. P., & Phillips, D. A. (2000). *From neurons to neighborhoods: The science of early childhood development*. Washington, DC: National Academy Press.

Stata Corporation. (2005). *Stata statistical software, release 9.0*. College Station, TX: Author.

Statistics Canada. (1995). *National Longitudinal Survey of Children and Youth: Overview of survey instruments from 1994-95 data collection cycle I*. Statistics Canada Catalogue no. 89F0077XIE. Ottawa: Statistics Canada. Retrieved from http://www.statcan.gc.ca/pub/89f0077x/89f0077x1996001-eng.pdf

Statistics Canada. (2005). *Microdata user guide: National Longitudinal Survey of Children and Youth*, Cycle 6 September 2004 to June 2005. Retrieved from http://www.statcan.ca/

St. Pierre, R. G., & Layzer, J. I. (1998). Improving the life chances of children living in poverty: Assumptions and what we have learned. *Society for Research in Child Development Social Policy Report*, **12**, 1–25.

Steiger, J. H. (1990). Structural model estimation and modification: An interval estimation approach. *Multivariate Behavioral Research*, **25**, 171–180.

Thomas, H., Micucci, S., Ciliska, D., & Mirza, M. (2005). Effectiveness of school-based interventions in reducing adolescent risk behavior: A systematic review of reviews. *Effective Public Health Practice Project*. Retrieved from http://old.hamilton.ca/phcs/ephpp/Research/Summary/2005/AdolescentRiskReview.pdf

Tolan, P. H., Guerra, N. G., & Kendall, P. (1995). Introduction to special section: Prediction and prevention of antisocial behavior in children and adolescents. *Journal of Consulting and Clinical Psychology*, **63**, 515–517.

Tremblay, R. E., Masse, L. C., Pagani, L., & Vitaro, F. (1996). From childhood physical aggression to adolescent maladjustment: The Montreal Prevention Experiment. In R. D. Peters & R. J. McMahon (Eds.), *Preventing childhood disorders, substance abuse, and delinquency* (pp. 268–298). Thousand Oaks, CA: Sage.

Tremblay, R. E., Vitaro, F., Bertrand, L., LeBlanc, M., Beauchesne, H., Boileau, H., et al. (1992). Parent and child training to prevent early onset of delinquency: The Montreal Longitudinal-Experimental Study. In J. McCord & R. E. Tremblay (Eds.), *Preventing antisocial behavior: Interventions from birth through adolescence* (pp. 117–138). New York: Guilford Press.

Tucker, L. R., & Lewis, C. (1973). A reliability coefficient for maximum likelihood factor analysis. *Psychometrika*, **38**, 1–10.

United Kingdom Government. (2008). *What is a children's trust?* Retrieved from http://publi cations.everychildmatters.gov.uk/eOrderingDownload/7965-DCSF-What_is_a_Children %27s_Trust_(6pp)_printing_version.pdf

United States Whitehouse. (2009). *Education.* Retrieved from http://www.whitehouse.gov/ agenda/education/

Veugelers, P. J., & Fitzgerald, A. L. (2005). Effectiveness of school programs in preventing childhood obesity: A multilevel comparison. *American Journal of Public Health*, **95**, 432–435.

Vitaro, F., Brendgen, M., Pagani, L., Tremblay, R. E., & McDuff, P. (1999). Disruptive behavior, peer association, and conduct disorder: Testing the developmental links through early intervention. *Development and Psychopathology*, **11**, 287–304.

Vitaro, F., Brendgen, M., & Tremblay, R. E. (2001). Preventive intervention: Assessing its effects on the trajectories of delinquency and testing for mediational processes. *Applied Developmental Science*, **5**, 201–213.

Waddell, C., Hua, J. M., Garland, O. M., Peters, R. D., & McEwan, K. (2007). Preventing mental disorders in children: A systematic review to inform policy-making. *Canadian Journal of Public Health*, **98**, 166–173.

Wandersman, A., & Florin, P. (2003). Community interventions and effective prevention. *American Psychologist*, **58**, 441–448.

Webster-Stratton, C. (1992). *The incredible years: A trouble-shooting guide for parents of children ages 3–8 years.* Toronto, Canada: Umbrella Press.

Webster-Stratton, C., Reid, M. J., & Hammond, M. (2001). Preventing conduct problems, promoting social competence: A parent and teacher training partnership in Head Start. *Journal of Clinical Child Psychology*, **30**, 283–302.

Webster-Stratton, C., & Taylor, T. (2001). Nipping early risk factors in the bud: Preventing substance abuse, delinquency, and violence in adolescence through interventions targeted at young children (0–8 years). *Prevention Science*, **2**, 165–192.

Weisz, J. R., Sandler, I. N., Durlak, J. A., & Anton, B. S. (2005). Promoting and protecting youth mental health through evidence-based prevention and treatment. *American Psychologist*, **60**, 628–648.

Willms., J. D. (Ed.). (2002). *Vulnerable children.* Edmonton, Canada: The University of Alberta Press.

Zins, J. E., Blodworth, M. R., Weissberg, R. P., & Walberg, H. (2004). The scientific base linking social and emotional learning to school success. In J. E. Zins, R. P. Weissberg, M. C. Wang & H. J. Walberg (Eds.), *Building academic success on social and emotional learning: What does the research say?* (pp. 3–22). New York, NY: Teachers College Press.

ACKNOWLEDGMENTS

We would like to dedicate this monograph to the memory of Urie Bronfenbrenner whose ecological theory of human development inspired our research and that of many others. He was a true pioneer in translating theory and research into effective public policy. Thank you, Urie.

Better Beginnings, Better Futures has been funded since 2007 by a research contract from Public Safety Canada (2007–2010). The project was previously funded by the Ontario Mental Health Foundation (2006–2008), Ontario Ministry of Children and Youth Services (2005–2006), Ontario Ministry of Health and Long Term Care (2000–2004), and Ontario Ministry of Community and Social Services (1990–2000). This report reflects the views of the authors and not necessarily those of the funders. We acknowledge the dedication of the Site Researchers, whose diligence and hard work have made this longitudinal research possible, and the central team for their support in helping this monograph come to fruition. We are grateful to the research families, youth, and teachers who have participated in the research over the past 11 years.

Correspondence concerning this monograph should be addressed to Ray Peters, Better Beginnings, Better Futures Research Coordination Unit, Queen's University, 98 Barrie St, Kingston, Ontario, Canada K7L 3N6.

Telephone: (613) 533-6672

Fax: (613) 533-6732

Email: ray.peters@queensu.ca

Ray DeV. Peters is an Emeritus Professor of Psychology at Queen's University in Kingston, Ontario. He has been the Director of the BBBF Research Coordination Unit since its inception in 1990 and is a leading expert in child development and prevention research and practice. His major research interests concern the promotion of children's well-being and the prevention of children's mental health problems. In the past 15 years, he has written extensively about effective programs for vulnerable children, prevention of childhood disorders, and early childhood development.

Alison J. Bradshaw is a Research Associate with the BBBF Research Co-ordination Unit. She is particularly interested in the effects of preventive interventions on the long-term health and well-being of disadvantaged children.

Kelly Petrunka has been the Associate Research Director of the BBBF Research Coordination Unit since its inception in 1990. Her major research interests include effectiveness and economic analyses of early childhood prevention programming for disadvantaged children and their families.

Geoffrey Nelson is Professor of Psychology and a faculty member in the graduate program in Community Psychology at Wilfrid Laurier University in Waterloo, Ontario. His research and practice has focused on housing and self-help organizations for people with serious mental illness and community-based prevention programs for children and families.

Yves Herry is Associate Vice-President (Teaching and Learning Support) at the University of Ottawa. His research interests include the impact of learning strategies on the development of self-concept and literacy. He conducts his research in the context of French language minority settings.

172

Wendy M. Craig is a Professor of Psychology at Queen's University. Her current research focuses on healthy relationships and the individual and systemic risk and protective factors associated with bullying and victimization. She is leading a national network, PREVNet (Promoting Relationships and Eliminating Violence Network), whose mission is to promote safe and healthy relationships for Canadian youth (http://www.prevnet.ca).

Robert Arnold teaches methodology, statistics and sociology of the family at the University of Windsor. He has been Project Methodologist for BBBF since 1990 and currently participates in a spinoff project, in which children from an Aboriginal community, who had been followed from birth to Grade 3 by BBBF, are followed to Grades 6 and 7. Another group of children on whom data were gathered at age 4 are being interviewed in Grade 12. The result, it is hoped, will be a fuller picture of health and development in an Aboriginal community than has yet been available in Canada.

Kevin C. H. Parker is a psychologist and Director of the Psychology Clinic at Queen's University. He is an Adjunct Associate Professor in Psychology and Psychiatry at Queen's University. He research has focused on measures, methods, and issues important in clinical practice including attachment, intelligence, ASD, and diagnosis.

Shahriar R. Khan (M.Sc., 1989; M.A., 1993, The Australian National University) is a Data Analyst with the BBBF Research Coordination Unit. His area of interest is analyzing and interpreting social and biosocial data, and he has research experience in the fields of child development, nutrition, and sociodemographic appraisals of family/household of developing nations.

Jeffrey S. Hoch works at the Centre for Research on Inner City Health in the Keenan Research Centre of the Li Ka Shing Knowledge Institute of St. Michael's Hospital. He teaches economic evaluation as an Associate Professor in the Department of Health Policy, Management and Evaluation at the University of Toronto. His research applies economic methods to challenges confronting society.

S. Mark Pancer is a Professor of Psychology at Wilfrid Laurier University. He has had a long-standing interest in working with children, youth and their families to develop and evaluate programs that help prevent social and emotional problems. He has been one of the principal investigators in the BBBF project since its inception in 1990. He is particularly interested in how community residents, particularly young people, are involved in the development of community programs such as BBBF.

Colleen Loomis is Associate Professor of Psychology at Wilfrid Laurier University. Her research focuses on how individuals and communities interact to promote inclusion and participation, particularly for immigrants and multicultural groups within educational settings. She has published on psychological sense of community, service learning, and related subjects, including self-help groups, gender and power, socioeconomic class, mentoring, and bilingual education.

Jean-Marc Bélanger has been the Director of the School of Social Work at the Université de Moncton since 2007. Previously, he was at Laurentian University in Sudbury for 17 years specializing, among other interests, in the area of community development. He has been involved with the Sudbury BBBF project since its inception in 1991, and has been a member of the BBBF Research Coordination Unit since 1997. He is also involved with the Father Involvement Initiatives—Ontario (FII—ON) as Chair of the Father Involvement in Educational Institutions (FI-EI) Action Group, looking at curriculum content pertaining fathers' involvement with their children.

Susan Evers is a Professor in the Department of Family Relations and Applied Nutrition at the University of Guelph. She is responsible for the growth status and dietary intake component of BBBF. Her primary research interests include dietary behaviors and overweight during childhood and adolescence and nutritional health during pregnancy.

Claire Maltais is the director of the French language teacher education program at the Faculty of Education at the University of Ottawa. She specializes in early childhood education and literacy. Her research focuses on the impact of full-time preschool programs on the development of children.

Katherine Thompson is a graduate student at the Faculty of Education at the University of Ottawa. She is interested in childhood education and the affective and cognitive development of children.

Melissa D. Rossiter is a Lecturer in the Department of Applied Human Nutrition at Mount Saint Vincent University, Halifax, Nova Scotia. Her research focuses on examining the risk factors for and trends in overweight and obesity among women, children, and adolescents.

STATEMENT OF EDITORIAL POLICY

The *Monographs* series aims to publish major reports of developmental research that generate authoritative new findings and uses these to foster a fresh perspective or integration of findings on some conceptually significant issue. Submissions from programmatic research projects are welcomed; these may consist of individually or group-authored reports of findings from a single large-scale investigation or from a sequence of experiments centering on a particular question. Multiauthored sets of independent studies that center on the same underlying question may also be appropriate; a critical requirement in such instances is that the various authors address common issues and that the contribution arising from the set as a whole be unique, substantial, and well-integrated. Manuscripts reporting interdisciplinary or multidisciplinary research on significant developmental questions and those including evidence from diverse cultural, racial, ethnic, national, or other contexts are of particular interest. Because the aim of the series is not only to advance knowledge on specialized topics but also to enhance cross-fertilization among disciplines or subfields, the links between the specific issues under study and larger questions relating to developmental processes should emerge clearly for both general readers and specialists on the topic. In short, irrespective of how it may be framed, work that contributes significant data or extends developmental thinking will be considered.

Potential authors are not required to be members of the Society for Research in Child Development or affiliated with the academic discipline of psychology to submit a manuscript for consideration by the *Monographs*. The significance of the work in extending developmental theory and in contributing new empirical information is the crucial consideration.

Submissions should contain a minimum of 80 manuscript pages (including tables and references). The upper boundary of 150–175 pages is more flexible, but authors should try to keep within this limit. If color artwork is submitted, and the authors believe color art is necessary to the presentation of their work, the submissions letter should indicate that one or more authors or their institutions are prepared to pay the substantial costs associated with color art reproduction. Please submit manuscripts electronically to the SRCD Monographs Online Submissions and Review Site (MONOSubmit) at www.srcd.org/monosubmit. Please contact the Monographs office with any questions at monographs@srcd.org.

The corresponding author for any manuscript must, in the submission letter, warrant that all coauthors are in agreement with the content of the manuscript. The corresponding author also is responsible for informing all coauthors, in a timely manner, of manuscript submission, editorial decisions, reviews received, and any revisions recommended. Before publication, the corresponding author must warrant in the submissions letter that the study was conducted according to the ethical guidelines of the Society for Research in Child Development.

Potential authors who may be unsure whether the manuscript they are planning would make an appropriate submission are invited to draft an outline of what they propose and send it to the editor for assessment. This mechanism, as well as a more detailed description of all editorial policies, evaluation processes, and format requirements, is given in the "Guidelines for the Preparation of Publication Submissions," which can be found at the SRCD website by clicking on *Monographs*, or by contacting the editor, W. Andrew Collins, Institute of Child Development, University of Minnesota, 51 E. River Road, Minneapolis, MN 55455-0345; e-mail: wcollins@umn.edu.

Note to NIH Grantees

Pursuant to NIH mandate, Society through Wiley-Blackwell will post the accepted version of Contributions authored by NIH grantholders to PubMed Central upon acceptance. This accepted version will be made publicly available 12 months after publication. For further information, see www.wiley.com/go/nihmandate.

CURRENT